Cities at War

Cities at War

Global Insecurity and Urban Resistance

Mary Kaldor

Saskia Sassen

EDITORS

Columbia University Press *New York*

Columbia University Press
Publishers Since 1893
New York   Chichester, West Sussex
cup.columbia.edu
Copyright © 2020 Columbia University Press
All rights reserved

Library of Congress Cataloging-in-Publication Data
Names: Kaldor, Mary, author. | Sassen, Saskia, author.
Title: Cities at war : global insecurity and urban resistance /
    edited by Mary K. Kaldor and Saskia Sassen.
Other titles: Global insecurity and urban resistance
Description: New York : Columbia University Press, [2020] |
    Includes bibliographical references and index.
Identifiers: LCCN 2019035766 | ISBN 9780231185387 (cloth) |
    ISBN 9780231185394 (pbk.) | ISBN 9780231546133 (e-book)
Subjects: LCSH: Urban warfare—Developing countries—Case studies. |
    Internal security—Developing countries—Case studies. | Metropolitan
    areas—Developing countries—Strategic aspects. | Urban violence—
    Developing countries—Case studies. | Political violence—Developing
    countries—Case studies. | Low-intensity conflicts (Military science)—
    Developing countries. | Human security—Developing countries—
    Case studies. | Sociology, Urban.
Classification: LCC U167.5.S7 K35 2020 | DDC 355.4/26—dc23
LC record available at https://lccn.loc.gov/2019035766

Columbia University Press books are printed on permanent and durable
acid-free paper.
Printed in the United States of America

Cover design: Lisa Hamm

Contents

Acknowledgments

This book was supported by the European Research Council programme "Security in Transition: An Inter-disciplinary Investigation of the Security Gap." We want to express special thanks to Ruben Andersson, who helped us organize a series of meetings to discuss the book and who helped to choose and edit the individual chapters. We also thank Dominika Spyratou, Amy Crinnion, and Makena Micheni for administrative assistance.

Cities at War

Introduction

Global Insecurity and Urban Capabilities

MARY KALDOR AND SASKIA SASSEN

Perhaps the worst suffering in Syria has been experienced in Ghouta, a suburb in Eastern Damascus that was under siege from the beginning of the war in 2012 until a cease-fire in April 2018. It has been continuously bombarded by the regime and is where several large-scale chemical weapon attacks have taken place. Government forces and the armed opposition controlled what went in and out and maintained exorbitantly high prices for food and necessities—the consequence was extreme deprivation and starvation. But Ghouta is also the site of a dairy factory, which supplies much of the dairy products consumed in Damascus. Because the rest of Damascus needs yogurt and other dairy products, the farmer has negotiated a deal with the regime, creating a small safe haven inside Ghouta. This is what we will refer to as the "yogurt run," a tiny opening in the siege that allows Ghouta's yogurt to reach places on both sides of the conflict.

We use the idea of the yogurt run as a metaphor to capture the presence of urban capabilities—the mutuality that underpins densely populated urban conurbations and that inherently provides a counter, however slight, to forcible fragmentation and closure, and to the dynamic of insecurity based on perpetual exclusions. A central argument in this book is that recognizing such urban capabilities—even where we can least expect them to be present—is one key to understanding cities facing war or profound insecurity. One important implication is a better understanding of how inhabitants can maximize whatever pertinent yogurt runs are present in their city. Conventional armies rarely see these capabilities embedded in urban space. Irregular combatants see and use them for their purposes, which do not always coincide with what residents might want. We want to use this notion of urban capabilities to detect embedded vectors that can lead to the diluting or unsettling of conflict in cities.

This is a book about insecurity in cities. Today, the most extreme form of such insecurity is war, and the most extreme form of war involves an often asymmetric combination of conventional forces and myriad irregular groups. Contemporary wars are increasingly urbanized, whether we are referring to full-fledged asymmetric wars, or to terrorist attacks in cities outside the war zones, or to violent organized crime.[1] In the past, conventional forces preferred to fight battles in open fields, and irregular groups based themselves in remote areas such as jungles or mountains. Today, the urban built environment has become the equivalent of jungles and mountains—both as a way to hide and evade fighting and as a source of succor and support.

Contemporary wars involve forced displacement on a massive scale, swelling the conurbations where the majority of the world's people now live. Newly arrived immigrants contribute to the vitality and creativity of the city, but they are also vulnerable to prejudice and frustration and the way in which traditions are reinvented, distorted, and instrumentalized in contemporary urban settings. Cities simultaneously nurture inclusive, cosmopolitan, and multicultural communities alongside old and new racisms; the politics of class based on growing income inequality and religious fundamentalisms; all of which leads to the active use of built environments to segregate, exclude, and worse. Today's insecure cities are crisscrossed by borders and divisions, walls and checkpoints, ghettoization and expulsions, sieges and violent attacks.

Much of the literature on cities and war focuses on the militarization or securitization of cities.[2] This book instead treats the city as a lens through which to understand contemporary violence as well as contemporary peace. We are interested in the granular character of contemporary insecurity and the ways in which the city itself in effect "talks back" (Sassen 2012). Wars are usually analyzed through the prism of the nation-state; yet, it is often pointed out that contemporary wars are global and regional as well (Kaldor 2012). Our case studies are empirical investigations of a variety of cities from the perspective of the inhabitants and, as such, shed new light on how to explain, interpret, and perceive twenty-first-century war without the blinkers of geopolitical preoccupations.

Our approach brings with it a recognition that women and children are also key actors in these wars—they are not just victims. Going beyond the notion of war as mere combat, we must recover the multiple ways in which women and children play a role. Capturing their participation is not easy. Guns and tanks are dominant factors in conflict zones, and men are still the dominant users of guns and tanks. Yet women often play major roles in these wars—with the Kurdish women fighters a powerful example. But any war requires sustaining the fighters.[3] Gathering food is the most familiar factor. What is often neglected in this aspect of war situations is the fact that women are key actors in making connections with other groups—including enemy groups—to secure food.

War zones are much more than guns and tanks. Several works in the literature capture this expanded role of women, including girls, works that too often are overlooked as the focus remains on the guns and tanks. Also often overlooked is the fact that the search for food, water, and medications in each case is likely to require a capacity to negotiate with friends and with the enemy. Women engage in negotiations with all sorts of actors, including the enemy.

These concerns are in line with an emerging scholarship that focuses on the margins—people and conditions that are not at the center of the discourse, people who are overlooked or flattened into the poor, the victims of colonialisms of all sorts, and similar groups. Postcolonialism begins to function as a way to capture the complexities involved in the making of such subjects. For instance, Robert J. C. Young, one of the pioneers of the study of postcolonial literatures and their cultures, examined marginalized peoples and histories that were overlooked in the traditional analysis of cultures (Young 1995 and 2015). This brings to the fore a set of new questions and interrogations of our societal and cultural analyses (Sassen 2003).

We now have a vast scholarship examining how we might revise the forms of knowledge that circulate in the academy, how we can retrieve the histories of people and struggles that have disappeared and whom we failed even to notice existed.[4] In this collection, the yogurt run represents a bit of those unrecorded histories.

We can think of the diverse forms of violence and the insecurities they generate in our case studies as signaling the existence of systemic edges deep inside a city. In fact, we might ask whether these types of urban conflicts are today's frontier spaces: has the frontier shifted from the erstwhile edges of empire to the systemic edge deep inside cities? And as with the old imperial wars that generated a massive demand for armaments, today's urban wars and insecurities are generating a self-reinforcing industry of security services that, more often than not, feeds more conflict and hence more insecurity.

In other words, this is a book about the rising power and importance of cities in relation to war and generalized insecurity—both as new sites of violence and division and as sites of resistance and of opportunity for the emergence of new norms and political arrangements, enabling the reconstruction of security.

The New Wars: Contemporary Urban Violence

We use the term *new wars* to include the full range of violent conflicts that find in cities one major site for their enactment.[5] Today's wars can be contrasted with the deep-rooted political contests of the past, whether we are talking about wars between the major powers or the classic civil wars between governments and rebels that took place mainly in the twentieth century. Rather, they are better described as a social condition or a culture (Kaldor 2018) or as an ecosystem (Kilcullen 2013). New wars involve both conventional forces and irregular combatants including militias, private security contractors, terrorists, paramilitary groups, warlords, and criminal gangs. These latter groups of combatants find in urban space a tool for war. The shadow effect of these wars extends well beyond the actual theater of war, as we can see in diverse terrorist attacks in cities often far from war zones.

But beyond this narrow meaning of war, there is a proliferation of forms of violence that find in cities a conducive environment. They include sectarian conflict, terrorism, acts of violent criminal gangs, genocide, ethnic cleansing, sexual violence, massive evictions of poor settlements to build office parks or gated communities, and other violations of human rights. Today's urban conflicts are often a mixture of all of these.

So-called old wars—the wars of the modern period from the late eighteenth to the middle of the twentieth century (both interstate and civil wars)—largely took place in the countryside, at least in theory. Battles were fought in fields. In the nineteenth and early twentieth centuries, strategists and tacticians advised against fighting in cities. According to the U.S. Capstone urban warfare manual, "Tactical doctrine stresses that urban combat operations are conducted *only* when required and that built-up areas are *isolated* and *bypassed* rather than risking a costly, time-consuming operation in this difficult environment" (United States Department of the Army, 1979, 1). During the cold war, military planners anticipated fighting on the north German plains, not in cities. And the same was true, by and large, of the insurgencies taking place outside the main imagined theater. Insurgents hid in mountains and jungles, coming out sporadically to weaken and disorient the ruling regimes.

Of course, there were urban battles: the centers of power were located mostly in cities. It is estimated that 40 percent of operations in World War II took place in cities. Images of Berlin, Dresden, Stalingrad, Tokyo, and Hiroshima are etched into our consciousness of that war. But cities played a somewhat passive role: they were bombed or under siege; they were not necessarily theaters of war in the way they are today. Occupation and liberation each produced urban combat, but not to the extent we saw, for instance, after the occupation of major Iraqi cities or in the recent combat against ISIS.

A shift began during the cold war period. The Battle of Algiers (1957), Hue in Vietnam (1968), and the "troubles" in Northern Ireland are but three examples of an emergent pattern of asymmetric war: regular armies confronting insurgencies fought by so-called irregular combatants who lacked airplanes and tanks but had only guns and bombs and thus found in urban space a strategic space for their types of operations. We have also come to understand how incapacitating this type of asymmetric conflict is for regular armies. These earlier forms of violence in cities can be viewed as forerunners of today's forms of violence.

If we think about the key characteristics of new wars, there are several reasons such wars are likely to be urban based. First, new wars are fought by networks of state and nonstate actors that are both global and local. Indeed, global circuits are critical in both political and economic terms. Often the individual combatants are recruited from rural areas or from recently arrived rural-urban migrants. However, they are incorporated into transnational networks, whose political communications and financial infrastructure are necessarily city based. This was the case in Syria, where armed opposition groups mobilized among the unemployed and frustrated rural poor using funding often provided by rich Gulf donors. The opposition groups promoted various versions of pan-Islamic ideologies and engaged in predatory activities, such as the smuggling of antiquities, that were integrated into global circuits. Indeed, the explosion of house prices in London can be explained partly in terms of the money-laundering activities of Syrian warlords. It is cities, therefore, that are integrated into the global economy and that host the infrastructure of global networks.

Second, the new identity politics is being nurtured in cities. Cities were always, to some extent, segregated. There are rich and poor neighborhoods. There are Chinatowns and Little Italys. It was Venice in the sixteenth century that established the first ghetto—an area allocated to Jews by the doge, called the Campo del Ghetto Nuevo. The social base of the new wave of identity politics tends to be young unemployed males, and this includes newly arrived urban immigrants who congregate in areas of similar ethnicity or religion. Examples include poor Shi'as in Baghdad or Basra, industrial workers with rural plots in the former Yugoslavia, and displaced persons and returned refugees in Kabul, not to mention the inner cities of the West. They often receive help and support from identity-based nongovernmental organizations (NGOs) or religious institutions and are often deeply insecure, yearning for an imagined traditional culture from which they came. Such people are vulnerable to identity-based ideologies that are used to win newly established elections. Indeed, the need to create homogeneous constituencies helps to explain social and ethnic cleansing, which fosters identity-based fear of the "other."[6]

Third, in new wars, military-style battles are avoided, and most violence is directed against civilians. In such wars, the aim is political control of territory, which is achieved through expelling or terrorizing those who might challenge political control. Contemporary communications are critical for recruitment, connectivity among disparate groups, and, above all, spreading fear. Hence we find ever-smaller territorial fiefdoms surrounded by borders, checkpoints, and walls—cities composed of archipelagos.

On the one hand, it is easier to evade new techniques of surveillance in cities, which is one reason that shantytowns and tower blocks are the twenty-first-century equivalent of mountains and jungles. On the other hand, cities are a suitable target either because of the vulnerability of twenty-first-century city infrastructure to terrorist acts such as suicide bombings and air strikes, or because of the spread of organized crime, and/or because of the political goal of ethnic cleansing. In many cases, ethnic or religious ghettoization explains why historic and cultural symbols are targeted, while in other cases, it is these symbols' insertion into global circuits of meaning that makes them prime targets for insurgent groups. Coward talks about how *urbicide* is used to describe the way in which new wars deliberately target the very fabric of the city—the notion of publicness and the idea of a civic community on which cities are based (Coward 2006).

The statistics of new wars tell a grim story. Although casualties (deaths) are, on the whole, lower than in the industrial wars of the twentieth century, the typical characteristic of contemporary wars is expulsion. Political control is established through the forced eviction of those with a different identity or those who disagree. Every year, the grand total of refugees multiplies; as of July 2019, the total number of people displaced by war and repression had reached an all-time high of 70.8 million, according to the United Nations High Commission for Refugees (UNHCR). This displacement can also be treated as forced urbanization—multiplying the population of cities such as Goma in eastern Congo, Pristina in Kosovo, or Kabul in Afghanistan—and further augmenting the causes of insecurity.

Finally, the economies of the new megacities are vastly different from the classic city described by Charles Tilly as the basis of the nation-state (Tilly 2000). Particularly in the third world, the dramatic growth of cities has not necessarily translated into the growth of productive wealth. Often the economies of cities are dependent on state provision financed through resource extraction and/or international aid. In these circumstances, taxation is low, as is spending on urban and social infrastructure. Unemployment is frequently high, and this is associated with the spread of an informal and often criminalized economy that is integrated into global circuits and networks of power—*la Ville Sauvage* (Goma case study) or the *feral city* (Norton 2003).

The disorder associated with violence provides a convenient cover for a variety of revenue-generating activities that include looting, extortion, so-called protection and hostage taking, as well as smuggling in drugs, antiquities, oil, diamonds, or people. It is this informal economy that both provides finance for new wars and, by the same token, flourishes within the environment of violence.

All these factors help to explain the persistence of contemporary urban violence and why it is so difficult to bring new wars to an end. The various warring parties—state and nonstate, regular and irregular—have a vested interest in violence both for political reasons (because violence is a way to construct extremist identities) and for economic reasons (because violence is a method of extracting resources). These factors also explain how this predatory social condition that characterizes many cities has a tendency to spread through the global networks that compose the new wars.

Global Security Interventions

It is possible to distinguish external interventions in terms of what Kaldor calls "security cultures" (Kaldor 2018). The terms *security* and *culture* are complex concepts. *Security* is profoundly ambiguous, in that it is supposed to refer to the safety of the individual or the state—the referent of security—yet at the same time, the word conjures up a set of capabilities or practices (military, police, or intelligence agencies) that are deeply embedded in notions of political authority. *Culture* is used to refer to the combination of a set of practices (security apparatuses and how they act) and to an objective (the safety of the nation or human beings). These various components or elements combine—not necessarily harmoniously—to produce and reproduce certain types of behavior. Whether such behavior is good or bad is a normative judgment that can be made on the basis of an empirical study of what constitutes a culture. Or to put it another way, such a culture is characterized by a set of social relationships that have their own specific logics and that open up or close down pathways for change.

New wars can also be described as a culture. Whereas old wars were understood as deep-seated political contests—and, indeed, interruptions in everyday life—new wars involve myriad armed actors and networks who reproduce themselves in both political and economic terms through violence, spreading tactics and practices along the vectors of insecurity and permeating everyday life over time. The insecurity experienced in cities comes primarily under the rubric of new wars. But these wars are deeply imbricated with the global. In all our studies, the globalized context, the nexus of global capital, crime, and communication are deeply intertwined at local levels. In addition, in several of our studies, local insecurities are overlaid by global security interventions, which, in this book, we describe in terms of two other types of security culture: the war on terror and the liberal peace.

The war on terror is about the use of military force to attack nonstate actors—it is the war of the manhunt, *par excellence* asymmetric war. The war on terror involves a sinister twenty-first-century combination of intelligence agencies, private security contractors, and regular military forces. Air strikes, drone attacks, and warfighting, the characteristic practices of the war on terror, exacerbate identity-based polarization and weaken the formal economy. Fallujah, Grozny, or Raqqa are examples of where battles were fought without restraint. Grozny was reduced to rubble and, at one point, pinned down some 130,000 Russian troops as opposed to 3,000–5,000 Chechens. Yet despite the formal victory in 2000, the conflict and the interconnection between terrorism and organized crime has not been severed.

Fallujah was destroyed twice by U.S. forces, and yet the Sunni insurgency was still able to regroup and reenter the city after the battle was over, leaving today's legacy of ISIS. Raqqa and other cities formerly controlled by ISIS have been totally destroyed, yet local people are angrier with the Western Coalition than with ISIS, because of the scale of death and destruction. Moreover ISIS fighters are reappearing in supposedly liberated areas.

Warfighting results in very high casualties, especially among civilians, even with the kind of precision attacks that were used by the Israelis in Lebanon and Gaza or by NATO in Libya. Even if such attacks do minimize civilian casualties, they provoke counterattacks by groups that have neither the capacity nor the legal requirement to minimize civilian deaths. The same argument applies to drone attacks that are supposed to avoid civilian casualties: mistakes are inevitable not only in continuing collateral damage but also in the identification of targets—so-called signature strikes, for example—and hovering drones are themselves a form of terror.

Even where direct attacks are avoided, the prevalence of these external interventions is characterized by partitions, security zones, and extensive surveillance, what is described in the Karachi study as a process of *enclavization*. The establishment of green zones in Iraq and Afghanistan provides heavily guarded and mostly peaceful areas for the international community. Outside the green zones, in the red zones, ordinary citizens are vulnerable to bombs and crime, broken infrastructure, unemployment, and mud or dust. Even after General David Petraeus introduced a new approach to security in Baghdad, setting up joint security stations all over the city and negotiating hundreds of local cease–fires, the city remained riddled with partitions and checkpoints.

In contrast to the war on terror, the liberal peace is about stabilization after a formal peace agreement and involves a combination of peacekeepers, civilian aid agencies, and NGOs. The liberal peace model of security is about implementing a peace agreement in which the participants in the peace agreement are the actors of new wars. It involves separating the sides and controlling heavy weaponry, demobilizing or integrating armed fighters, as well as numerous other so-called peace-building programs. But it cannot control the ability of the armed actors to prey on ordinary people, because the armed actors are the key agents in implementing the agreement. This model of security does reduce the overall level of violence through physical segregation and surveillance and other measures, but it fails to establish law and order and everyday security.

As the chapters in this book show, this model of security can be seen as a way of living with perpetual war. The walls and checkpoints become emblematic of threats, and physical distance increases the suspicion and fear that is the bedrock of identity politics. This model of security is also expensive, given that partitions have to be constructed and monitored; checkpoints have to be manned, and often infrastructure has to be duplicated on both sides of the partition. The model creates an industry of insecurity that may self-perpetuate and add to existing insecurities.

Where the liberal peace coexists with the war on terror, as in Bamako, Kabul, or Baghdad, insecurity is pervasive. This is also the case in Karachi, where localized insecurity—a version of the new wars culture—is overlaid by the war on terror, leading to a ceaseless process of enclavization. It is also the case in

Ciudad Juárez, where the war on terror on the U.S.-Mexico border intersects with criminal violence and violence resulting from privatization of security, similar to the enclavization to be found in Karachi.

Where the liberal peace is less overshadowed by the war on terror, it is more likely to take advantage of urban capabilities, including local civic activities, and to contribute to the role of city as safe haven in the midst of war, as the study of Goma demonstrates. In the two cities where no global security intervention is present (Bogotá and Novi Pazar), security in the sense of safety is linked to how the complex conjunction of violent activities and urban capabilities in a broader globalized economic context plays out.

Table 0.1 summarizes the combinations of new wars with global security interventions that characterize the case studies in this book. It is these differences in the way that insecurity is experienced and the possible openings that are investigated in the following chapters.

Table 0.1 Cities and Security Cultures

	War on Terror	Liberal Peace
Bamako	x	x
Kabul	x	x
Baghdad	x	x
Ciudad Juárez	x	
Karachi	x	
Goma		x
Bogotá		
Novi Pazar		

Urban Capabilities

While cities increasingly provide the ideal setting for the flourishing of new wars, the city itself also might provide the elements of an alternative security culture. Urban spaces possess the capacity to make new subjects and identities that would not be possible in, for example, rural areas or a country as a whole. A city's sociality can bring out and underline the urbanity of subject and setting and dilute more essentialist signifiers. This shift often happens when cities confront major challenges and need new solidarities. For instance, cities have increasingly begun to pass their own ordinances to contest national policy norms. Examples include the passing of more progressive environmental laws and designating cities as sanctuaries for undocumented immigrants. The joint responses required to address and solve urban problems place emphasis on an urban—rather than individual or group (such as religious or ethnic)—subject and identity.[7]

Nevertheless, as the chapters of this book show, cities can also provide the impetus for new divisions that draw on the vulnerability of newly arrived migrants, as well as the growing precariousness of older inhabitants, in the face of evictions, inequalities, and armed conflict. Violence tends to split a city's people along often reinvented or instrumentalized divisions, such as happened in Baghdad.

Still, movements composed of disparate groups with a variety of grievances have managed to coalesce in increasingly legitimate ways as they are confronted with extreme challenges. They can generate subnational struggles for self-governance at the level of the neighborhood and the city. The commingling of diverse struggles that is inherent to urban spaces can cultivate a broader and deeper push for a new normative order.

Beyond war, cities have often enabled struggles that aim to go beyond the conflicts and racisms that mark an epoch—partly because urban residents simply had to do so to make the city function, and partly because of the cosmopolitan traditions of cities such as Baghdad, Novi Pazar (Serbia), or Aleppo (Syria). Such initiatives simultaneously emerge from and further develop urban capabilities.[8] It is out of this type of dialectic that arose the open urbanity that historically made European cities spaces for expanded citizenship. One factor feeding these positives was that both the modest middle classes and the powerful found in the city a space for their diverse life projects. For the poor and powerless, the city has increasingly become the space of last resort, their having been expelled by the corporatizing of land and the destruction of villages.

Today, two types of acute challenges facing cities tell us something about how urban capabilities can alter hatred and conflict, as the yogurt run illustrates. One is the urbanizing of war, and the other is the hard work of *making* open cities—that is, urban societies that are open to diverse groups with flexible mechanisms in place to resolve differences. An achievement of this in Western cities might be the repositioning of the immigrant and the citizen as above all *urban* subjects rather than essentially different subjects, as much of the anti-immigrant and racist commentary does.

These are among the features that make cities a space of great complexity and diversity. The enhanced inclusion they make possible lends them civic capability. But cities also confront major conflicts that threaten to reduce that complexity to little more than a cement jungle. Extreme racism, government-led wars on terror, and pending crises of climate change, to name a few, demand that we expand urban capabilities and the meaning of civic membership.[9]

The city, then, is uniquely capable of nurturing novel partial orders.[10] The new strategic role of cities versus states in international economic dealings suggests growing power for cities and makes it possible for us to imagine a return to the dominance of urban over national law. Cities are one of the key sites where new norms and identities are made. They have been such sites at various times and in various places, and under vastly diverse conditions. With globalization and digitization—and all the specific elements they entail—global cities emerge as strategic sites for making norms and identities. Some of these norms and identities reflect extreme power, and others reflect innovation under duress: notably, much of what happens in immigrant neighborhoods.

Whereas strategic transformations are sharply concentrated in global cities, many are also enacted (besides being diffused) in cities at lower orders of national urban hierarchies. Beyond economic functions, there is the potential for cities to make informal norms and identities, often resulting from urban challenges and dynamics that force residents and leaders into crafting innovative responses and adaptations. In short, cities combine constraints and possibilities that push urban residents into action when such constraints might not push a nation into action.

In all our case studies, it is possible to identify examples of urban capabilities. Novi Pazar, in Serbia, succeeded in remaining outside the Balkan wars during the 1990s as a consequence of determination on the part of the city elites, even though its fragile order is under threat from the external environment of violence and neoliberal economic policies. Farza, a suburb of Kabul, offers an example where local residents, along with security forces, have found ways to negotiate differences to exclude violent actors from the area. And Goma in eastern Democratic

Republic of the Congo (DRC) has, in the midst of war, provided a sort of refuge for a combination of displaced persons, armed groups, and liberal peace actors.

The militarization and securitization of cities can push residents into action because those actions override the welfare function. The imperative of security means a shift in political priorities. It implies a cut or a relative decrease in budgets dedicated to social welfare, education, health, infrastructure development, economic regulation, and planning. This trend challenges the very concept of citizenship and suggests that cities still must find new ways to transcend conflict and harness the power of the challenges they face.[11] Under these conditions, recovering urban capabilities is essential for the city to remain a diverse and inclusive space despite ideological and actual war, and racism and xenophobia.

The partial resilience of urban capabilities, then, also implies the possibility of making new subjectivities and identities. For instance, often it is the urbanity of the subject and of the setting that mark a city, rather than ethnicity, religion, or phenotype. But that urban marking of subject and setting does not simply fall from the sky. It frequently comes out of hard work and painful trajectories. One question is whether it can also come out of the need for new solidarities in cities that are confronted by major challenges, such as violent racism, armed conflict, or environmental crises. The acuteness and overwhelming character of the major challenges cities confront today can serve to create conditions in which the challenges are bigger and more threatening than a city's internal conflicts and hatreds. This might force us into joint responses and, from there, to the emphasis of an urban, rather than individual or group, subject and identity—such as an ethnic or religious subject and identity.

Outline of the Book

This book focuses on cities that are not considered part of the advanced industrial world, even though they are connected through numerous global circuits. They are part of what is sometimes described as the "global south" or the third world, even though they are located east, west, south, and even north, and even though they vary considerably in levels of income and degrees of globalization.

The book begins with three deeply insecure cities where the global presence comprises both the war on terror and the liberal peace. In chapter 1, about Bamako in Mali, Ruben Andersson vividly describes the remapping of urban space as a consequence of international interventions. He describes how this remapping creates dangerous divisions between Bamako and the no–go hinterlands as well as between internationals and local city dwellers—an ever-spiraling, pervasive insecurity caused by a combination of bunkerization and remote-controlled intervention.

Chapter 2 on Kabul by Florian Weigand contrasts two areas of Kabul: one rural and one urban. He shows how a low-key, inclusive communally based approach to security in the rural area has minimized levels of violence. By contrast, proximity to terrorist targets, lack of trust in security forces, and a complex of walls and checkpoints have produced a deep sense of insecurity in the urban area. His depiction of bunkerization and remote intervention in Kabul echoes some of the elements of the Bamako study.

Chapter 3 by Ali Ali on Baghdad tells the story of what he calls the "systematic discarding" of people in Baghdad after the U.S. invasion in 2003 through the lived experience of individuals.

He takes the reader through the various phases of discarding—first, the dismantling of the army and the de-Ba'athification process, then the ethnic cleansing that took place during the civil war, and finally, the exclusion of Sunnis with the establishment of a Shi'a-dominated government.

Chapters 4 and 5 are about cities where the war on terror intersects with a range of localized forms of violence. Ciudad Juárez is a town on the U.S.-Mexican border characterized by extreme drug violence that has many of the characteristics of a new war. Mary Martin shows how criminal violence intersects with the war on terror that is enacted on the border, as well as the neoliberal privatization of security in relation to economic enterprises—a neoliberal security culture. She shows how the authorities, with mixed success, confronted these deadly forms of violence through the construction of a public security approach aimed at regenerating a sense of civic solidarity.

Sobia Ahmed's chapter on Karachi provides a granular account of what she calls the "process of enclavization" that has developed in the context of the combination of criminality, ethnoviolence, and the war on terror. She describes an enclavization, similar to the privatization described in Ciudad Juárez, that seems only to perpetuate and exacerbate the sense of insecurity experienced by residents of Karachi.

In chapter 6, Karen Büscher shows how the city of Goma in eastern DRC has been transformed as a consequence of war from a small administrative center into a large urban conglomeration. She focuses on the way in which an international liberal peace presence, together with urban capabilities, have produced a variety of zones of protection: a place of refuge, a safe haven for rebels, an international humanitarian industry, and a hub of transregional trade.

Finally, the last two chapters are about cities where an international presence is minimal. Chapter 7 by Johannes Rieken and colleagues about Bogotá provides an example of the way in which urban capabilities can be nurtured through the construction of civic spaces and communal activities, improvements in city infrastructure, and efforts to diminish socioeconomic inequalities and increase respect for the rule of law. The model has its shortcomings, which are outlined in the chapter, but it can be contrasted to the physical and privatized approach to security involving walls and checkpoints that tends to make things worse.

Chapter 8 portrays the compelling story of Novi Pazar, a predominantly Muslim city in Serbia. Vesna Bojicic-Dzelilovic shows how urban capabilities were deployed to resist war and violence and how this has become increasingly difficult in the context of industrial decline, poverty, large-scale population movements due to the influx of refugees, the emergence of exclusionary identity politics, and clientilistic forms of governance.

In the brief conclusion, we reflect on the spaces for tactical urbanism—how the widespread manifestations of urban capabilities, however minor, might provide the opening for an alternative way of imagining how to reduce violence.

This book offers the perspective of the urban subject as one compelling answer to contemporary wars. On the one hand, we argue that political violence has become increasingly urbanized partly as a consequence of displacement that expands the cities and partly as a result of the way in which newly reinvented exclusive identities prey on the vulnerable as a consequence of inequality, deprivation, and displacement, while the built environment offers a haven for irregular groups in both physical and economic terms. In the coming chapters, we describe the ways in which cities have been partitioned, segregated, and damaged materially and spiritually. At the same time, what we call the yogurt run is intrinsic to cities. Cities cannot offer a haven or even a ghetto without certain types of public services and connectivities—these are the capabilities of the city that shape a different kind of urban or civic subjectivity that is the main way in which security can be constructed or reconstructed.

Notes

1. See, for example, Abrahamsen, Hubert, and Williams 2009; McKilcullen 2013.
2. See, for example, Graham 2010.
3. The multiple roles women take on in war zones has long been overlooked in the literature on "mankind" and war. The current development of this literature now includes questions of identity and selfhood. In specific situations, these factors are also present in war zones, even though war zones are, for now, not the current focus in the literature on the many instantiations of womanhood. See, for example, Compton, Meadow, and Schilt 2018, Phoenix 2017; Chinkin and Kaldor 2013.
4. See, for example, Loomba 2015, Tricoire 2017.
5. For a full theorization of new wars, see Kaldor 2012.
6. Akar and others have demonstrated how this happens in Beirut; for example, Akar 2012; Fawaz, Harb, and Gharbieh 2012.
7. For a longer discussion of urban subjects, see Sassen 2012.
8. See Sassen 2008, 277–319. All subsequent citations refer to this edition.
9. In previous research, Saskia Sassen has explored in depth the resurgence of urban lawmaking and its significance. The emergent landscape described here promotes a multiplicity of diverse spatiotemporal framings and diverse normative miniorders, where once the dominant logic was toward producing grand unitary national spatial, temporal, and normative framings. (See Sassen 2008, chaps. 2, 6, 8, and 9).
10. One synthesizing image we might use to capture these dynamics is the movement from centripetal nation–state articulation to a centrifugal multiplication of specialized assemblages.
11. See Graham 2010, Marcuse 2002, and Sassen 2008, chapter 6.

References

Abrahamsen, R., D. Hubert, and M. C. Williams. 2009. "Guest Editors' Introduction" in "Special Issue on Urban Insecurities." *Security Dialogue* 40 (4–5): 363–72. https://doi.org/10.1177/0967010609343301.

Akar, H. B. 2012. "Contesting Beirut's Frontiers." *City & Society* 24 (2): 150–72. https://doi.org/10.1111/j.1548-744X.2012.01073.x.

Beall, J., T. Goodfellow, and D. Rodgers. 2013. "Cities and Conflict in Fragile States in the Developing World." *Urban Studies* 50 (15): 3065–83. https://doi.org/10.1177/0042098013487775.

Compton, D'Lane, Tey Meadow, and Kristen Schilt, eds. 2018. *Other, Please Specify: Queer Methods in Sociology.* Oakland: University of California Press.

Chinkin, Christine, and Mary Kaldor. 2013. "Gender and New Wars." *Journal of International Affairs* 67 (1): 167–87.

Coward, M. 2006. "Against Anthropocentrism: The Destruction of the Built Environment as a Distinct Form of Political Violence." *Review of International Studies* 32 (3): 419–37. https://doi.org/10.1017/S0260210506007091.

Fawaz, M., M. Harb, and A. Gharbieh. 2012. "Living Beirut's Security Zones: An Investigation of the Modalities and Practice of Urban Security." *City & Society* 24 (2): 173–95. https://doi.org/10.1111/j.1548-744X.2012.01074.x.

Graham, Stephen. 2010. *Cities Under Siege: The New Military Urbanism.* London: Verso.

Kaldor, Mary. 2012. *New and Old Wars,* 3rd ed. Cambridge: Polity.

Kaldor, Mary. 2018. *Global Security Cultures.* Cambridge: Polity.

Loomba, Ania. 2015. *Colonialism/Postcolonialism (The New Critical Idiom).* London: Routledge.

Marcuse, Peter. 2002. "Urban Form and Globalization After September 11th: The View from New York." *International Journal of Urban and Regional Research* 26 (3): 596–606.

McKilcullen, D. 2013. *Out of the Mountains: The Coming Age of the Urban Guerrilla.* London: C. Hurst.

Norton, Richard J. 2003. "Feral cities." *Naval War College Review* 56 (4): 97–106.

Phoenix, Ann. 2017. "Unsettling Intersectional Identities: Historicizing Embodied Boundaries and Border Crossings." *Ethnic and Racial Studies* 40 (8): 1312–19. https://doi.org/10.1080/01419870.2017.1303171.

Sassen, Saskia. 2003. "The Repositioning of Citizenship: Emergent Subjects and Spaces for Politics." *New Centennial Review* 3 (2): 41–66. https://muse.jhu.edu/article/48301/pdf.

———. 2008. *Territory, Authority, Rights: From Medieval to Global Assemblages,* 2nd ed. Princeton: Princeton University Press.

———. 2012. "Urban Capabilities: An Essay on Our Challenges and Differences." *Journal of International Affairs* 65 (2): 85–95.

Tricoire, Damien. 2017. *Enlightened Colonialism: Civilization Narratives and Imperial Politics in the Age of Reason.* London: Palgrave Macmillan.

United Nations High Commission for Refugees (UNHCR). Figures at a Glance. www.UNHCR/Figures-at-a-glance. accessed September 16 2019.

United States Department of the Army. 1979. *Military Operations in Urbanized Terrain (MOUT).* FM-90-10, Washington, DC.

Young, Robert C. 1995. *Colonial Desire: Hybridity in Theory, Culture and Race.* London: Routledge.

———. 2015. *Empire, Colony, Post-colony.* London: Wiley Blackwell.

1

Bamako, Mali

Danger and the Divided Geography of
International Intervention

RUBEN ANDERSSON

"No other mission in contemporary times has
been so costly in terms of bloodshed." This was
how Hervé Ladsous, undersecretary-general
for peacekeeping from 2011 to 2017, summed up a dreadful year
for the United Nations mission in Mali to the Security Council
in January 2015. In the West African country's war-hit north,
peacekeepers were facing almost daily assaults by improvised
explosive devices, ambushes, and suicide attacks, and the fatali-
ties were swiftly adding up. Their mission was peacekeeping
with no peace to keep; their blue helmets were themselves prime
targets.[1]

In early 2012, Tuareg separatists had taken up arms in Mali's
desert north in what was to be the opening shot for prolonged
insecurity in the region.[2] A coup d'état led by disgruntled officers
followed in the country's capital, Bamako, while in the north,
jihadists joined forces with—and eventually elbowed aside—
the separatists who were clamoring for an independent state of
Azawad. To cut off the advance of the jihadists, France launched
a military campaign, Operation Serval, followed by a UN peacekeeping mission, the Multidimensional Integrated Stabilization
Mission in Mali (MINUSMA), in 2013. MINUSMA's presence

has consolidated since that time, and a peace accord has briefly held out the promise of better times in Mali. Yet pervasive insecurity has proliferated in ways that are sadly emblematic of many international interventions of recent times, including Somalia and Afghanistan.

In this chapter, I explore how international actors have grappled with the situation in the Malian hinterland, casting a critical eye on the various forms of remote intervention that have enabled them to retain a presence amid mounting insecurity. I focus on the uneven mapping of danger and intervention—that is, the interaction between designated no-go zones and safe zones, and between the interveners and locals who are circulating in these spaces. The drawing of distance to remote danger, I will show, has come to define much of the international presence in Mali, yet it has largely failed to provide a sense of security and it has had negative impacts on Mali's prospects for recovery from war.

Bamako, a sprawling city of about two million, is a key site on this danger-driven map of intervention. Far from the conflict-hit north, the capital has come to act as a hub for the various actors, including peacekeepers and small European nongovernmental organizations (NGO)s, who descended on the country from 2013 onward. Risk aversion led many of these international workers to remain in Bamako rather than deploy up north, which in turn meant that the spatial divide between capital and dangerous hinterland—already mapped onto Mali's territory by foreign militaries and travel advisories in the preconflict days—was gradually reinforced. This partial presence in the country was accompanied by the imposition of a somewhat alien security model on Bamako itself (imported to a large extent from Kabul: see Florian Weigand's chapter in this volume).

Although the Bamako base of the interveners strengthened the existing divide between headquarters and hinterland, risk management practices within Bamako itself deepened the divide between local city dwellers and the internationals. These dual forms of risk avoidance via growing distance on national as well as local/urban scales were to have negative consequences for intervention and the quest for peace and local acceptance, in a trend with broader implications for the organization of interventions in global crisis or conflict zones today.

In the first section, I consider international actors' various means of managing risk and insecurity in the safe zone on Mali's map of danger—that is, in their Bamako headquarters—before looking at how these attempts at drawing distance to danger easily crumble. Next, I sketch the broader geography of intervention, showing how the "dangerous" north came to stand in uneasy relation to the capital's bunkered headquarters while danger kept eluding this neat geographical division and filtered into the city space, not least as Bamako was hit by high-profile terror attacks in 2015 (violence would also spread from the north into central Mali from this time onwards; these more recent developments are not covered in this chapter). Building on the headquarters–hinterland divide and its various tensions and overlaps, I conclude the chapter by asking what alternatives to remote-controlled intervention might be available, as well as what kind of social capabilities may be drawn upon to minimize the distance between intervener and intervened-on that has come to characterize international efforts in Mali and other crisis zones.

City of Risk: Bamako and the Mapping of Intervention

In 2014, my plane was descending toward Bamako's Senou airport amid the heat-induced haze of May: fieldwork was finally beginning. The preparation had been drawn out, involving elaborate risk assessments and steep insurance payments at my university. Now, as I stepped onto the hot runway, already it was clear that some things had changed radically since my previous visits in 2001 and 2010–11. On the tarmac stood seven black-painted UN military planes, lined up in waiting for the cargo and personnel making their way to Mali's war-scarred north. Inside the airport terminal, a Western woman scuttled between the police booths, overseeing Malian officers grappling with newly installed biometric equipment. Police aimed infrared pistols at us, screening for Ebola.

Mali, it was amply clear after only a few minutes back on its soil, was now a country under international tutelage, its security assured by UN and French soldiers and its borders controlled by Western devices and expertise. It was also marked by an edginess I had never experienced before, I thought, as I finally found a taxi in a remote corner of the airport parking lot. As we drove on empty streets toward central Bamako, I kept looking over my shoulder, as if on guard against an unlikely ambush.

As my taxi weaved its way into the busy city center, the French embassy reared into view. Unlike in earlier years, it was now clad with antiblast HESCO bastions (of the kind first used in Afghanistan) to shield against attacks, their bulky frames a reminder of the extensive French counterter-ror operation expanding from Mali across the wider Sahel region. White SUVs drove around on Bamako's streets, "UN" emblazoned on the sides. At times, foreign soldiers in uniform strolled past. Bamako played host to a new set of visitors, military officers, UN workers, humanitarians, and security contractors. "Peaceland"—as Autesserre (2014) has called the self-contained world of international missions—had descended on Bamako like an extraterrestrial ship unloading its cargo and personnel, all according to the well-established global template of what Kaldor (2018) and Duffield (2001) have termed "liberal peace."

On the face of it, Malians should have been happy with UN intervention. MINUSMA had arrived on the back of large promises of aid for Mali as the country returned to democracy and civilian rule. The arrival of the UN and associated actors was also welcome in another sense, as the departure of most aid workers during the conflict had caused havoc for Mali's aid-dependent economy and local job prospects. Yet as I walked Bamako's streets that May, eavesdropping on youths gathering for tea on street corners, discontent was palpable. Among the tea-drinking friendship groups *(grins)*, the white UN four-wheel-drive vehicles rumbling through town failed to inspire confidence. "They are just here to eat," said many locals I talked to, meaning the peacekeepers were in it only to gain something for themselves rather than help Mali recover from conflict.

This was perhaps an unfair assessment, but the mission's setup in Bamako did its best to reinforce the mistrust. To Mali's government, the decision to locate UN mission headquarters in the capital was a provocation, indicating the state's failure to manage its own affairs. To the UN, however, the reason behind a Bamako base was simple: insecurity in the war-scarred north—that is, precisely the insecurity it was there to prevent. The UN agencies and peacekeepers had been slow to deploy up north; and as they did so, the protective measures there were even starker than in the capital. Although, in hindsight, such measures might have seemed reasonable given the mounting attacks on peacekeepers, initially the threat was less pronounced. In the northern towns of Gao, Timbuktu, and Kidal, peacekeepers and civilian UN staff lurked behind high walls, from where—or so locals complained—they rarely emerged to keep the people safe from attacks by rebels, jihadists or the Malian armed forces. Distance between local realities and the fortified "archipelago" of intervention (Duffield 2010) was growing wider.

The large UN presence in Bamako, meanwhile, was awkwardly detached from the existing urban fabric. As it was set up in mid-2013, MINUSMA had commandeered the five-star Hotel l'Amitié, which rose from the quarters of central Bamako. While locals complained about how much Mali paid for the UN's highly visible presence, the hotel itself—whose pool on my last visit had been a favored haunt of the local elite—was now off-limits behind its cement vehicle barriers, curls of razor wire, and tanks operated by armed blue helmets. As UN staff drove up to the gates at lunchtime, they clogged the busy road outside, frustrating local drivers, much as the French embassy's antiblast bastions did a few streets away.

The Bamako bunkering was indicative of a trend toward fortification of international missions that has existed since the 1990s, whether by the UN or by interveners such as the United States in postinvasion Baghdad (Chandrasekaran 2006). As noted in a growing body of studies (e.g. Duffield 2010; Fast 2014; Andersson and Weigand 2015), bunkering and buffering have increased distance to local society in a dangerous spiral that risks generating novel risks as contact points diminish and resentment stirs. This was also to be the case in Mali in 2014–16, the period of concern to this chapter.

It was not just the UN and Western governments that geared their operations toward the unseen dangers. Some international NGOs in Bamako had situated their offices close to easy evacuation routes should the worst happen. One large French aid organization had a map on its wall showing no-go zones where staff were not allowed to stop after 6:00 P.M.: two areas in town, plus anything beyond the Bamako city limits. "Stay in the Radisson," one officer formerly involved in the EU military training mission in Mali (EUTM) had advised me before I left for Bamako, in words that now sound eerie following the 2015 terror attack there. "It's the only hotel with armed guards." Meanwhile, the hotel commandeered by EUTM in one of the capital's leafier districts was now surrounded by fenced-in walkways and barriers to protect against attack; still, the military officers, many of them arriving fresh from Afghanistan, complained that protection was too basic compared with that in Kabul.

At night, EUTM officers holed up in Bamako's posher restaurants along with other, largely Western, internationals. Their daytime and nighttime haunts constituted a circuit that was separate from mainstream Bamako life yet that affected the city's workings in significant ways. In Bamako's postdevelopment and posttourism days, the stopovers on this circuit were the cashpoints to which local entrepreneurs and workers were drawn. And it was one of them, the nightclub La Terrasse in a popular entertainment area, that was to be the first Bamako terrorist target in 2015, the year in which the "danger of the north" seeped south toward the capital and (more severely) the country's central regions.

The consequence of those attacks would be further bunkering and separation, yet the key point here is that by that time, the international interveners already had distanced themselves from local society because of perceived insecurity, using templates imported from Afghanistan and the bunkerized UN presence elsewhere. This distance-making process involved physical barriers (HESCO bastions, bollards, fences) as well as subtler social means of separation (the circumscribed circuits of nightlife and daily work). Gradually, if imperfectly, Bamako was starting to exhibit something akin to the enclavization described in Sobia Ahmad Kaker's chapter on Karachi in this volume. The international archipelago of intervention was creating its own discrete community spaces that were set apart from the diverse urban fabric around them.

Meanwhile, downtown Bamako still teemed in its urban ways. Its ramshackle central markets overflowed with imported Chinese goods and assorted magical charms, just as it had in 2001 on my first visit to the city. Bamako's shared *sotrama* vehicles still plied the potholed routes, where new passengers still greeted strangers on board with *"Ani sogoma"* (good morning) or *"Anoullah"* (good evening), followed by long strings of inquiries into relatives' health, as they squeezed onto the rickety benches. Bamako has sometimes been referred to as the world's largest village, a sprawling collection of communities drawn from the rural base. Indeed, the city's pronounced "urban capabilities" (Sassen 2012) for conviviality, as seen among *sotrama* passengers each day, depended greatly on the broader civic capabilities so characteristic of the postcolonial Malian nation as a whole (Pes 2011).

Amid the war and political shifts of 2012, key values associated with the Malian nation-building project functioned as partial bulwarks against the perceived sense of disintegration and corrosion of trust among conationals. Whitehouse (2013) has identified some of these capabilities that have helped to ensure good-neighborliness among different groups, including *mɔgɔya*, or "the eagerness to engage with other people socially in almost any situation"; *danbe*, or dignity, honor, and reputation—in short, a deep sense of rootedness in one's own social past—*faso kanu*, "love of father's house" or Malian patriotism; and *senenkunya*, or joking relations, at times including elaborate ritual insults. International visitors to Mali have long had a taste of this, and I sometimes found myself at the sharp end. As Amadou Diarra, the Malian moniker I acquired in 2001, during my first visit to the country, I have endured no end of taunts from my joking relations the Traorés, including the most profane assertions that I subsist on bush meat alone.

Besides such much-debated joking relations, anthropologists such as Pes (2011, 30) have shown how the flexibility and openness of less visible forms of group membership—in terms of age, descent, and residence longevity—have allowed for a peaceful social fabric to develop in many parts of Mali. This is not an *urban* capability per se (Pes's study is rural), but it is clear to any casual visitor to Bamako how much of this interpersonal interaction has traveled into the "world's largest village." This included the thousands of internally displaced people (IDPs) who came to the capital after 2012. Reaffirming their strong civic ethos, Bamako residents took pride in their tradition of *djatiguiya* (welcoming) as they hosted IDPs for months or even years in their own homes. In the courtyard of a friend of mine in southern Bamako, for instance, some eight families had squatted for well over a year; elsewhere richer IDPs helped by hosting their fellow northerners in spare rooms. Even as the initial warm welcome ebbed amid strains on resources, the displaced, rather than bringing conflict into the city, were by and large integrated into its urban fabric.

That was not the case, however, for the much more privileged international interveners descending on Bamako in the IDPs' wake. Instead of integrating into the urban fabric, as earlier generations of mostly Western expatriates had tried to do when Mali was pictured as a "donor darling" and key development partner, the new interveners largely sidestepped it. In their set-aside "safe" locations (offices, hotels, poolside homes, and expensive restaurants), the expats clustered at one remove from local society. The new arrivals had little interest in or even knowledge of the joking relations that developed among Malians and earlier generations of visitors—understandably so, perhaps, as many were likely to leave soon anyway on another assignment in "Peaceland." Instead, the interveners tended to cement relations among themselves, leading to growing proximity among military, aid, and peacebuilding sectors while distance to local realities grew.

This failure to participate in the urban and civic fabric of Bamako fueled mistrust. In Bamako, fingers were pointed at the white four-wheel drives; look, they are out hunting for girls again, or heading for another glitzy party! Some aid workers and UN officials sometimes tried their best to mitigate local resentment, but given the risk-averse structure of the international presence, this was a losing prospect. One UN adviser had tried to get a taxi scheme in place for MINUSMA staff, to spread some of the benefits of the mission to local drivers rather than rely on UN-provided, supposedly secure, transport to and from work. This failed, however, he recounted with frustration, owing to a combination of strict risk management protocols and the usual UN bureaucracy. In the end, most expatriates resigned themselves to the restrictions while finding temporary escape in the bars and restaurants of the international scene.

The expat bubble of Bamako that resulted was in many ways a cut-price version of the "Kabubble" in Afghanistan (Andersson and Weigand 2015). Instead of integrating into the urban fabric, the expat community developed its own separate dynamics: loud parties and poolside dinners behind guarded gates, followed by a drive home to the international compound by employer-vetted drivers. At my guesthouse, one night a worker displaced from his native Dogon country, where he had worked as a tourist guide before the conflict, asked as the reggae started booming and glasses clinking on the terrace upstairs: "If you're in a country to help it, you don't go out like that at night, no, you spend all your time thinking about it, right? How is this helping Malians?"

As other authors have emphasized in recent years—notably Autesserre (2014), Smirl (2015), and Duffield (2010)—we need to pay close attention to the everyday organization and infrastructures of intervention to understand its impact and consequences. This brief look at the physical and social organization of intervention in the urban milieu of Bamako has highlighted two features: first, the spatial clustering of privileged (often Western) internationals in the headquarters of the capital, distanced from the northern frontlines; and, second, the peculiar distance developing between Bamako residents and this latest generation of international visitors. Yet this leaves us with an incomplete picture of Mali's geography of intervention and conflict. For a fuller view, we need to look toward the country's north and to the workers tasked with bringing peace to it in a faltering manner.

Remotely Uncontrolled: Protests and Peril in Mali's North

As the UN mission commenced in mid-2013, Mali's map was divided into zones of danger and deployment. While the French counterterror forces—first under Serval and then under the regionwide successor mission, Barkhane—lurked in the northern hinterlands, other interveners remained unevenly spread across Malian territory, corralled in bastions and cocooned by their SUVs. Their lopsided presence helped congeal Mali's geography of intervention into red and green zones while imposing a division of labor between local, "regional" (African), and "international" staff.

A quick traipse around the lobby of the MINUSMA headquarters hotel—clad with pictures of African peacekeepers, I discovered as I finally made it past the bollards and guards—made clear that the northern frontline tasks had been left largely in the hands of regional forces. Their task was a tough one, and more trouble was brewing for them during that tense May of 2014.

In the restive regions of Kidal and Gao, low-ranking African soldiers had been thrown in at the deep end while the mission's groaning civilian support system frequently failed to supply them with food and water. UN salaries were not being paid because of administrative glitches, adding to the chaos. The frontline Africans had no armored cars, scant protection, and little preparation for the dangers ahead; sitting atop their open pickups, they were low-hanging fruit for armed factions wishing to make a violent impact. Some European military officers asked in private whether the UN leadership was racist, as it exposed these soldiers to risks that would be unthinkable for Western or even Asian troops, the former stalwarts of peacekeeping missions.

In stark contrast to the mission overkill down in the bloated Bamako headquarters, frontline soldiers from countries including Guinea and Chad were largely left to fend for themselves behind their crumbling camp walls—and fend some of them did. In 2014, reports surfaced of soldiers deserting and even attacking the local population.[3] Still, the UN and its member states were content that *someone* was up there "keeping the peace," not least since MINUSMA's African soldiers highlighted the so-called regional ownership of crises that new missions were supposed to be all about.

The Chadians, who had joined the Malian frontlines first as part of the French counterterror operations, only to be eventually (and partially) incorporated into the UN peacekeeping force, were exemplary of this trend toward Africanized deployments. "They are savages, but they are good," was how one peacekeeping officer in New York bluntly described them to me. Unsurprisingly, they would also end up being the largest takers of casualties on Mali's postintervention frontlines.

While African deaths racked up, Western troop contributors kept swelling the ranks of the new intelligence functions of MINUSMA, initially at a safe distance in Bamako. Despite their secure existence in a hangar outside the airport during 2014, the soldiers' arrival was preceded by media reports back home about the risks they faced. Some Europeans—first Swedes and Dutch—did eventually deploy to the north as part of a bid by their governments for an upcoming Security Council seat. However, unlike their northern-deployed African counterparts, the Europeans were Special Forces–equipped with armored cars, Apache helicopters, surveillance drones, and their own mobile medical teams. The Europeans' role was to complement the non-Western forces with intelligence and Special Forces capabilities, not to supplant the latter in their patrolling duties, for which they remained woefully underprepared. The result was a constant withdrawal behind camp walls by the Africans, leading to more local anger about UN inaction.[4]

In sectors other than peacekeeping, a similar Africanization of northern operations was under way. European military trainers with EUTM were not allowed to venture into northern Mali, where the Malian battalions it trained were posted as soon as the soldiers completed their drills. Meanwhile, in the aid sector, Malian and regional workers—that is, black or otherwise "Malian-looking" staff—almost exclusively maintained the operations of UN agencies and international NGOs.[5]

This racial and regional division of labor was not altogether new. Rather, it expanded on arrangements put in place a few years before the 2012 conflict, as international staff had increasingly been withdrawn from the north because of security risks (Bergamaschi 2014, 354). Yet although it was true that jihadists had kidnapped Westerners, killing some and demanding huge ransoms for others, Malian staff also were at risk of attacks, as aid workers emphasized in interviews. Even if no spectacular murders of Malians had yet taken place, four Malians working for the International Committee of the Red Cross had been kidnapped in early 2014. Besides, the fear of attacks on internationals did not correspond with the limited such attacks until that point: as one UN officer collating these data told me that May, "Mali's not Afghanistan." However, in a reflection of the moniker "Africa's Afghanistan" that some security pundits had assigned to Mali after 2012, the measures rolled out in the country, from bunkering to subcontracting, already resonated with arrangements in the simmering Afghan war well before the violence started escalating.

To return to the topic of mapping of insecurity and danger, deployments in Mali were unequally spread across its unevenly risky territory. The division of labor in the military and aid sectors reinforced the distance between categories of interveners: African peacekeepers on patrol versus Western military trainers in Bamako and intelligence gatherers equipped with drones; Malian and West African frontline workers versus international (to a large extent Western) aid managers in the capital.

To the aid managers, however, the distance between headquarters and hinterland could be overcome through "remote management" and related techniques. Previously applied in Somalia and other conflict-hit countries, such procedures enabled project managers in Bamako to check in with partner organizations or lower-ranking employees in the field via e-mail, phone, or occasional "flash visits." In the UN mission, a similar remote relationship developed between headquarters and the hinterland. The danger zone remained at a distance yet comfortably within reach through modern technology and administrative procedures—or so went the story before the worst possible news hit the headlines in May 2014, in which the northern danger would end up encroaching on the capital, not for the last time.

The trouble started with a visit by the Malian prime minister to Kidal. The northern town had been left as the bastion of the rebels from the National Movement for the Liberation of Aza-wad (MNLA) after the French intervention, much to Bamako's chagrin. The French were playing a double game in the north, keeping the MNLA rebels as allies while routing jihadists in the hinterland. The premier now wanted to give this arrangement a push as he arrived in Kidal on May 17 with the intention of showing support for patriotic locals and state administrators.

He failed. As the prime minister tried to make it into central parts of Kidal, armed men took officials at the town's governorate hostage. Then, as Malian forces attacked and French and UN soldiers stood by, the hostages were executed.

Soon, protests began. On our grainy guesthouse television, I saw protesters screaming into the night in downtown Bamako: rumor had it that a UN vehicle had been torched. The next day aid workers were scrambling to exit the north, but no flights were leaving. Anger against perceived UN and French inaction in Kidal was mounting, as was anger against northern Tuaregs and Arabs, who were seen as partial to the separatist cause. Mali was yet again a tinderbox about to ignite; yet the Kidal events were only the start of the cruelest week Mali had seen for some time.

"Have you heard the news?" I was in a plush hotel in northern Bamako on the night of May 21 when a European researcher broke the latest developments to me. Malian forces, some of them recently trained and equipped by the EU, had attacked the rebels in Kidal without informing the French or MINUSMA, then the MNLA had routed them. Kidal had fallen, followed by Menaka farther south. "The Malian soldiers just ran away," the researcher said; she reported that they hid in the UN camp while the rebels stole their EU-provided vehicles. We walked upstairs to the hotel restaurant, set on a terrace brimming with soldiers and UN workers, to dine with a friend of ours from an NGO. What would the implications be here in Bamako?

Over dinner, our friend looked out over the gathered men in uniforms. "I shouldn't really be here," she said, but let it be. Bamako's expat humanitarians tried to keep separate from the military, yet socially speaking, this was proving impossible; they mingled on the same circuit, stuck in the same high-end haunts. Our researcher colleague was nervous, too; she was not allowed to go anywhere on foot, according to new security instructions from somewhere (her embassy? Intelligence? She would not say). Instead, she borrowed our friend's designated driver and left, as the NGO worker confided that she, too, was not really allowed to move around this area after dark.

The next day, I awoke to a Bamako in lockdown mode. Angry crowds gathered outside MINUSMA's headquarters and the French embassy's antiblast barriers. My meetings were canceled. International organizations told their staff to stay indoors and away from the center. An interviewee from EUTM could not meet with me, he explained, because they were in "alternative planning" for the foreseeable future. Military officers such as himself could not leave their barricaded hotel without security escort, and their barracks outside the capital were under curfew. Up north, further protests were brewing, and aid workers started evacuating the city; the situation was swiftly getting out of hand.

The protests and the rekindled northern troubles, which were eventually quelled as the Malian government softened its tone, revealed the fragile hold of international interveners on the north. Having failed to capitalize on initial local trust, the UN and France had instead built more distance from local society, paving the way for a spiral of negative rumors and resentment about their role in stabilizing the country. Meanwhile, the Malian state was withdrawing its scattered presence in the north, reducing any lingering administrative hold even further. The efforts toward breaking the northern deadlock had faltered, and the divide between south and north—and between operational headquarters and the northern hinterland—was growing deeper.

A Giant on Clay Feet

Even before the Kidal events that May, frustration was running high among the frontline soldiers facing the dangers up north, as well as among headquartered military officers in Bamako. Some soldiers and civilian staffers saw MINUSMA as the "most chaotic UN mission ever." Its structure was uncommunicative; its offices were disconnected, sometimes literally so; and its logistics chain was faulty.

One Swedish soldier, Mikael, summed up the predicament by calling MINUSMA "a giant with a bloated head and clay feet." By this he meant that large numbers of bureaucrats had congregated in Bamako's Hotel l'Amitié while the dangerous sections of the north were in the hands of unprepared African soldiers. This division, it was clear to Mikael, had contributed to the protests, killings, and chaos of May 2014. MINUSMA's chain of command was faulty, he said; the mission should have supported the French as they planned to liberate the hostages in Kidal, but this did not happen—and for that reason the French would not enter either, leading to the atrocity.

For this Mikael blamed inept African leadership. In the UN, "everyone's supposed to be the same," he said, echoing many of his Western military colleagues. By this he meant that officers who were inherited from an earlier West African military mission of 2013 were seen as on par with highly trained NATO counterparts.[6] In a face-saving exercise, the military commanders of MINUSMA were all African, Mikael said, even though some could barely use a computer; other officers mumbled similar complaints. Yet the fundamental problem was not simply about a few bad apples: rather, it was about much wider questions around the politics of intervention—including the rollout of a division of labor and of an unequal risk template unsuited to Malian realities, as discussed in this chapter.

In sum, the so-called multidimensional and integrated MINUSMA mission was beset by multidimensional problems. For a start, it could easily be accused of inhabiting a gray zone between counterterror and "liberal peace" approaches to security, in addition to being hobbled by the various political problems attached to integrated missions since the 1990s (see, e.g., Duffield 2010; Charbonneau 2017). On a practical level, it was stymied by ill-equipped soldiers and officers, bad communication, social divisions, dreadful logistics, and bureaucratic overhang. The efforts of the many highly able military and civilian staff in HQ were bludgeoned by a chaotic system at every turn—a system, moreover, imported from templates that had failed elsewhere and that has been applied without much thought.

In the politically hostile Mali context, this chaos spelled disaster both for the prospect of peace and for the more immediate safety of those at the sharp end of intervention, whether locals, blue helmets, or humanitarians. Cowed by fear of external threats, the UN mission had not addressed its *internal* mess (Fast 2014), which was now adding greatly to the risks for staff and locals, along with political questions around MINUSMA's awkward role.

Among these risks was one that had been left to linger amid the obsession with insecurity: political risk. As noted, it was becoming amply clear that most Malians had had enough of the international presence. "The Africans among them come here with deals," alleged one local aid worker. "They might pay 20 percent to their boss [for being sent on a mission], so why would they take any risks?" In this critique, shared by other workers, a bunkered existence in the north meant that the money just kept rolling in (in theory, at least, given that pay was sometimes withheld by superiors). To make up for the shortfall or simply to moonlight, soldiers sold their supplies—including UN-provided water bottles—to middlemen. These later ended up on markets in the north, undercutting merchants.

Besides the financial side effects of deployment, there were also more insidious social consequences. Prostitution was becoming rife in a country with a limited market to begin with, according to some aid workers. In Gao, one NGO worker recalled in dismay, poor young women had been coming to a clinic for AIDS tests. They were not the typical profile for these tests, so the doctor asked them why—and was told it was because the soldiers asked them to show their paperwork before sleeping with them. The implications of all this were dire in a once-proud and deeply Muslim country, which was moreover trying to recover from a jihadist takeover.

If the military and political sides of the mission were languishing, the humanitarian efforts of the UN and the NGOs were doing only marginally better. Accusations flew about frittered-away assistance. In Bamako, aid for displaced people had disappeared into the pockets of partner staff or false beneficiaries. Up north, the wastage was worsened by the division of labor created by "remote programming," expat aid workers said when speaking in private. One recalled a flash visit of hers to a northern town, where an NGO had organized distributions of supplies via the head of the village, who simply had given everything to his own relatives. "I was shocked!"

This should not be shocking. The squandering of aid is a long-standing problem, as is to be expected when vast humanitarian supplies suddenly enter a crisis-hit area. In northern Mali, this had been the case since the 1970s droughts—yet now the corruption was worsened by lack of oversight, as headquarter staff remained in Bamako, at one remove from the scramble for funds.

Some donors were becoming increasingly skeptical and outspoken about the failed aid efforts. One representative of a major European funding body said: "It's incredible . . . in Kidal, Gao, and Timbuktu, there's a frustration [with the UN] that is turning toward the humanitarians, but no one talks about this!" To him, one key problem was the "self-limitation" imposed on NGOs: "it's security that justifies everything." When he took field trips to remote parts of the north, NGO managers rarely joined him. Instead, they stayed in Bamako, with its endless meetings, parties, and paper-pushing. "They eat all resources, produce reports, and create new little strategies," he said, echoing Malian complaints about the inaction of peacekeepers. "They have to justify their salaries!" The "absorption capacity" of these remotely managed NGOs was "nonexistent," he said, which in turn limited the sums that funders were willing to cough up for new projects. "We see cartons of Plumpy'Nut [a nutritional supplement] in the market of Gao, and the supplies that are distributed just disappear." Worse, there was a lack of "accountability toward beneficiaries." To him, remote management was all about more remoteness and no management, creating a huge acceptance problem.

"Who was attacked when [rebels] entered Menaka?" he asked, referring to the armed groups' entry into this northern town after the Malian forces' routing in Kidal in May 2014. It was two large international NGOs with little local acceptance, he said, rather than Médecins du Monde, which had built up a strong local presence since the conflict. "It's the ones that don't have a grounding in the community who are being attacked." As with the UN peacekeepers, the humanitarians had let an obsession with external threats to expat staff drive their strategies, with severe consequences for their operations and local workers' safety.

Soon after the May protests in Bamako and Gao had receded, the attack came that aid agencies had long feared. Two Malian humanitarian workers were killed in the north when their vehicle was blown up by a remote device. Their employer was a frontline partner to the UN High Commission for Refugees and had been using one of UNHCR's white vehicles. The NGO's global head flew in to pay his respects, but as expected, little news reached Western audiences of this tragedy, unlike what would be the case if Western workers had been killed. A week later, a suicide bomber rammed his way into a crumbling peacekeeping camp, leaving four Chadian soldiers dead, again gaining minimal media coverage. In the coming months, attacks on peacekeepers escalated via suicide bombs, lobbed missiles, and improvised explosive devices. By the end of February 2015, there were forty-six dead in the mission; five were Asian and forty-one were African, with eighteen of these from Chad alone. And the numbers swiftly rose.[7]

It was amid this bloodshed that the UN peacekeeping chief stepped in to the Security Council to deplore the violent attacks. Casualties could mount for only so long before eyebrows were raised, including by the otherwise steadfast Chadian government.

While discussions unfolded in New York, back in Mali it was clear by late 2014 that the UN—poised between the resentment of southern Malians for their seeming inaction and renewed targeting by supposed jihadist fighters in the north—had been drawn into the Mali conflict, not as keepers of an elusive peace but as hapless combatants and soft targets while the French reorganized their forces. Instead of distancing themselves from the northern danger zone, they had been pulled right into it.

The barriers erected to shield the internationals from local society and regional threats kept failing to bring security. In early 2015, as protests against the UN unfolded yet again, peacekeepers fired into the crowds outside the MINUSMA camp in Gao, killing three and stirring yet more protest. Meanwhile, as noted, insecurity kept spreading across the north and into Mali's central regions as the peace process between rebels and government faltered. In 2015, terror attacks pierced the Bamako bubble before extending farther across the region, hitting neighboring Burkina Faso and its capital, Ouagadougou, in 2016.

As other chapters in this volume show, diffuse danger and bunkering often develop hand in hand in a vicious cycle. The initial mapping of danger onto Mali's territory and the unequal portioning of risky tasks across this map of intervention had partly "insured" more powerful Western interveners against the risks, yet the costs were significant, too, as seen in the political blowback of mounting protests and in the Bamako attacks of 2015. If the interveners had somehow shifted tack and tried to integrate into the urban fabric—as previous generations of development workers had done—perhaps the political and security risks could have been contained as tensions rose. Instead, once trouble hit, separation grew. Instead of outreach to local society came more bunkering and further withdrawal. One European intelligence officer, reflecting on the eventual move of UN military headquarters from Amitié to Senou airport, recalled Somalia, where the African Union and UN have clustered for years in a high-security compound next to the Mogadishu airfield, as far removed from local society as possible and always with one eye on the exit route. Using a metaphor deployed by drone warriors, he described the international interveners as looking down on northern Mali through a soda straw, seeing only a tiny portion of its social terrain without managing to escape their heavily protected yet fundamentally fragile ivory tower.

Conclusion: The Quest for Connection

The Mali story since 2013 is a sobering one but perhaps should be expected. In part, it is a story of the blurry UN mandates and ill-applied mission templates that academics and officials have long criticized. It is clear by now that traditional peacekeeping models do not fit the "new wars" of the post–cold war era, characterized by a multitude of armed factions working from predatory and exclusivist agendas (Kaldor 1999), nor do they work well alongside the war on terror and its regional and local iterations. In Mali, security involves not only an array of international forces via MINUSMA but also foreign counterterror operations and externally imposed border security, all of which interact with the often violent Malian security apparatus. In addition to these official constellations, an ever-expanding range of armed factions, jihadist groups, and government-sponsored militias compete to control key smuggling routes through the desert, or patches of central and northern Mali, while individuals often switch sides and hold multiple allegiances in a confusing array of constellations (Strazzari and Whitehouse 2015). In this context, the UN is dealing with something more akin to criminal syndicates, which requires a vastly different type of intervention from that adopted during the cold war.

Instead of squaring up to this challenge, however, the reaction has been to withdraw from it—both in the political sense of sticking to the wider UN template and in the physical sense of drawing distance to the problem. One adviser to the UN deputy secretary-general, frustrated with the lack of progress, asked me in New York, "If the price to be up north is essentially that we have to hunker down in bunkers, then what's the point?" No stabilization, no policing, no securing of areas could happen from within the fortress, he said—and much less so when the biggest fortress of all was a thousand kilometers south, in Bamako.

Worse, and to return to the key theme of this chapter, the fortress model and its associated division of labor is at best a clumsy protection mechanism against asymmetric warfare tactics that, as the editors of this volume put it in the introduction, "find in cities one major site for their enactment." The enemy is swift on its feet, dominating social media and spreading news of even the most distant attack on peacekeepers far and wide within hours or minutes. In this game, the biggest prize with the most "juice" (to cite one international worker) was precisely the well-guarded compounds and plush hotels such as the Radisson: they ensured instant coverage across international media.[8] By contrast, the UN operated a creaking machinery. Reusing the Swedish soldier's description, MINUSMA's clay feet were, by 2014–15, wobbling from asymmetric attacks, as well as from the resentment besetting its very presence in Mali.

Two caveats are in order. First, armed groups had their own interests in continued violence that would persist no matter what the interveners did or did not do. Second, Western internationals *were* present in the north, as noted, but in a very limited sense. The Swedes and Dutch (and, later, Germans) handled intelligence, while the latter plus the French conducted violent raids. Yet this kind of military engagement remained bare-boned. Tuareg groups sometimes referred to the Dutch forces as "tourists" as a means of disparaging them after their raids, which moreover could lead to severe negative blowback for the less well prepared—and non-European—parts of the UN mission. The risks, in other words, were real, yet the ways in which they were handled, mapped, and *distributed* were shaped by the political geography of danger, distance, and withdrawal.

A very different path for Mali and its interveners could be chosen. Instead of strengthening the divide between headquartered capital and dangerous hinterland, interveners must take risks and deploy into areas where they can make a difference and start building genuine relationships with local groups that hold the key to ending conflict. Instead of strengthening bunker walls, risk protocols, and unequal divisions of labor, interveners have broad scope for weaving themselves into the social fabric on a more equal footing. Here, the solution to Mali's troubles must, to a large extent, be found in the very civic capabilities mentioned earlier in this chapter. Taking us back to the discussion of urban subjects in the introduction to this volume, we must note, however, that urban modes of conviviality in Bamako are part of a much larger sociocultural fabric that has sustained Mali throughout the postcolonial period. Further, in the deserted north, *connectivity* has long been a "precondition for human survival" (Scheele 2012, 14). Establishing connections that have been torn apart by conflict and competing economic interests, while building new ones among northerners, southerners, and interveners, is essential for moving out of the impasse of confrontation, protest, violence, and withdrawal.

Besides building on Mali's varied civic capabilities, those of the interveners themselves also need to be thrown into the mix.

Indeed, many international interveners were acutely aware of the limitations of the disconnected mode of business in Mali and actively tried to go beyond it, as noted in passing above. Some aid workers and UN officials skirted stringent security protocols to travel north on missions. Others tried to tweak or subvert UN rules within Bamako—including by venturing out of the fortified hotel headquarters to talk to protesters and listen to their views. One leader of a Swedish peacekeeping contingent explained to me in spring 2016 how he had actively gone beyond the risk-averse strictures of his Timbuktu mission and helped to defend the town against attackers while meeting rebel leaders. Another UN worker recalled how she had almost single-handedly been running one of the most dangerous camps in northern Mali. In other words, the civic capabilities of workers can be harnessed and tied into Mali's civic fabrics, which remain paramount.

To return to one key example from this chapter, the Bamako hosts of northern IDPs stand as a model of hospitality in times of adversity. Their city of open compound doors, rather than the divided city of barricaded enclaves, can perhaps lead the way toward a different model of engagement with a supposedly Malian conflict that at its heart is a *globalized* problem searching for a global as well as a local solution.

Notes

This article draws on materials from the author's monograph *No Go World* with University of California Press (Andersson 2019) and from his article in *Current Anthropology* (Andersson 2016). University of California Press and *Current Anthropology* are gratefully acknowledged.

1. See Associated Press reports of the meeting on January 6, 2015.
2. Space constraints preclude a longer discussion of the history and dynamics of Mali's conflict. For one multiauthored intervention, see Lecocq et al. 2013; on MINUSMA, see also Charbonneau 2017.

3. See Tham Lindell and Nilsson 2014 on logistics problems and reports of attacks on local communities.

4. For more on the division of labor and its consequences, see a series of reports by the Danish Institute of International Studies, https://www.diis.dk/en/region/mali.

5. The policy on using nonwhite staff in the north was rarely formalized explicitly but was common among all the UN agencies and NGOs I interviewed. Sometimes it included deploying black Western staff north as well, some workers said. Local (Malian) staff also would include northern Tuareg; that is, not only black Africans.

6. Sweden is not part of NATO, but its military forces have become closely aligned with NATO, including through participation in both Libya and Afghanistan.

7. In March 2015, two Dutch peacekeepers died when their helicopter crashed in an accident. Figures are available from the DPKO Web site, https://peacekeeping.un.org/en/fatalities.

8. For similar reflections (if not conclusions) regarding the security risks inherent in MINUSMA's bunkering approach, see the security analysis by Bruxelles2, http://www.bruxelles2.eu/2016/06/02/la-minusma-severement-attaquee-a-gao-et-sevare-une-strategie-a-revoir/.

References

Andersson, Ruben. 2016. "Here Be Dragons: Mapping an Ethnography of Global Danger." *Current Anthropology* 57 (6): 707–31.

——. 2019. *No Go World: How Fear Is Redrawing Our Maps and Infecting Our Politics*. Oakland: University of California Press.

Andersson, Ruben, and Florian Weigand. 2015. "Intervention at Risk: The Vicious Cycle of Distance and Danger in Mali and Afghanistan." *Journal of Intervention and State Building* 9 (4): 519–41.

Autesserre, Séverine. 2014. *Peaceland: Conflict Resolution and the Everyday Politics of International Intervention*. Cambridge: Cambridge University Press.

Bergamaschi, Isaline. 2014. "The Fall of a Donor Darling: The Role of Aid in Mali's Crisis." *Journal of Modern African Studies* 52 (3): 347–78.

Chandrasekaran, Rajiv. 2006. *Imperial Life in the Emerald City: Inside Baghdad's Green Zone*. London: Bloomsbury.

Charbonneau, Bruno. 2017. "Intervention in Mali: Building Peace Between Peacekeeping and Counterterrorism." *Journal of Contemporary African Studies* 35 (4): 415–31.

Collinson, Sarah, and Mark Duffield, with Carol Berger, Diana Felix da Costa, and Karl Sandstrom. 2013. *Paradoxes of Presence: Risk Management and Aid Culture in Challenging Environments.* Humanitarian Policy Group report, March. http://www.odi.org/sites/odi.org.uk/files/odi-assets/publications -opinion-files/8428.pdf.

Duffield, Mark R. 2001. *Global Governance and the New Wars: The Merging of Development and Security.* New York: Zed.

———. 2010. "Risk-Management and the Fortified Aid Compound: Everyday Life in Post-Interventionary Society." *Journal of Intervention and Statebuilding* 4 (4): 453–74.

———. 2019. *Post-Humanitarianism: Governing Precarity in the Digital World.* Cambridge: Polity.

Fast, Larissa. 2014. *Aid in Danger: The Perils and Promise of Humanitarianism.* Philadelphia: University of Pennsylvania Press.

Kaldor, Mary. 1999. *New and Old Wars: Organized Violence in a Global Era.* Cambridge: Polity.

———. 2018. *Global Security Cultures.* Cambridge: Polity.

Lecocq, Jean Sebastian, with colleagues. 2013. "One Hippopotamus and Eight Blind Analysts: A Multivocal Analysis of the 2012 Political Crisis in the Divided Republic of Mali." *Review of African Political Economy* 40 (137): 343–57.

Pes, Luca Giuseppe. 2011. "Building Political Relations: Cooperation, Segmentation and Government in Bancoumana (Mali)" (PhD thesis, London School of Economics and Political Science).

Sassen, Saskia. 2012. "Urban Capabilities: An Essay on Our Challenges and Differences." *Journal of International Affairs* 65 (2): 85–95.

Scheele, Judith. 2012. *Smugglers and Saints of the Sahara: Regional Connectivity in the Twentieth Century.* Cambridge: Cambridge University Press.

Smirl, Lisa. 2015. *Spaces of Aid: How Cars, Compounds and Hotels Shape Humanitarianism.* London: Zed.

Strazzari, Francesco, and Bruce Whitehouse. 2015. "Introduction: Rethinking Challenges to State Sovereignty in Mali and Northwest Africa." Special issue, *African Security* 8 (4): 213–26.

Tham Lindell, Magdalena, and Claes Nilsson. 2014. "Utmaningar för FN: s stabiliseringsinsats i Mali." *FOI Report,* October.

Whitehouse, Bruce. 2013. "What's to Love About Mali? Four Things", *Bridges from Bamako* (blog), February 4, http://bridgesfrombamako.com /2013/02/04/whats-to-love-about-mali/.

2

Kabul

Bridging the Gap Between the State
and the People

FLORIAN WEIGAND

Flying into Afghanistan's capital, Kabul, airplane pilots must navigate a mountain range that surrounds the city, which lies 1,800 meters above sea level. In winter the mountains are covered in snow, creating a stunning panorama on sunny days. From the window of the plane one can see how the houses spread upward on the slopes of the mountains. Many of the smaller huts and houses have the same sandlike color and blend seamlessly with the terrain. The streets are narrow and bumpy, and from above, the traffic seems to be flowing slowly. Although Kabul might look like a large village from far away, it is actually a buzzing urban space. An estimated 4.2 million people live in Kabul Province (OCHA 2014), which is divided into 22 urban municipalities and 14 rural administrative districts (*Pajhwok Afghan News* 2014). In all of the predominantly rural Afghanistan, Kabul Province has the largest proportion of urban population (Belay 2010, 47).

Afghanistan's political and geographical landscape has been shaped by the war on terror, during which the Afghan state and foreign forces have tried to fight a growing insurgency. Even though most of the fighting happens in rural parts of the country, the war can be felt in Kabul; security is omnipresent. The pairs of helicopters that fly over my house several times per day at low altitude interrupt every conversation and make the windows shake. The green Afghan National Police's (ANP) pickup trucks are everywhere; a "ring of steel" of checkpoints surrounds the inner city center; and many roads are sealed off by the police and can be accessed only with a special license. With these and other security measures, the Afghan state responds to threats such as the growing number of insurgency attacks and criminal activities. However, despite all these and many other security practices, many people in Kabul City feel insecure.

Just a stone's throw from looming checkpoints and barriers, people's experience is different. From the city center it is only a short car ride to the more rural administrative district of Farza in the northern part of Kabul Province. After passing the last security belt of checkpoints, one observes fewer and fewer security measures. Far fewer police and army vehicles can be seen. Farza was comparatively secure in previous years, but the influence of insurgents and criminals is on the rise. Still, people in this part of Kabul Province are much more confident about their security.

In this chapter I explore the reasons that people's perceptions of security between certain rural and urban parts of Kabul Province differ so much. The chapter is based on field research in Afghanistan that I undertook from May 2014 to December 2015. I describe and compare people's experiences in two zones of (in)security in Kabul Province: Kabul City and the more rural district of Farza. On the basis of this comparison, I develop ideas about the mechanisms linking security practices with perceptions of (in)security. I argue that inclusive security practices can help to enhance the level of perceived security and legitimacy of the state, whereas exclusive security practices and segregation contribute to increased perceptions of insecurity for most residents and delegitimize the state.

In Kabul City, the Afghan state is geographically close to the people and highly visible. It features a large number of symbolic buildings associated with the state, such as ministries and headquarters for security forces. This setting provides numerous attractive targets for frequent insurgency attacks similar to those in Baghdad. In response to this threat, the state protects itself with walls, and security forces, separating it from most of the people and segregating the city. People who are associated with the state and/or can afford to do so hide behind blast walls and armed guards, shifting the risk to less influential and poorer people.

The majority of people, who cannot afford a high level of protection, have become the main victims of insecurity. If a bomb goes off in front of a barrier, it tends to kill and injure the people on the street rather than those behind the wall. For instance, in January 2018, a bomb hidden in an ambulance detonated at a police checkpoint on a shopping street known as Chicken Street, close to the Ministry of Interior in Kabul, killing more than 100 and injuring more than 200, most of them civilians. Thus being close to potential targets such as state buildings, government officials, or security forces makes people less secure.

Because of the focus on protection, the police lack the resources to deal with the growing number of kidnappings and other criminal activities that affect residents on a daily basis. In addition, many police officers and other state officials rely on bribes to supplement their low salaries. As a consequence, people perceive the state as ineffectual—or even detrimental—to their security. In the vicious cycle of increasing security measures in response to attacks without providing security for most of the people, the state is increasingly delegitimized.

Conversely, in the rural district of Kabul Province, Farza, people feel secure despite the small number of security forces. Here the threat of insurgent attacks is lower due to a lack of attractive targets. However, also the response to threats in Farza is different from that in Kabul City, making it more difficult for insurgents to gain a foothold and less likely for threats to be carried out. Residents cooperate with the police, helping one another to fight crime and provide security. In this way both residents and security forces are more secure, allowing the state to gain its legitimacy.

This chapter investigates and explains this divergence in how threats are addressed in Kabul City versus Farza. I describe the specific threats, the application of security practices, and the resulting perception of (in)security.[1]

Zone of Insecurity: Kabul City

Geography of (In-)Security

The last official master plan for Kabul City dates from 1978; it concerned how to accommodate a growing population of up to two million in an area of 32,000 hectares (Konishi 2011, 16–17). Today about 3.6 (OCHA 2014) to 4.5 million (Konishi 2011, 20–21) people live in the 22 municipality districts that form Kabul City in an area that spreads over 102,270 hectares (Konishi 2011, :20–21). Almost 80 percent of these areas have remained informal settlements (Konishi 2011, 18). Kabul is still one of the fastest-growing cities in the world (Rasmussen 2014; Setchell and Luther 2009). A car ride without at least one major traffic jam is surprising and usually occurs only on Fridays and at night. Almost everyone seems to own a car, and the city is packed with Toyota Corollas.

Despite the growing population, airy public spaces exist in Kabul City. There are a number of parks where people go for walks or picnics, as well as the zoo—built during the earlier kings' modernization drive—which has survived decades of violence. But the more public the spaces, the more they tend to be dominated by men. It is clearly men who define life on the streets. In the vacant spaces between houses one can often find groups of boys or men playing football, volleyball, or cricket. When walking through Shahr-e Naw Park in the city center, one rarely sees women. However, in more restrictive spaces, such as the zoo and Bagh-e Babur garden, where people have to pay an entrance fee, women and families are more commonly seen. Farther from the main paths in Bagh-e Babur garden, one can even see teenage couples sitting together behind bushes. Indeed, their presence is an indication of subtle changes affecting public spaces in the city, alongside an emerging street art scene. For instance, enormous painted eyes appeared on a blast wall outside the presidential palace, a political message against corruption.

Security practices and measures are the main defining feature of Kabul City today. Security shapes not only the appearance of the urban space but also daily life within the city. For instance, public places have been turned into securitized spaces that only certain people can enter. Leaving the airport and entering the buzzing city, one is immediately exposed to security measures. Armed police officers guard the gate of the airport, frequently checking all vehicles and people entering the area. When driving by car to Kabul from one of the neighboring provinces, one must pass the security belt of checkpoints that surrounds the city. Police officers pull over some of the cars to check both vehicles and passengers.

There is a further ring of steel of smaller checkpoints around the city center. The city is permeated with blast-resistant walls

Figure 2.1 Street in Kabul, November 2016.

Source: Photograph by author.

and HESCO bastions, containers filled with soil or sand, often blocking parts of the street (figure 2.1.). In some cases, entire streets—for instance, those with important government agencies such as the Ministry of Interior or Ministry of Foreign Affairs— are sealed off and can be entered only with an approved numbered license plate or pass. The green Ford Ranger police pickup trucks can be seen at every corner, and the sand-colored vehicles of the Afghan National Army (ANA) are common. Convoys of armored cars transporting wealthy or important people and their accompanying armed guards on pickup trucks often cause blockages as they try to make their way through the slow-moving traffic faster than drivers who are perceived as less important.

But, as in the case of Bamako discussed elsewhere in this book, the international interveners have also helped shape the geography of the city. Walls, armored cars, and armed security contractors separate the people of Kabul from the employees of the various civilian international organizations (Andersson and Weigand 2015; Weigand and Andersson 2019). The headquarters for the international military mission, NATO's Resolute Support Mission, which replaced the International Security Assistance Force (ISAF) in 2015, still occupies a large part of the quarter called Shash Darak. The visibility of the foreign military forces, however, has decreased year after year, and the massive MRAPs (mine-resistant ambush protected vehicles), which replaced Humvees, are spotted on the streets of Kabul less often. Most of the transport of foreign military forces now happens by air. U.S. helicopters commute between Bagram Air Base in the north of Kabul and the headquarters of NATO's Resolute Support Mission, as well as between the airport and the United States, which causes constant noise and window rattling in the city center.

Threats and Sources of Insecurity

During the time of my research in 2014–15, attacks were frequent. The number of improvised explosive device (IED) attacks, targeting mainly members of the Afghan National Security Forces (ANSF), reached a new peak. There was also an increase in criminal incidents such as armed robberies and kidnappings of Afghan businessmen and foreigners. This trend was reflected in the interviews I conducted. The main concern raised by residents of Kabul City was the growing insecurity caused by both insurgents and criminals. My interviewees not only blamed the sources of insecurity (insurgents and criminals), but they were also dissatisfied with the authorities' response. Most people in Kabul City view the Afghan government and security forces as responsible for their security. Although these forces are highly visible in Kabul, my interviewees did not feel protected by them. From their perspective, the security forces not only failed to provide security but, being corrupt and predatory, were often even a source of insecurity. Their objective was protecting the state, prioritizing state security over the security of citizens.

News of attacks such as explosions spread quickly in Kabul. Within seconds, the incident is reported on social media, triggering discussions regarding the target and exact location. Although most people depend on TV and radio reports, word of mouth also plays a central role. After hearing the sounds of an explosion, before returning quickly to business, many people call and check on friends or relatives who might have been affected. Without exception, all the people I interviewed in the city center voiced security concerns; most of them emphasized that insecurity was the most pressing issue they were facing. All interviewees in Kabul City also agreed that they felt increasingly insecure. For instance, one interviewee explained: "Before 2001 our security was reinforced, but we had severe economic problems. After 2001 the government solved the unemployment to a large extent. But over the past four years, the security situation has become worse, and in addition the unemployment is becoming a problem again."

The perceived main sources of the growing insecurity were attacks and crime. In interviews people mainly blamed insurgents for the deteriorating security situation. They perceived insurgent groups as the masterminds of the IED attacks, suicide bombings, and rocket-propelled grenade (RPG) shelling, which killed foreigners, officials, and a large number of civilians. Many people expressed thoughts similar to those of Farhad,[2] who works as a security guard: "The Taliban and other insurgency groups are the main source of insecurity here." However, the interviewees did not think that these groups were isolated actors. It is a common perception that neighboring countries, particularly Pakistan and its Inter-Services Intelligence (ISI), support the insurgents.

Like student Adeeb, most interviewees thought that "Pakistan has always been our enemy." But the interviewees in Kabul City clearly distinguished the Pakistani people from the government. Although many interviewees expressed their sympathy for the people—for instance, because of the hospitality they experienced while in Pakistan as refugees during the civil war—they voiced their frustration over the perceived Pakistani influence in Afghanistan, seeing it as the root of all insecurity. For example, many interview subjects thought that the Taliban were a Pakistani group used to destabilize Afghanistan.

In addition to the insecurity caused by insurgency groups, the people were also afraid of crime. Many interviewees reported that the number of robberies and kidnappings in their neighborhood was growing steadily. They were particularly worried about the increasing number of kidnappings in the center of Kabul that were targeting people regardless of their political orientation, motivated only by the hope for ransom money.

As a consequence of the growing insecurity, coupled with economic stagnation, many interviewees looked back at past regimes with positive feelings. The achievements of former President Hamid Karzai were frequently emphasized. Hameed, a shopkeeper, explained: "We liked the Karzai regime because there were rules and regulations." But others had reference points further back in history. For instance, security guard Farhad praised the achievements of the last Communist president (1987–1992), claiming that "the only person who has ever provided security for us was Dr. Najibullah."

Security Practices and Perceptions

The people I interviewed in Kabul City were extremely disappointed by the failure of the government and the ANSF to provide security. They clearly distinguished between the behavior of different actors. The ANA is generally considered to act in the interest of the country and the people. University student Adeeb said: "I think just the ANA should be providing security in the future, because they have been working well so far." This positive perception can be explained by the limited interaction between the people and the army in Kabul. Even though the army is visible throughout the city, it does not intervene in citizens' daily lives. For example, soldiers usually do not check people or cars. Adeeb considered the main responsibility of the army to be defending Afghanistan against potential enemies such as Pakistan. Others also believed that the army is fulfilling this role well.

Compared with perceptions about the ANA, those of the Afghan National Police (ANP) are different in Kabul City. Many people explained that they consider the police to be the main force responsible for ensuring their security. Some were indeed grateful for the presence of the ANP, believing that those forces help to mitigate the risks of crime and attacks. One interviewee was pleased that the "police patrol in the city, especially at night." However, most people thought that the police are failing to achieve their primary mission of ensuring security.

Many interviewees reported that they were afraid of encountering police officers. People often felt they were treated as potential threats or as an additional source of income for the officers. A police general shared the perception of the citizens of Kabul in an interview: "Seventy percent of the police officers do what they want. They neither follow orders nor do they respond to the needs of people. They arrest whom they want and release them once enough money has been paid." He saw the recruitment of criminals and limited training as the core of the problem, complaining that almost all officers had a criminal record and were trained poorly to serve as low-paid fighters rather than effective police officers: "When people were recruited for the police, in the past they were trained for six months. The training was only about code of conduct, not fighting at all. . . . The Americans and British train the officers for two weeks and then call them 'experts of the battlefield.'" This illustrates the prevailing focus of creating a police force that can fight to protect the Afghan state but is incapable of protecting and supporting its citizens, as they are not actually trained in policing.[3] Hence residents often do not see the police as a stabilizing force but, instead, complain that they are a source of insecurity. "If you see a police officer on the street, you want to go another way," an interviewee in Kabul—ironically, a prosecutor—told me.

Another set of actors who play a role in the provision of (in)security are foreign military forces. The perception of these forces varies widely; Karlborg (2015, 16), in her study on the perceived legitimacy of the international forces in Kabul, concluded: "In certain respects, the ISAF presence is evaluated through a liberation frame, while in others, it is evaluated through an occupation frame." Many people think that the international military is crucial for the survival of the Afghan state. For instance, one interviewee stated that "the international forces shouldn't be leaving the country but should stay to support the people and the government." Similarly, student Temur explained: "The international forces brought a lot of change and improvement to our country. . . . They play a big role in providing security." Nevertheless, there also are more critical voices in Kabul, often criticizing the behavior of the international military forces. The police general explained his rejection of the international military forces, saying that "any member of ISAF can search any house and kill anybody. They can do what they want."

Finally, the Taliban was also perceived by interviewees in Kabul City as playing a role as a security provider—despite the dominant perception of insurgents as the main source of insecurity. Some interviewees grew up in other parts of the country or commute between their home province and Kabul to work or study. Often these provinces are fully or partly under the control of Taliban groups, enabling the interviewees to compare different authorities in light of their own experience. Although some who are working for the government or international organizations are too frightened to return to their home cities and prefer remaining in Kabul, those who are not directly affiliated with one of the authorities in the city in some cases prefer the authority of the Taliban. An interviewee from Wardak Province who studies in Kabul told me: "We don't like the Afghan security forces . . . such as the ANP because they aren't able to provide security for us. I think the Taliban are better than the ANP for us." Another student from Wardak explained further: "We don't like the Afghan security forces because they often treat people badly and sometimes bother innocent people." His vision therefore was that "just the Taliban should be providing security in the future."

Kabul City can be characterized as a zone of high-profile security measures but perceived insecurity. This urban insecurity is driven both by attacks on the large number of targets with a symbolic value that represent the state or the foreign forces, and the increasing number of criminal activities. The interviewees were generally disappointed by the way in which security forces were dealing with these threats. Even though security practices are highly visible in Kabul City, they have failed to contribute positively to residents' perceived security. Ironically, being close to the Afghan security forces or the foreign military forces often can increase the risk of becoming a collateral casualty of an insurgent attack. Further, people often consider the security forces themselves to be a source of insecurity. Although the army is still widely accepted, possibly also because of its limited scope for causing insecurity, the police often are seen as a threat. In many cases, the remaining support for the ANSF does not seem to be based on trust in the forces or ideology but simply a lack of alternatives. Shopkeeper Edris summarized his frustration: "Security belongs to the nation, not to the government." In the Afghan capital, however, the state is busy protecting itself and failing to provide security for its citizenry.

Zone of Security: Farza District

Geography of (In-)Security

Driving out of Kabul City to the north of the province, one sees rapid changes in the geography. Traffic on the main road that goes all the way to the provinces of Balkh and Kunduz remains hectic, but the number of houses decreases the farther one drives. More and more often, large gardens can be spotted behind mud walls. In addition to the people in the urban areas of Kabul City, a rural population of around 700,000 in the wider province (OCHA 2014) live in the 14 administrative districts that surround Kabul City.

Turning left off the main road after driving about half an hour, one enters the small road to Farza District. Farza is one of the more rural districts of Kabul Province. With a population of around 21,500 people in 18 villages, Farza District is also one of the smallest in Kabul Province (OCHA 2014;

Pajhwok Afghan News 2014). The road connecting Farza with the main road is narrow but in good shape. There are only a few cars on the road and green gardens spread out next to small houses across the flat land on both sides of the road. Even though the drive from the city center to Farza is short, it feels like one has entered a different world.

Farza is situated in the northwest of the Shomali plain at the foot of the Hindu Kush, an area once known as Kabul's garden. It had been a lush, fertile area and a popular destination for weekend picnics for people from Kabul. But heavy fighting and the Taliban's scorched-earth policy turned the area into an uninhabitable desert (Schetter 2005, 15; Snow et al. 2009, 8; Isby 2010). Throughout the late 1990s, the people of Farza were living on the frontline between the Taliban and the Northern Alliance, as the forces of Ahmad Shah Massoud were based close by in the Panjshir Valley (Snow, Dennys, and Zaman 2009, 8). The Taliban's summer 1999 offensive leveled Farza. According to Snow et al (2009 8), the military operation "was marked by summary executions, the abduction and disappearance of women, the burning of homes, and the destruction of other property and agricultural assets, including the cutting down of fruit trees." Many people were deported, and much of the remaining population fled to Panjshir, Kabul, or neighboring countries (Snow et al. 2009, 8). Only after the U.S.-led invasion in 2001 did people start to return and recultivate the land (Meek 2001). Today many fruit trees are flourishing again, and life has slowly returned to the villages of Farza.

Life in Farza appears to be somewhat peaceful nowadays. In contrast to Kabul City, security forces are not highly visible here. One rarely sees police or army officers on the streets of Farza, nor are there many armed people to be seen in general. I encountered police officers only on my first trip to the district.

Driving down the small road toward the district center, I was stopped at a small checkpoint. The officers were surprised to see a foreigner and invited me in for tea. I declined and continued my journey to the district center, where I met another police officer, who invited me for lunch. Not wearing a police uniform but plain clothes, he took me to his house in his old and dented green police pickup truck and asked how he could help me with my research.

Threats and Sources of Insecurity

Spending time in Farza in 2014 and 2015, I felt secure and never at risk when walking around in the district. Most of the people I interviewed in Farza had experienced a high level of insecurity during the Taliban time and had been forced to move to Panjshir or Pakistan. They had only returned after 2001. Today they are generally happy with the security situation in the district, instead demanding improvements to other services, such as health care. People reported an increasing number of criminal and insurgency activities in the provinces but thought that the growing danger was targeted successfully despite a smaller number of security forces in the district. The interviewees explained that they manage to achieve security through close cooperation with and coordination between security forces and the people living in the district. The members of the elected community *shuras* (councils) and the police meet on a regular basis. So just a short drive from the center of Kabul City, people trust, support, and are satisfied with the work of the police.

The most essential needs that Farza's residents raised in the interviews were basic services such as electricity and better health care. But although most people were not entirely happy with the status quo, many interviewees acknowledged that things were moving in the right direction. For example, a shopkeeper from Qala-e-Karim village pointed out: "Our most essential need is electricity and asphalted roads. Before we had a lack of drinkable water. But this problem has already been solved." Not a single interviewee in Farza mentioned security as a major concern. This perception stands in stark contrast to their earlier experiences. Mahmood recalled: "During the time of the Taliban, it was very insecure. Our gardens were burned down, our houses were robbed, and the fruits in our gardens were stolen." Similarly, Abdul from Hassan Khail village said: "During the Taliban regime, people were dishonored, houses were robbed, gardens were burned down, and the values of humanity were called into question. Now, fortunately, things have changed for the better. People's rights are observed, their property is secure, and they live in a peaceful environment."

All the people I talked to confirmed this view of Farza as being very secure. Many interviewees expressed thoughts similar to Mahmood's: "In Farza District, insecurity does not exist at all. While some people might still be armed, they hide their weapons." The comparatively good security situation in Farza almost certainly can be explained in part by the different kinds of threats in the districts, as many insurgent attacks in Kabul Province now appear to be targeting sites with high symbolic importance, such as highly secured ministries, hotels, or military convoys. Hence Farza as a rural district with no prominent institutions is a far less attractive target for insurgents than Kabul City. Similarly, there are more incentives for insurgents and criminals in Kabul City, where many of the wealthy Afghans and foreigners live.

Nevertheless, most of the fighting in Afghanistan takes place in rural areas. The Taliban is successfully expanding its control in many parts of the country. Increasing insurgency, therefore, is also a potential threat for districts such as Farza, although of a different kind compared with the attacks conducted in Kabul. Indeed, my interviewees reported a growing number of criminal and insurgency activities in the district from mid-2015 onward; no security incidents were reported to me in the year before. Some interviewees pointed out, though, that petty crime continued to occur at a low level. For instance, Zabi complained: "Here are some drug addicts who cause insecurity." However, interviewees also reported more serious threats. For instance, an interviewee from Hassan Khail village said in summer 2015: "One of my relatives here is a businessman. Some days ago he received a letter saying 'If you don't give us 50,000 USD we will kidnap your son or another member of your family.'" An interviewee from Fainda village also reported a potential threat: "One day I was at the local school and saw a person with explosive material. I called the police and they arrested him." But despite the growing danger, the interviewees from Farza were satisfied with the current security situation.

Security Practices and Perceptions

Several reasons explain why people continue to feel secure in Farza despite the growing threats. Some people I talked to outlined the relevance of history. They emphasized their longing for peace after experiencing so much violence and destruction. One interviewee argued: "Three decades of war and the extremist Taliban regime made people hate violence. Therefore, people prefer not to start or get involved in conflicts." This is unusual, as in many cases the war destroyed the sense of community and traditions of providing security in Afghanistan.

Aside from how the sense of community evolved in Farza, all interviewees agreed that the key to success was a more cooperative way of providing security, which works despite or because of the small number of security forces. According to the interviewees, the number of police officers for the entire district is only around 50. They are trained the same way that all other police officers are trained, including those in Kabul City. But the people with whom I talked pointed out that the small number was sufficient to provide security because residents were coordinating closely with the security forces. This indicates that police officers' training is not the only factor; rather, the overall culture of security provision at a certain duty station also matters. One of the community authorities explained: "Security reinforcement is designed in a way that involves all community members. . . . Security is the result of close cooperation between the people and police, while neither of the parties would be able to achieve security alone."

Almost all the other interviewees explained this success in a similar way. For example, the principal of a local school said that "security is provided by both people and police," and another interviewee said: "Security is provided by the people in close coordination with the security forces. . . . As there are only 50 police officers, they couldn't ensure security without the support of the people." The head of the development council further outlined what collaboration between the people and the police looks like: "We patrol the main road ourselves. If we see suspicious individuals or groups, we chase them, report them, and, if we realize that they might escape before the police arrive, arrest them ourselves." In addition, people in Farza viewed the composition of the police as a success factor, in that it combines local expertise with external neutrality. Mahmood explained to me: "The ANP consists of residents from this area as well as some outsiders. Having people from this area in the police force helps to assist the police to find the right targets."

Citizens' perception of the security forces in Farza is also different compared with that in Kabul City. All interviewees in Farza expressed their satisfaction with all security forces, including the police, despite the small number of officers. For instance, a shopkeeper in the district center said: "We like all security forces in the area, and I always supported them." An interviewee from Qala-e-Karim village confirmed: "We are convinced by all security forces because they are the main source of security." Whereas interviewees in Kabul City distinguished carefully between the different actors in the security sector, most of the people I interviewed in Farza were happy with all of them, while some expressed a preference for the ANA over the ANP. Only the international forces are perceived mainly negatively. For example, an interviewee from Hassankhell village told me: "I don't like any international forces because they haven't achieved anything substantive for our country in the past 15 years." Others, like Shafiq, were indifferent: "If the international forces are present or not, it does not make a difference to our lives."

Policing in Farza appears to be similar to what the Afghan Local Police (ALP), a U.S.-sponsored village-level defense force, was supposed to achieve; however, it failed to do so in many cases, as the program often was co-opted by local power dynamics (Vincent, Weigand, and Hakimi 2015). Conversely, in Farza, policing appears to be driven by a collective interest in security rather than only the authorities' objectives. The people in Farza trust and feel respected by the police, and the officers appear to be interested in providing human security—that is, security for the people in the district that is also officers' home. This close cooperation between security forces and residents is driven in part by the shared history of violence under the Taliban and the small size of the district, resulting in community oversight, mutual dependencies, trust, and willingness to cooperate. That the police are partly sourced locally is likely to contribute positively to this relationship, as is the contingent of more neutral officers from other parts of the country. Forces from the outside, such as the foreign military, however, are perceived more as a threat than a source of security.

These conclusions on Farza need to be researched and developed further, also considering the changes that may have occurred in the district since 2015. My impression was that most people I talked to were happy to have the chance to state their opinion, but it is difficult to say to what extent they always felt secure and confident enough to share with me their honest views. The conclusion that emerged from the interviews I conducted is that the feeling of being included or considered in security practices helps to construct a perception of security and state legitimacy. But that does not mean that everyone in Farza is equally happy. I might have talked only to more or less influential people in Farza, who are content with the kind and degree of coordination, and it is possible I did not have sufficient access to marginalized people who would dare to speak up. For example, my access to female interviewees in rural Farza was more limited than in Kabul City. Further research is necessary to gain a deeper understanding—for instance, by looking at other zones of security and insecurity in the country more broadly, and paying more attention to the perspective of women.

Conclusion

People in Kabul Province have lived through times of conflict, destruction, and insecurity continuously over the past few centuries. Today insecurity again affects and alters daily life in the province. But comparing Kabul City with Farza District illustrates that the degree of (in)security people experience differs greatly between the urban center and the rural outskirts of the province. The interviews I conducted indicate that not only the kinds of threats but also the security practices and objectives contribute to the differences in perceived (in)security.

On the one hand, negative self-reinforcing dynamics are in place in Kabul City. Here the security forces are numerous and highly visible, but most people do not consider them to be helpful. Although the army is respected far more than its forces are encountered, the opposite appears to be the case for the police. People come across police officers at every corner but often feel less rather than more secure in their presence, as the officers are seen as predatory and corrupt. Some interviewees think that police officers are not trained to do so-called real policing, such as investigating crime, but are little more than poorly trained soldiers.

The relevance of international forces is decreasing and perceived differently. Some believe that they are essential for stability, but others see them as destructive occupying forces. Even though the various potential security providers and other authorities have different and competing objectives, they create a perception of the state as a network of national and international actors that defends itself but has no capacity for or interest in providing security for its citizens. Consequently, many people feel alienated from the state and see a large gap between the state and themselves. Still, most hope that the state will provide security, often because of a lack of alternatives. This perception also indicates that the insurgents' strategy is successful. By keeping the state busy with attacks, it is neglecting its citizens, resulting in decreasing trust in the security forces and, ultimately, in a reduced legitimacy of the state.

On the other hand, more positive self-reinforcing dynamics are in place in Farza District. Here, compared with residents of Kabul City, people are happy with the work of the Afghan security forces. Their satisfaction appears to be based on a perception of an inclusive security practice that rests on strong cooperation between residents and the security forces. The officers and the people trust one another, cooperate, and try to enforce human security for all. Taking the history of the district into consideration, this is surprising, as war tends to destroy traditions and community relationships. However, people in Farza once again have developed a strong sense of community and see their history as an incentive to provide security more successfully in the future. However, although authorities from Farza are perceived positively, the external foreign forces are viewed with a far greater degree of mistrust. In Farza the state and the people are part of the same community and jointly take care of their security.

The success in Farza rests not only on the willingness of the state authorities to cooperate with the people but also on the ability of the people to organize themselves and cooperate with state authorities. This is much easier to achieve in a rural setting, where the community is small and defined and includes state authorities as integrated members, and in which the threat is perceived to be external. In contrast to "urban capabilities" (Sassen 2012) in cities, this ability of rural communities perhaps can be termed *rural capabilities*. Rather than being an essential characteristic of Afghan culture, this term simply points to the broader civic potential of small-scale communities in the face of conflict.

However, the foregoing comment does not mean that we can conclude that rural security provision or community policing is necessarily better for people. The case of the Afghan Local Police illustrates the unpredictability of what can happen if policy blueprints are inserted onto a dynamic rural landscape on the assumption that the so-called pristine locale is more efficient or legitimate. The sense of community in Afghan villages often was destroyed by war and displacement or became fragile with ongoing conflicts over land rights. Further, the "enclavization" of any community—whether rural or urban—might have negative side effects, as the case of Karachi illustrates in this volume.

By and large, in Farza the local dynamics appear to have been beneficial. The case illustrates that cooperation between the state and the people in the interests of achieving security for all depends on developing a sense of community and an inclusive and participatory strategy, and on having authorities with a genuine interest in achieving human security rather than extracting protection money. As in Farza, an inclusive and human-centric security strategy might help to establish a virtuous cycle of state legitimacy and improved security. Achieving the same undoubtedly is much more difficult in a large urban area such as Kabul City, which, in addition, is the capital and therefore a symbolically attractive target for insurgent attacks. Trapped in a vicious cycle, the state in Kabul City protects itself through distance from its citizenry, not only failing to provide security but also becoming a source of insecurity itself, which delegitimizes the state and might foster further instability and insecurity.

Notes

I would like to thank Mary Kaldor, Saskia Sassen, Ruben Andersson, Jörg Friedrichs, Abe Simons, the authors contributing to this volume, and other friends and colleagues for their critical comments and valuable suggestions. My sincere appreciation goes to the interviewees and to Maiwand Rahimi and Mirwais Wardak for making my research in Afghanistan possible. This work was supported by the UK Economic and Social Science Research Council (ESRC grant number ES/J500070/1).

1. The chapter reflects the situation and perceptions in Kabul during my research in 2014–15. Since the time this research was conducted, the security situation in Afghanistan has deteriorated further. In addition, progovernment forces have become increasingly responsible for civilian deaths in the country, exceeding the number of civilians killed by antigovernment elements in the first quarter of 2019; see UNAMA 2019.
2. The names of all interviewees were changed for their protection.
3. See also Weigand 2013.

References

Andersson, R., and F. Weigand. 2015. "Intervention at Risk: The Vicious Cycle of Distance and Danger in Mali and Afghanistan." *Journal of Intervention and Statebuilding* 9 (4): 519–41. http://dx.doi.org/10.1080/17502977.2015.105 4655.

Belay, T. 2010. "Building on Early Gains in Afghanistan's Health, Nutrition, and Population Sector." Washington, DC: World Bank. https://elibrary.worldbank .org/doi/abs/10.1596/978-0-8213-8335-3.

Isby, D. 2010. *Afghanistan—Graveyard of Empires. A New History of the Border- land.* London: Pegasus.

Karlborg, L. 2015. "Enforced Hospitality: Local Perceptions of the Legitimacy of International Forces in Afghanistan." *Civil Wars* 16 (4): 425–48. https:// doi.org/10.1080/13698249.2014.984383.

Konishi, K. 2011. *Draft Kabul Master Plan.* Accessed August 9, 2019. http://pdf .usaid.gov/pdf_docs/PA00JMMJ.pdf.

Meek, J. 2001. "Scorched Earth Legacy of Vanished Regime." *Guardian,* November 17, 2001, http://www.theguardian.com/world/2001/nov/17/afghanistan .terrorism7.

OCHA (United Nations Office for the Coordination of Humanitarian Affairs). 2014. "Afghanistan: Population Statistics." Accessed 10, 2015. https://www .humanitarianresponse.info/en/operations/afghanistan/dataset/afghanistan -population-statistics.

Pajhwok Afghan News. 2014. "Kabul Administrative Units." http://www.elections .pajhwok.com/en/content/kabul-administrative-units.

Rasmussen, S. E. 2014. "Kabul—The Fifth Fastest Growing City in the World— Is Bursting at the Seams." *Guardian,* https://www.theguardian.com/cities /2014/dec/11/kabul-afghanistan-fifth-fastest-growing-city-world-rapid -urbanisation.

Sassen, S. 2012. "Urban Capabilities: An Essay on Our Challenges and Differences." *Journal of International Affairs* 65 (2).

Setchell, C. A., and C. N. Luther. 2009. "Kabul, Afghanistan: A Case Study in Responding to Urban Displacement." *Humanitarian Exchange Magazine* Issue 45 (December). http://www.odihpn.org/humanitarian-exchange -magazine/issue-45/kabul-afghanistan-a-case-study-in-responding-to -urban-displacement.

Schetter, C. 2005. "Ethnoscapes, National Territorialisation, and the Afghan War." *Geopolitics* 10 (1): 50–75. https://doi.org/10.1080/14650040590907712.

Snow, C., C. Dennys, and I. Zaman. 2009. "Conflict Analysis: Farza and Kalakan Districts, Kabul Province." Cooperation for Peace and Unity (CPAU),

March. Accessed August 9, 2019. http://cpau.org.af/manimages/publications /Conflict_analysis_farza_and_kalakan_district.pdf.

UNAMA (United Nations Assistance Mission in Afghanistan). 2019. "Quarterly Report on the Protection of Civilians in Armed Conflict. January to 31 March 2019." Accessed August 9, 2019. https://unama.unmissions.org/sites /default/files/unama_protection_of_civilians_in_armed_conflict_-_first _quarter_report_2019_english.pdf.

Vincent, S., F. Weigand., and H. Hakimi. 2015. "The Afghan Local Police— Closing the Security Gap?" *Stability: International Journal of Security & Development* 4 (1): article 45. http://dx.doi.org/10.5334/sta.gg.

Weigand, F. 2013. "Human vs. State Security: How Can Security Sector Reforms Contribute to State-Building? The Case of the Afghan Police Reform" (LSE International Development Working Paper Series 13-135). http://eprints.lse.ac.uk/62690/1/WP135.pdf.

Weigand, F., and R. Andersson. 2019. "Institutionalized Intervention: The 'Bunker Politics' of International Aid in Afghanistan." *Journal of Intervention and Statebuilding* (February 1). https://doi.org/10.1080/17502977.2019.1565814.

3

Baghdad

War and Insecurity in the City

ALI ALI

The 2003 U.S. military intervention in Iraq divided the city of Baghdad into two zones, green and red, green being the safest area in the city. The actions of the occupation authorities contributed to the creation of "hot zones" within the Red Zone. Hot zones were, in Baghdadi parlance, sites of intense armed conflict. They were areas in which armed groups sought to impose their own zones of control, fighting U.S. forces or other armed groups. They often targeted civilian populations, expelling those whom they believed would challenge their identity-based claims to power and extorting money and goods from those who remained.

In this chapter, I tell the story of how insecurity was experienced by people living in Baghdad in the aftermath of the U.S. invasion—a story that shows how insecurity is inextricably linked to exclusion, which is expressed through zoning. I focus on the neighborhood of Al Ghazaliyya in the western outskirts of Baghdad, bordering on Anbar province. It became a site of intense conflict between U.S. forces and armed groups emanating from various hinterlands that earlier had provided a refuge, based on kinship ties, from the intense bombing campaign that preceded the invasion.

Broadly speaking, there were two main processes of exclusion,[1] which were part of a process I describe in detail elsewhere as the systemic discarding of populations[2]—because they become superfluous, and possibly threatening, to political regimes that emerge from systemic transformations. First, the dismantling of the army and the de-Ba'athification undertaken by Paul Bremer, the head of the Coalition Provisional Authority (CPA) established after the invasion, involved systemically discarding the majority of those who had worked in both military and civil capacities for the former regime. Second, as Shia exile groups came to dominate the Iraqi government that was supposed to replace the CPA, Sunnis were systemically discarded from many public positions as a consequence of an emerging sectarian politics. Sunnis became a marginalized minority in a system that apportioned power in Iraq on the basis of communal identity, favoring Shias and Kurds.[3]

The discarding process led to the rise of armed groups, most of whom engaged in violent identity politics, criminal activities, and efforts to control space in the city through the violent demographic reordering. They attempted to establish zones of control within the Red Zone, challenging the presence of U.S. forces and rival armed groups and attacking populations that they believed were likely to challenge their identity-based claims to power. The initial U.S. response was to engage in brutal military tactics under the guise of the war on terror, transforming those areas into hot zones.

The peak of the violence took place in 2006–7—a mixture of insurgency and counterinsurgency, sectarian conflict, and violent organized crime. Then came the so-called surge, an American plan to return security to the country by increasing troops and applying a shift in counterinsurgency strategy toward what was known as a population-centric approach that was relatively and surprisingly successful, considering the odds (ICG 2008). From mid-2007, some of the militias were defeated, but the effects of their violence—the separation of Baghdad into communally unmixed zones—have been frozen into place by a network of concrete walls. Today some neighborhoods remain encircled with concrete walls three meters high and with only a handful of access points guarded by police or soldiers.[4] To the division of Baghdad into Red and Green Zone was added a new set of sectarian zoning arrangements.

The testimonies of Iraqis in this chapter provide case studies of how Baghdadis experienced the violent zoning in the city.[5] They were collected using narrative interview methods during fieldwork in Syria in 2010 about their experiences of daily life in Baghdad between 2003 and 2010. The narratives of Adnaan, Um Ahmed, and her daughter, Baan, are featured at length in this chapter as illustrative, but not representative, case studies. Adnaan, a former military officer, was discarded by the new postinvasion order but later worked with U.S. forces in his neighborhood to counter the dangers caused by armed groups. The narratives of Um Ahmed and Baan relate the dangers of living in a hot zone in more detail. They show how they addressed those dangers and how they eventually decided that leaving the neighborhood was the safest option. Less detailed testimonies from other Baghdadis are also presented in the chapter.

The Baghdad Context

Iraq's capital, like others, is a melting pot for the rest of the country. Before the Gulf wars, people moved there to work, study, and enjoy a life in the metropolis that was unavailable elsewhere in the country. The city was populated by rural migrants, residents from other cities, Kurds, Arabs, Christians, Mandaeans, professional classes, working classes, traders, refugees, students from Arab states that did not provide free education, and migrant laborers from Sudan and Egypt.

The 1991 Gulf War and the subsequent period of sanctions stripped the city, and the country, of most of its foreign residents. There had been a large number of Egyptian laborers, a legacy of the labor shortages from the Iran–Iraq war. But in 2000, a few remained, along with Sudanese migrant workers. There remained a population of Palestinian refugees at that time, although most had resided in the city since the 1950s and were very much a part of the city's fabric.[6] Also remaining were students from Arab states—especially neighboring Jordan—who came to Baghdad University for the low tuition fees it charged while offering a qualification that was still respected at that time. That qualification was a legacy of the huge resources that had been invested in public educational institutions over many decades.

Although the round City of Peace[7] was commissioned in 758 AD by the Caliph Mansur, little remains of ancient Baghdad, compared with other cities in the region, such as Damascus and Cairo, both of which retain extensive old cities with features from ancient eras. Historic buildings still stand in Baghdad, among them Al Mustansariyya school (1234), one of the first universities in the world.[8] But contemporary Baghdad, the inhabited space of the city, is modern. The population in 1947 was around 515,000 (Batatu 2004, 35, 133; Al-Qazzaz 2019). The 2004 estimate was 6.5 million.[9] The vast majority of its residential units are thus twentieth-century constructions that accommodated the rapidly expanding population of the capital after 1947.

After Iraq became a republic in 1958, Iraqi architects embraced Western building designs and materials such as concrete, iron, and cement, all of which are unsuited to the intense heat of the local climate (Al-Taie et. al 2012) and increase the urban heat island effect. British architects introduced these materials to Iraq during the British Mandate (1920–32), as well as modern urban planning. As a result, houses were built in straight lines adjacent to new streets; the English-Baghdadi style saw houses built far from one another along the banks of the Tigris, in contrast to the narrow alleyways of the Ottoman era, when houses were made of clay, gypsum, and wage—materials that naturally repelled heat (Al-Taie et al 2012). In 1980 the city had a $7 billion facelift as the government prepared to host the Non-Aligned Nations conference in 1982, though the group did not convene there because of the Iran–Iraq War (Al-Qazzaz 2019). Across the city, the government built new highways, wider streets, five-star hotels, and high-rises, as well as new bridges across the Tigris (Al-Qazzaz 2019).

High-rises are present in the central areas of the city, but the residential areas outside the center are low-rise, except for the minarets of mosques that dot the urban landscape, the towers of churches in Christian neighborhoods, and the majestic date palms to which many Baghdadis feel an emotional attachment. Most residential units outside the city center are houses rather than apartments, although this is changing because of the steep increase in land prices. In poor neighborhoods, houses are small and tightly packed, some with tiny yards. In the middle-class and wealthy neighborhoods, the houses are larger and there is more space between them, owing in part to the larger gardens, almost every one of which has a date palm. The houses have flat roofs, on which Baghdadis used to sleep at night when they felt safe enough to do so.

The streets are wide, and most offer little respite from the blazing sun. Baghdad's autumns and winters are short, and the spring and summer months are long and oppressively hot. The mean daily temperature from June to September is above 40°C with no rain.[10] August temperatures regularly hit the high 40s and can reach 50°C. Before the 2003 war, and after the recent improvements to security in the city, most socializing took place after sunset for respite from the scorching heat. The heat is a strong feature of the lived experience in Baghdad.

Despite Baghdad's being a large city, its residents maintain relations with their neighbors, ranging at the positive end of the scale from regular conversations to relations that resemble family ties. Commonly relations involve sharing food and visiting during Eid, and the children of the households play together. However, the Baghdadis I interviewed said this dynamic has changed since the "events"—the euphemism they use to describe the collection of horrors the city experienced under military occupation. As displacements took place, some neighbors protected one another's homes, but in some cases neighbors were involved in the expulsions. There was a climate of fear and generalized violence that led to neighbors of years—sometimes decades—being replaced with new households, the extent of whose relationship to a militia was unknown. Neighbors were a source of both security and insecurity, as later examples in this chapter illustrate.

Exit from the City: Safety in the Hinterlands

Many residents expected the entire city to be unsafe during the period of bombing and the battle to dislodge Saddam Hussein in 2003. However, there was no immediate mass exodus from Iraq, despite expectations from the United Nations High Commission for Refugees (UNHCR) in the run-up to the invasion.

UNHCR established emergency camps at the border regions of neighboring countries to deal with a million anticipated refugees (Marfleet & Chatty 2009). But "no substantial movements" were reported across Iraq's international borders in March 2003, and only "small numbers" were "trickling into Jordan and Syria" in April (UNHCR 2003a and 2003b). UNHCR prepared to supervise refugee returns and reintegration until general insecurity in Iraq prompted changes to the agency's policy statements in 2004 (Marfleet 2007, 406). The Iraqis I interviewed in Syria recalled that the major exodus was from Baghdad to the hinterlands, to escape the threat of bombing.

The city changed in the run-up to invasion. Majeed and other Baghdadis I interviewed described the changes, such as oil fires being lit by the Iraqi army. Plumes of smoke covered the sky over Baghdad, which the Iraqi army hoped would disrupt U.S. Air Force radar.[11] There was an increased military presence in the city; positions were manned by the Popular Army, a reserve force that included older men. News programs reported intensive diplomatic activity with world leaders who were visiting Saddam Hussein.

Mohsin, one interviewee, observed changes in Baghdad, noting a heavily increased security presence, which indicated to him that war was imminent. He also observed Baghdadis leaving the city in large numbers for the provinces. Anwar, another interviewee, recalled how the highways leading out of Baghdad were full of cars heading to the provinces. For a time, his own street was almost deserted. Mohsin's relatives left for an agricultural area near Ramadi, where his uncle owned land. Najmeh's family fled to Al-Qadisiya in southern Iraq, where her relatives owned agricultural land. Anwar's relatives left for Salah ad-Din province. Farah's family spent two months away from Baghdad in their village of origin in northern Iraq.

Zoning: Green and Red

When they returned to their city, Baghdadis found it divided between the Green Zone and the Red Zone. The Green Zone was a secure space equipped like an American suburb. People living there were sheltered from the lawlessness and privations that plagued the rest of Baghdad, what they referred to as the Red Zone (Chandrasekaran 2007, 18–19). Life in Baghdad's Red Zones contrasted sharply with that of the Green Zone. Only a few months into the occupation, "security officers insisted that Baghdad was insecure. The only safe place was inside the walls. That's why they called it the Green Zone" (Chandrasekaran 2007, 18). The U.S.-led coalition chose an already gated area in central Baghdad in which to base itself. On the western bank of the Tigris river stood a compound that included Saddam's Republican Palace, government buildings, and villas for his aides and bodyguards. The streets were greener and cleaner, and fewer people lived there than in the rest of Baghdad (Chandrasekaran 2007, 13). Saddam had built a tall brick wall around it with three guarded entrances. The Americans expanded the neighborhood by a few blocks and "fortified the perimeter with seventeen-foot-high blast barriers made of foot thick concrete topped with coils of razor wire" (Chandrasekaran 2007, 8–13). They quickly made it into "Baghdad's Little America"; a mural of the World Trade Center adorned one of the entrances to the main canteen, which served only American food (Chandrasekaran 2007, 8–13). The rest of Baghdad was a Red Zone of major insecurity.

Life in the Red Zone was extremely dangerous. Deaths, injuries, and destruction of infrastructure and housing were commonplace, and daily life was disrupted by the violence and the collapse of the state, in terms of essential public services and the security it provided. Many of the country's public institutions were systematically looted. The security situation immediately after the fall of Saddam's regime varied between different areas of Baghdad and of the country overall, but the general picture was one of decline. That decline reached a nadir from early 2006 until late 2007 after the bombing of the Shia Al-Askari Shrine in Samarra and a confluence of factors led to a state of violence in Iraq, in contradistinction to a state of law (Harling 2011). Basic services such as electricity and water supplies, the ordering of traffic, and law enforcement were no longer guaranteed by the state for some years after 2003.[12] Although the city's capacity to maintain such services had been weakened during 13 years of a harsh international blockade, Baghdadis could, for example, still expect electricity from the national grid. Mohsin's neighborhood expected between four and six hours a day of power cuts before 2003 but received only two hours' worth of electricity from the national grid after 2003.

Mobility was constrained by the prevailing circumstances. The climate of insecurity led people to make fewer and fewer outings after dark, and many women stopped driving because of the stories of carjacking and kidnapping. The growing number of checkpoints, concrete blast barriers, and dividing walls in the city increased journey times significantly. This was exacerbated by the reported flood of new cars arriving in the country, and the armored patrols of U.S. forces, which, said Baghdadis, after six months into the occupation began shooting at vehicles that approached too closely or too quickly.

Najmeh described her shock at the rampant crime, insecurity, and the presence of U.S. military forces on the city's streets: "there was no going out at night at all. . . . It was a whole month till we got some electricity." Shaykh Rami's sister lived close to a government compound where vehicles were stored; they were stolen by criminal gangs. Gangs were robbing and killing residents and one another. The growing insecurity and the number of armed checkpoints meant that outings were restricted to daytime and to those of absolute necessity. This restricted travel was highly problematic for a city like Baghdad, where the weather is hot and the evenings represent a period of relative respite from the oppressive heat of the day. This was compounded by the collapse of electricity provision from the national grid in many areas. Residents were compelled to depend on private generators, either purchasing their own or subscribing to a larger street generator, although the generators were not always reliable.[13] The city was thus defaced with ugly generator cables that weaved across the streets of many neighborhoods, sagging clumps of metal and plastic, an ever-present reminder of the ineptitude and corruption of successive Iraqi governments and occupation authorities. This was daily life in the occupied Red Zone.

A Hot Zone: Al Ghazaliyya and the Relationship to the Hinterlands

Al Ghazaliyya became part of the Red Zone after 2003. As Iraq descended into a state of violence and rival armed groups sought to impose their control through violent demographic transformations, Al Ghazaliyya became a hot zone.

The area was originally a mixed and sprawling residential neighborhood built on land given to government employees during the 1960s and 1970s. Its original inhabitants included officers from state security and armed forces, many of whom sold their properties soon after receiving them (Harling 2011, 53). The area was "punctured by large avenues and devoid of any deep economic or interpersonal neighborhood ties" and would have been vulnerable to a takeover by the Mehdi Army militia had it not been for its close relationship to the hinterland of Anbar, a hub of Sunni insurgent activity (Harling 2011, 53). Before the U.S. invasion, migrants from Anbar settled there, given that it was the urban setting closest to their places of origin. During escalating U.S. counterinsurgency operations in Anbar in 2004, an influx of displaced people sought refuge there; similarly, when violence escalated in Ghazaliyya, residents fled to nearby places in Anbar, such as Abu Ghraib (Harling 2011, 53).

The U.S. forces' approach to security in Iraq was shaped by the narrative of the war on terror and an outdated military logic (Kaldor 2012). In the early years after the invasion, they used brutal counterinsurgency methods similar to those seen in Vietnam and Algeria (Kaldor 2012, 166), including

> excessive use of force, widespread detention and torture and abuse as a means of extracting information, and the attempts to destroy the safe havens of the insurgents through the attacks on places such as Fallujah, Samarra, Najaf, or al-Sadr City. (Kaldor 2012, 166)

The war on terror spilled over from the hinterlands of Anbar into Al Ghazaliyya, and vice versa. Insurgent groups fought back. They used Al Ghazaliyya as a gateway into Baghdad, and consequently it "progressively fused with Anbar"; "its connection to the rural hinterland ensured the flow of resources necessary to hold off a determined Sadrist attempt to cleanse the area" (Harling 2011, 53).

The Sadrists' loosely organized militia, the Mehdi Army, largely composed of poor Shi'ia, also had its origins in the hinterlands. Their strongholds in Baghdad were the former *sarayif* of Sadr City, Shu'la, Washshaash, and Fudhayliyya (Harling 2011, 49). The *sarayif* were once shantytowns in Baghdad with poor sanitation and populated by southern Iraqis thought to be landless peasants from Amara. The *sarayif* were turned into residential units with sanitation in the 1950s (Batatu 1986 2004). Their populations remained on the socioeconomic margins, and hostility toward them was mobilized in instrumental ways by the regime of Saddam Hussein during the 1990s (Haddad 2011). The Mehdi Army recruited many of its Baghdadi members from these areas. Intensive fighting in Ghazaliyya, between the Mehdi Army in neighboring Shu'la, and Sunni insurgent groups based in Ghazaliyya, turned it into a hot zone. Ghazaliyya was strategically important in the battle for Baghdad because it was the gateway to the city from Anbar. To its immediate north was the Shu'la neighborhood; a canal with crossing points separated the two. U.S. forces had outposts in Ghazaliyya but were aloof when it came to the fighting between the Mehdi Army and armed groups fighting them, and the American forces did not proactively defend civilians from militias until later during the surge.

After the attack on the sacred Shi'ia symbol, the Al-Askari Shrine in Samarra in February 2006, the Mehdi Army embarked on a campaign of sectarian cleansing, expanding from the *sarayif* neighborhoods to mixed and middle-class areas (Harling 2011, 49–50). The Mehdi Army's methods were systematic. Harling (2011) noted that they established offices to ensure residents of their commitment to protecting the area, supported neighborhoods to form vigilante groups, and brought in reinforcements from other Sadrist strongholds to defend the area. Further, methodical attacks on shopkeepers aimed at disrupting the social fabric of neighborhoods, forcing residents to leave because of a lack of supplies (Harling 2011). They turned urban capabilities in on themselves. Mehdi Army forces aimed to isolate Sunni neighborhoods from each other and from the hinterlands of Anbar, particularly on the lifelines between Ghazaliyya and Al A'amiriya—another Sunni bastion in western Baghdad—and the nearby district of Abu Ghraib in Anbar (Harling 2011, 49–50).

Adnaan: Systemically Discarded

Adnaan was an officer in the Republican Guard. He lived with his family in an apartment that was part of a residential compound owned by the government in the heart of east Baghdad. It was close to the Tigris river, which meanders and divides the city between east and west. He told me that when the occupation began, he was prepared to give the United States a chance to fulfill the promises it had made about democracy and prosperity. "I thought that Iraqis might be living with the prosperity of the Gulf States, but that they would control their own destiny." However, as an army officer, his security was immediately affected by the Coalition Provisional Authority's dissolution of the Iraqi army, Adnaan was systemically discarded. He lost his income and became convinced that armed resistance was the solution to end the occupation, but later he changed his outlook.[14]

Shortly afterward, he had to leave his apartment in central Baghdad, after an exile party—the Iraqi National Accord (INA)—opened an office in the residential compound. There were six buildings in the compound, nine floors high with 38 apartments in each building, inhabited mainly by officers and their families. The threats came six months after the occupation began, on the basis that the apartments were distributed to people who were "part of the former regime." Although some of Adnaan's neighbors joined the INA, they warned his family that its members were looking for him because he was an army officer. "They started asking around: where is so and so? *That* question asked in *that* situation means that they are looking for you. . . . So I left the apartment, but my family remained."

INA members continued to inquire about him, asking his wife where he was. Later his family rented an apartment elsewhere.

In 2004 he bought a house in Al Ghazaliyya. But with no salary or pension, Adnaan earned money by using his private car as a taxi. He had lost his military position and pension through different phases of the purge of the old order, and it was a segment of the new order, the INA, that forced him to leave his home.

The legitimacy of the nascent state was violently contested and was manifested in the streets. Government ministers and employees received frequent death threats. In addition to the exclusions from purges, Adnaan suffered from the side effects of this heightened sense of insecurity resulting from the new order. One day he waited with a passenger by a mosque where he had arranged to meet someone. Little did Adnaan know that the mosque was close to the home of the then–Minister of Justice, who had received death threats. The cigarette sellers nearby, who spotted Adnaan and his passenger waiting, were from the Secret Police. Armed men in civilian clothes soon arrived and detained Adnaan and his passenger at the Serious Crime Office. He was held by Iraqi forces for four days, then detained by U.S. forces for eight months. After his release he returned to Al Ghazaliyya.

The purge of Adnaan did not end there. He later worked with U.S. forces to secure his neighborhood from criminals and terrorists. His story continues after Um Ahmed and Baan explain what it was like living in the hot zone.

Living in the Hot Zone: Um Ahmed and Baan

Um Ahmed lived with her husband, two daughters, and son in Al Ghazaliyya. Her husband worked in the information technology section of the Iraqi army, creating and operating administrative databases. He had retired some years before the invasion, partly out of concern that if he had risen too high in the ranks, someone would make problems for him because he was a Shia. He opened a bookstore in nearby Amiriya while Um Ahmed worked as a teacher.

The school her teenage daughter, Baan, attended was in a hot zone in Khadhraa', just southeast of Ghazaliyya on what locals called "the road of death." Along its northern and southern edges ran two important highways going eastward into central Baghdad and westward to Anbar, leading to Abu Ghraib, Fallujah, and Ramadi and toward the border with Jordan and Syria. One of the highways ran along Camp Liberty, a vast U.S. military base, immediately to the south of which lies Baghdad International Airport, where U.S. forces also based themselves.

Baan's school was on a road that ran north to south between the two highways, with residential streets branching off on both sides. Frequent clashes between U.S. forces and different armed groups took place in Al Khadraa', which affected Baan's school. "We had an indoor playground, and we all had to stay on the ground. I remember there were bullet holes in some of the windows." One pupil survived a stray bullet that hit her leg. Many firefights took place around the school, prompting Baan's parents to move her to an inferior school that was closer to their home, reducing the time spent traveling.

It was while moving from place to place that Baghdadis felt most insecure. That was the reason given to Baan for her parents' refusal to take her to basketball sessions in the evening. "It was about survival at this time, they didn't want to take risks for 'play.'" But Baan's brother, a young man who was able to drive, was allowed to venture out alone. However, for many Baghdadis at this time, leaving the house entailed too much risk for unnecessary trips. Many remained in their homes except for journeys to school and workplaces or to buy food and medicine. While driving home past the school, Um Ahmed was at the front of the row of traffic when a U.S. Humvee emerged, chasing a black Opel with armed men inside. The Humvee was firing its mounted rotating cannon at the car while chasing it through the streets, mounting the pavement before crashing into the vehicle. "They were shooting at them, until we could see it in front of us, the Humvee climbed on top of the Opel. They killed them on the spot."

Baan often saw armed men hiding in the side streets dressed in black and carrying rocket-propelled grenades (RPGs) while on the bus to and from school. One day, armed men boarded the bus and attempted to take her away because she was the only student on the bus not wearing a head scarf. The driver begged them not to, assuring them she was from a "good family"; luckily, they were persuaded. Her all-female school enforced a compulsory head scarf dress code for all students, apparently after religious fundamentalists threatened the school.

Baan also saw two corpses that had been left in the street. Baghdadis learned to leave bodies alone and to wait for the National Guard to pick them up. Armed groups often targeted those who approached corpses, even setting snipers to shoot at people who approached the corpses at sites that became dumping grounds for the dead.

Al Ghazaliyya became an extremely violent place. Baan's brother and his friends routinely stood on the street outside their homes to socialize and observe the changes. Baan told me there was little else to do at times, especially when electricity was unreliable and their generator could not provide enough power to cool the whole house. However, as a young woman she was not permitted to spend time watching events on the street. Her brother witnessed armed men killing an entire family in their car. Armed men on the streets from Ghazaliyya pressured them to carry weapons and fight "because the people from Shu'la are coming to attack, you must be ready to defend this area."

The reference was to the Mehdi Army but also to Shias more generally.

Posters supportive of al-Qaeda in Iraq, "Omar Al Baghdadi's Brigade," appeared in Al Ghazaliyya, as did anti-Shia slogans. The groups marked their territory this way and struck fear into the Shia families who remained. Mortar fire was exchanged between groups in Shu'la and Al Ghazaliyya, killing a neighbor's daughter a few roads away from Um Ahmed's home.

One by one, the Shia families on their street left after receiving threat letters. Um Ahmed's family were shocked to realize that in one case, it was one of their neighbors who had been leaving the notes. This action was illustrative of the puzzling dynamics of civil violence in which private and personal vendettas mix with the master cleavages of a conflict (Kalyvas 2003). "He hated Shias, but he liked my husband and our family. It was strange, he would say that he didn't like Shias, but that we were okay." Um Ahmed wanted to move quickly to another neighborhood, out of the hot zone, but her husband refused, believing they would be fine because they had not been threatened. However, she did not want to wait, fearing they would have to leave hastily if they were threatened and had to abandon all of their belongings.

There were four or five Shia families on their street. When Um Ahmed saw the last family leaving, her husband finally agreed that they could go. That they had to wait for her husband's permission was telling of the power imbalance in gender relations—*he* had the veto. At times I felt that she was making a point to her husband while telling me this story: he was the "ghostly audience," not physically present but strongly present in the narrator's conscience (Langellier 2001,174, in Andrews 2007, 17). The point was that Um Ahmed's actions saved the family, and her husband's inaction put the family at risk.

In order to relocate securely, Um Ahmed devised a plan to move in secret. She told me that her son had witnessed a Shia family's belongings being burned as they moved out of Al Ghazaliyya. She decided to pack their belongings and furniture gradually. At night they loaded the car. In the morning, after driving Baan to school, they drove to Baan's grandfather's house and unloaded the belongings; they completed the process after ten days. What remained were large items of furniture and white goods. To move those items, they employed a driver who specialized in taking the belongings of Shia families out of Al Ghazaliyya to other neighborhoods.

Although one neighbor made them feel insecure, others helped and protected their home while it was empty. Across Baghdad, participants reported that empty houses were seized by armed groups to house "their" people—those who had been displaced from elsewhere—or to store weapons. At times the police would break into empty houses to check for explosives.

Armed men came to Um Ahmed's home when it was empty and demanded that their neighbors tell them if the house "belonged to Shias." Their neighbors denied this and the armed men left, believing Sunnis owned it. Elsewhere in Al Ghazaliyya and Shu'la, Baghdadis temporarily swapped homes with others to protect each other's properties. Um Ahmed told me that Sunni and Shia families temporarily exchanged houses by mutual agreement to safeguard each other's properties and lives.

After staying temporarily with relatives, Um Ahmed chose to live in an apartment close to her place of work in a relatively safe area away from the main road. It was a mostly Sunni neighborhood where several Shia families lived. Her husband was not comfortable with the idea, fearing further displacement. However, she persuaded him and created the impression for their new neighbors that they were Sunnis from Mosul. Their family name was attributed to both sects, and Um Ahmed made sure to speak loudly in Mosul dialect with her sister, which added to the illusion. Her identification card was issued in a part of Iraq associated with having a Sunni population, and this helped maintain the idea that they were Sunnis.

The Sons of Iraq in Al Ghazaliyya

Meanwhile, in Al Ghazaliyya, violence continued. Adnaan recounted how he and a number of others—former officers, doctors, and engineers—approached U.S. forces in one of the outposts that had been set up in Al Ghazaliyya. They proposed ways to improve security through the creation of a civilian force to monitor the streets for suspicious activity.

The Iraqi government rejected the proposal, considering it to be a militia. At this point the government would allow only its own militias to be present in the field. Adnaan believed the government feared that those militias might work against the government in the near future and "wreck its project of displacement, of separation." Soon after, U.S. forces provided the men with salaries as well as night-vision and photographic equipment. The men used cameras to collect evidence of events when U.S. forces did not believe their accounts. The American forces also provided uniforms, which Adnaan designed. "We called ourselves the Sons of Iraq." The project was formalized in July 2006. The men had no helmets or bullet-proof armor. After earning the trust of U.S. forces, Adnaan and his colleagues were permitted to carry a small number of rifles for self-defense.

The benefits of the security project were quickly felt as the Sons of Iraq group helped U.S. forces capture Mehdi Army and al-Qaeda groups infiltrating Al Ghazaliyya. Each street had a checkpoint, and the militia and criminal groups ceased operations in the area, knowing they would likely be caught. With security returning to the area, the Iraqi government and U.S. forces were able to provide services. They started cleaning up the area, building schools, and fixing the water delivery, electricity, and sewage systems, among other actions. Adnaan said that businesses started opening and some displaced families returned to their homes. The success of the project surprised everyone, according to Adnaan, who also said everyone involved was afraid of it at first. After its success he was visited by the U.S. ambassadors to Iraq and Afghanistan and by U.S. and Iraqi generals, including David Petraeus. The Iraqi minister of defense visited to show the world that on the whole, things were getting better.

The sense of security was short-lived for Adnaan and his Sons of Iraq unit as they were soon targeted by the security forces of the nascent Iraqi state.

The Purge Continues

Adnaan and the Sons of Iraq unit continued working successfully with U.S. forces until 2009, when operations were handed over to the Iraqi government. "I was immediately arrested by the Iraqis. . . . Seven allegations including terrorism and murder." The Americans intervened to fast-track his case to court, where it emerged that the only evidence was a 2006 report written against him by a "secret informer."

Adnaan's men were harassed by Iraqi forces, expelled from their sleeping quarters, and accused of terrorism. Iraqi forces frequently raided the Sons of Iraq's quarters in Al Ghazaliyya where his men rested when off duty, smashing furniture each time they "searched for explosives." Iraqi forces arrested many of them.

Iraqi Special Operations raided Adnaan's home at 1:30 in the morning; men with rifles broke into his home and handcuffed and interrogated him in front his wife and children for several hours, and searched the house for explosives. They found nothing incriminating, then said that they had actually been looking for someone else and left. Adnaan contacted U.S. forces for assistance but was told they could no longer intervene in internal Iraqi matters. "That was a signal to me that it was over."

Adnaan rented a house in Baghdad in a location he disclosed to none of his men, for the sake of everyone's security, and secretly moved into it with his family at the end of Ramadan in 2009. His men phoned him that evening: Iraqi Special Operations had broken into his Ghazaliyya home again, smashed the quarters of the Ghazaliyya Sons of Iraq, and arrested all of its members. They had asked specifically for Adnaan and his whereabouts. When Adnaan contacted the Iraqi army in Ghazaliyya for clarification, they said they were looking for someone else and he had nothing to worry about. "That was the end of it as far as I was concerned. I cut off all communications with them and changed my number."

With his family, Adnaan left the city for the safety of the hinterlands, to Salah ad-Din province, where his brother lived. In March 2010, a friend in the *mukhabarat* (intelligence) services contacted his brother to warn him that orders were issued to arrest Adnaan and that he should leave the country. Adnaan moved to Syria shortly afterwards He was purged by the new order for belonging to the old one and deemed a threat to the "new" state-building project taking place in Iraq.

The U.S. military intervention had multiple tremendous implications for security in the city. The immediate effects of zoning were felt across Baghdad, most of which had become a dangerous Red

Zone, in contradistinction to the secured enclave of the Green Zone. The exclusionary processes associated with the postinvasion period produced armed groups whose members contested the new political order and some of whom engaged in sectarian and criminal activities, with the main victims being civilian populations. Militias attempted to impose their own control over areas in the Red Zone—the Green Zone was almost impenetrable—contesting the authority of U.S. forces and of rival militias.

In places where this array of armed forces clashed violently for control, neighborhoods became hot zones, sites of intense armed conflict within the Red Zone. Al Ghazaliyya was one such neighborhood, and I have shown how specific Baghdadis managed the threats that pervaded these highly dangerous zones within a wider danger zone. I have also shown the implications of the hinterlands for Baghdadis' security, before and during the invasion, and argued that the war on terror, as practiced by U.S. forces through brutal military tactics in the hinterlands of Anbar, spilled over into Baghdad in the gateway neighborhood of Al Ghazaliyya.

A tentative conclusion might be that security is achieved only through bottom-up inclusion and engagement, noting, of course, the catastrophic consequences that the invasion had for security in the first place. The most stable period for Al Ghazliyya under the occupation was during the surge, when American forces stationed in Baghdad responded to locally based initiatives, such as that proposed by Adnaan, to protect their neighborhoods. However, these limited achievements were not sustained, and the exclusionary sectarian practices of the Iraqi government after 2009 completely negated this approach. Although this is not part of the story told in this chapter, the continuance of systemic discarding helps to explain the subsequent rise of new extremist groups, most notably ISIS.

Notes

This chapter was supported by a number of generous research grants. I am grateful to the Arts and Humanities Research Council, the University of East London, the British Institute for the Study of Iraq, and the European Research Council for their support. I also thank Mary Kaldor, Saskia Sassen, Ruben Anderson, Sobie Ahmed, Mary Martin, Vesna Bojicic-Dzelilovic, Florian Weigand, and Johannes Rieken for their comments and feedback on earlier versions of this chapter. I am also grateful to to all the Iraqi participants for sharing their stories of life under occupation.

1. The transformation of the Iraqi state brought about by so-called regime change produced numerous forms of exclusion, often with lethal consequences. See Ali 2011.
2. See Ali forthcoming.
3. This was amplified when many Iraqi Sunnis appeared to boycott the 2005 national elections, protesting—understandably—that parliamentary elections should not take place under foreign occupation.
4. Many blast walls were removed during the spring of 2019, opening up roads in the city, although some neighborhoods remain walled.
5. The names of participants have been changed to protect their anonymity.
6. Many were forced to leave Iraq after they were targeted by the nascent Iraqi state for alleged and, in some cases fabricated, involvement in terrorist attacks. See Zaman 2011.
7. See https://web.archive.org/web/20040902224710/http://islamicceramics .ashmol.ox.ac.uk/Abbasid/baghdad.htm.
8. See http://iraqheritage.org/iraq-heritage.php, link for *Madrasa Al-Mustansiriya*.
9. These are figures from the Arabic Wikipedia page for the Governorate of Baghdad, which cites the Iraqi Ministry of Planning: https://ar.wikipedia .org/wiki/%D9%85%D8%AD%D8%A7%D9%81%D8%B8%D8%A9 _%D8%A8%D8%BA%D8%AF%D8%A7%D8%AF#.D8.A7.D9.84 .D8.AA.D8.B1.D9.83.D9.8A.D8.A8.D8.A9_.D8.A7.D9.84.D8.B3 .D9.83.D8.A7.D9.86.D9.8A.D8.A9
10. World Meteorological Organization, http://worldweather.wmo.int/en /city.html?cityId=1464.
11. This is a reference to the oil fires lit by the Iraqi army in an attempt to disrupt the advanced guidance systems of the American Air Force. They were thought to have been oil pools created from pipelines. See Reed 2003, http://www.geotimes.org/may03/geophen.html. Images by Bruno

Stevens can be seen at http://bruno.photoshelter.com/gallery-image
/Iraq-2003-During-the-War/GoooocVnrF4iOWSk/IooooMyey3eoIdrs
and at http://bruno.photoshelter.com/gallery-image/Iraq-2003-During
-the-War/GoooocVnrF4iOWSk/IoooohBCKWf_vOpw.

12. Today, traffic police have restored some semblance of order to the city's
roads, and security has been much improved since the defeat, for now, of
the so called Islamic State. However, electricity from the national grid is
still limited to a few hours per day, and residents rely on subscriptions to
privately run neighborhood generators of varying reliability.

13. The documentary film by Rashed Radwan and Carmen Marques, *Generator Man*, about the owner of a neighborhood generator in Sadr City,
shows one example of this arrangement.

14. Adnaan did not say whether he was directly involved in armed resistance.

References

Ali, Ali. 2011. "Displacement and Statecraft in Iraq: Recent Trends, Older
Roots." *International Journal of Contemporary Iraqi Studies* 5 (2): 231–45.
http://doi.org/10.5334/sta.gd.

———. Forthcoming. "Displacement and State Transformation: The Coercion
and Systemic Discarding of the Mandaeans and Palestinians of Iraq 2003–
2010." In *Iraq After the Invasion: People and Politics in a State of Conflict*, ed. R.
Hinnebusch, P. Marfleet, K. Sakai. Abingdon: Routledge.

Al-Qazzaz, Ayad. 2019. "Baghdad." *Encyclopedia of the Modern Middle East and
North Africa. Encyclopedia.com.* Accessed September 17, 2019. https://www
.encyclopedia.com/places/asia/iraq-political-geography/baghdad.Al-Taie,
Entidhar, Al-Ansari, Nadhir and Sven Knutsson. 2012. "The Progress of
Buildings Style and Materials from the Ottoman and British Occupations
of Iraq." *Journal of Earth Sciences and Geotechnical Engineering* 2 (2): 39–49.

Andrews, M. 2007. *Shaping History: Narratives of Political Change*. Cambridge:
Cambridge University Press.

Batatu, H. 1986. "Shi'i Organizations in Iraq: Al-Da'wah al-Islamiyah and al-
Mujahidin." In *Shi'ism and Social Protest*, ed. J. R. Cole and N. R. Keddie,
179–200. New Haven, CT: Yale University Press.

Batatu, H. 2004. *The Old Social Classes and the Revolutionary Movements of Iraq:
A Study of Iraq's Old Landed and Commercial Classes and of Its Communists,
Ba'thists, and Free Officers.* London: Saqi.

Chandrasekaran, Rajiv. 2007. *Imperial Life in the Emerald City: Inside Iraq's
Green Zone.* New York: Penguin Random House.

Chatty, D. 2010. *Displacement and Dispossession in the Modern Middle East.* Cambridge: Cambridge University Press.

Haddad, F. 2011. *Sectarianism in Iraq: Antagonistic Visions of Unity.* London: Hurst.

Harling, P. 2011. "A State of Violence: A Sociological Reading of the Battle for Baghdad." In *Uncovering Iraq: Trajectories of Disintegration and Transformation*, ed. C. Toensing and M. Kirk, 43–66. Washington, DC: Center for Contemporary Arab Studies, Georgetown University.

ICG (International Crisis Group). 2003. *Baghdad: A Race Against the Clock.* Middle East Briefing. Brussels: International Crisis Group.

——. 2007. *Shiite Politics in Iraq: The Role of the Supreme Council* Brussels: International Crisis Group.

——. 2008. *Iraq After the Surge I: The New Sunni Landscape.* Middle East Report No. 74. Brussels: International Crisis Group.

Kaldor, M. H. 2012. *New and Old Wars: Organised Violence in a Global Era*, 3rd ed. Cambridge: Polity.

Kalyvas, S. N. 2003. "The Ontology of 'Political Violence': Action and Identity in Civil Wars." *Perspectives on Politics* 1 (3): 475–94.

Marfleet, P. 2007. "Iraq's Refugees: 'Exit' from the State. *International Journal of Contemporary Iraqi Studies* 3 (1): 397–419.

Marfleet, P., and Chatty, D. 2009. *Iraq's Refugees: Beyond Tolerance.* Forced Migration Policy Briefing 4, December, Oxford: Refugee Studies Centre.

Niva, S. 2008. "Walling Off Iraq: Israel's Imprint on U.S. Counterinsurgency Doctrine." *Middle East Policy* 15 (3): 67–79.

Radwan, R., and Marques, C.2012. *Generator Man.* Al Jazeera English: Witness Episodes, http://www.aljazeera.com/programmes/witness/2012/06 /2012618132430953572.html.

UNHCR (United Nations High Commissioner for Refugees). 2003a. Iraq region: No substantial movements reported. Geneva: UNHCR.

——. 2003b. Iraq: Small numbers trickling into Jordan and Syria, Geneva: UNHCR. Available: http://www.unhcr.org/cgi-bin/texis/vtx/iraq?page =briefing&id=3e92ef1f4.

Zaman, T. 2011. "Lessons Learned: Palestinian Displacements from Iraq. *International Journal of Contemporary Iraqi Studies* 5 (2): 263–75.

4

A Tale of Two Cities

Ciudad Juárez, El Paso, and Insecurity
at the U.S.–Mexico Border

MARY MARTIN

C iudad Juárez is Mexico's fifth largest city, with 1.3 million people. It cannot be separated from its so-called alter ego, El Paso in Texas, on the other side of the Rio Grande; both cities lie in a flat desert valley that divides Mexico and the United States. The hub of this border metropolis is a series of looping concrete bridges across the river. They arch into the air at intervals across the horizon, linking the dense and sprawling cityscape of Ciudad Juárez, which is dominated by its miles of shanty dwellings (*colonias*) with the neat urban contours of El Paso. Together they form the largest binational metropolitan area in the world.

The international boundary divides and defines these two cities. Although they share geographies and histories, they have markedly different understandings and experiences of security, well-being and governance. The gulf between them was highlighted when President Donald Trump arrived in El Paso in February 2019 for a rally of 6,000 supporters and warned of dangers lurking on the other side of the Rio Grande. Leading chants of "Finish that Wall!" Trump used the visit and rally in the run-up to declaring, days later, a national emergency over central American migration in order to access billions of dollars to pay for his promised border wall.

Yet few in either city sensed any crisis that would justify Trump's rhetoric, or his urgent call to forcibly separate cities like El Paso from their southern egos. For the inhabitants of this cross-border metropolitan area, the danger that Trump referred to had already passed.

Between 2007 and 2012, Ciudad Juárez experienced a wave of violent killings that reached 10,000 deaths in five years, accompanied by other violent crimes such as carjacking, extortion, torture, and disappearances. Most of this violence was linked to competition among drug cartels, but its roots were in the "subsoil" of corrupt and dysfunctional public administration and rule of law in Mexico. The killing spree itself was exacerbated by the Mexican army troops and federal police who were deployed to halt the narco-traffic turf battles. In contrast, El Paso basks in its reputation as one of the five safest U.S. cities. Downtown Ciudad Juárez is a tense, no-go area with too many broken windows, derelict buildings, and rubbish-filled streets, safer than it was a decade ago yet still prone to eruptions of violence.

This chapter explores the explosion of civil warfare in Ciudad Juárez through the changing nature of the border and the relationship between Juárez and El Paso in the decade since 2005, when another U.S. president, George W. Bush, began building the first fixed barrier in the shape of a border fence between the two cities. I look at why the historically binomial relationship ruptured and how everyday life in Ciudad Juárez diverged from that in El Paso, becoming securitized through a combination of wars against drugs and terrorism, and continues today as part of the discourse that frames migrants as a threat to U.S. national security.

As a result of this securitization, the period from 2006 to 2013 saw the emergence of three distinct, competing security cultures comprising different practices, values, and goals. Kaldor described a security culture as a "style or a pattern of doing security that brings together a range of interlinked components (narratives, rules, tools, practices, etc) and that are embedded in a specific set of power relations" (Kaldor 2018, 38). In Ciudad Juárez, there is a border security culture, a public or citizen security culture, and a neoliberal security culture. Each seeks to describe the city's predicament differently, articulate a particular set of threats and risks, identify distinct referent objects as requiring protection, and prescribe responses to the violence. In their narratives each culture constructs its own account of the ways in which the city is insecure; each has its geographic specificity, reifying and seeking to protect a different type of urban space, along with key symbols and markers. From each culture emerges a set of practices that include border checks, human rights defenders, and private security guards.

In section 2, I look at how these cultures emerged, shaped by events both within and beyond the city, principally the war on terror and the war on drugs, and how these wars broke long traditions of cross-border harmony. Sections 3, 4 and 5 explore how the cultures map onto regional, national, and global trends and enact different portrayals and practices of security and insecurity. Even after peak violence in Ciudad Juárez abated after 2012, these cultures have persisted, in tension with one another, compounding the challenge of normalizing life in the city.

Section 6 looks at attempts to recover Juárez's urban capabilities that have to navigate these cultures. The conclusion is that insecurity in Ciudad Juárez can be seen in terms of a failure to reconcile the tensions among security cultures, to harmonize the use of public spaces and align policies, and to develop a consensus attitude toward the frontier that both unites and divides Ciudad Juárez from El Paso.

The Fence

Ciudad Juárez sits at a historic crossing point between Mexico and El Paso, Texas, midway along the 2,000-kilometer-long national border. For more than a century, it has been where armies, traders, and migrants moved back and forth. Juárez's main park, El Chamizal, is on land returned to the Mexicans by the United States in 1964 after decades of disputes about the boundary line. Giant Mexican flags fly along the edge of the road to show where the United States ends and Mexico begins, but in reality the demarcation in Juárez has never been that clearcut. Since Mexican independence at the start of the twentieth century, the frontier has been the crossover between tides of Mexicans seeking work north of the Rio Grande and a contraflow of U.S. consumers heading south in search of alcohol, cheap drugs, divorces, dentists, and colorful entertainment.

The fence is eighteen feet high and has three layers of steel mesh. It extends another six to eight feet underground and is held in place by concrete blocks set on the desert floor. Cameras and lights are poised to track any attempt on the fence, and the sandy ground is dotted with sensors to detect the slightest movement. The sand is swept every day by U.S. border guards as carefully as any up-market beach resort. Why? So it can reveal fresh footprints. It is hard to see how a costly new structure made of concrete could provide any additional deterrence.

We are in a wide, flat no-man's land between the Rio Grande and the fence, which marks the boundary between Mexico and the United States. Ahead is a deep concrete culvert built to contain the river when it is in flood. The currents are so treacherous when this happens that most of the migrants who die crossing here die of drowning. We watch two young boys—so-called *halcones* (hawks) or lookouts—on the Mexican side of the river, who in turn are watching U.S. border guards as they patrol the fence in their SUVs. It feels like a desolate place from which to survey the "promised land."

As is the case with other cities in this volume, Ciudad Juárez became (re)defined through a catastrophic and sudden security failure. The process of seeing the city as an insecure environment came not only, and not even principally, from its citizens but also from external actors and national, regional, and global trends. Ciudad Juárez today is, more than ever before in its history, a city fabricated by the perceptions and understandings of outsiders. This is particularly true of the border security culture, which emerged as part of the Global War on Terrorism (GWOT) with its spin-off domestic practices under the imperative of U.S. Homeland Security. The key space in this culture is the U.S.-Mexico border, designated by U.S. federal policy makers as an unsafe space following the terrorist attacks of 9/11, and reimagined by Trump as the key entry point of a tide of immigration that threatens American culture, identity, and safety.

The second culture, struggling to assert itself, is public or citizen security. It emphasizes the need to protect and empower citizens against drug violence as well as forms of structural violence, particularly oppression of women, made graphically visible in a series of murders—femicides—in the 1990s. Public security has been advanced by civil society groups as a rights-based culture that draws attention to high levels of poverty, deprivation, and human rights abuses. The key spaces in this culture of violence and fear are public areas: streets, parks, and public monuments. They became symbols of insecurity, where individuals were likely to suffer violence. But they also served as sites of resistance, with citizens using street furniture, such as lampposts, to post memorials and demand protection.

The third security culture, which is distinctive though not unique to Ciudad Juárez, is a neoliberal framing of security in which the object to be protected is explicitly not the state (as in national security) nor the population or individuals (as in public/citizen security). It is the operation of the free market. In the case of Ciudad Juárez, this means securing and enabling the unfettered operation and growth of manufacturing. The key space surrounds the industrial plants, known as *maquiladoras*. These are the defining features of the cityscape, where transnational corporations (TNCs) transform raw materials into electronics and automotive, plastics, and engineering components for export across the border.

International businesses have turned Ciudad Juárez into a workshop of global products. Their presence has changed not only the aesthetics of the city but also its social relations. These businesses have created an underclass of manufacturing labor populated by immigrant workers in Ciudad Juárez and a management elite largely based in El Paso. The *maquiladoras* create their own security dynamics through a set of practices such as private security guards and bespoke transport arrangements and concessions, all designed to protect the manufacturing plants and to ensure a steady flow of new investment and output. The neoliberal security narrative in Juárez is a powerful counterculture. It asserts a pro-business agenda as the authentic representation of the city's capabilities and its hope of future security and prosperity.

These three cultures are grounded in different kinds of urban space: the border crossing, the manufacturing plant, the public and private habitats of citizens, and the protection of diverse urban capabilities. Although distinct, they also overlap in terms of the daily experience for residents who must navigate combinations of them. A confused visitor is tempted to ask: "Will the real Ciudad Juárez please stand up?" How can a city that attracts the headline "Murder Capital of the World" be the same one that gives rise to headlines such as "The City of the Future," "U.S. Companies Are Still Rushing to Juárez," or "Big Businesses Boom in an Unlikely Mexican City"?[1]

Past and Present: Juárez at the Crossing Point of People, Drugs, and Power

The explanation for the paradox that business is still attracted to the city despite the violence starts with the fact that Juárez sits on a frontier. For decades workers from rural areas in Mexico and Central America have sought the key transit point of Juárez—whose original name, *Paso del Norte*, means "Gateway to the North." After the enactment of the North American Free Trade Agreement (NAFTA) in 1994, preferential tariff arrangements encouraged the development of new manufacturing plants and jobs to serve the North American market. U.S. agricultural producers were able to flood the Mexican market with cheap produce, undercutting local firms. As a result, an estimated 1.3 million Mexican agricultural jobs were lost,[2] fueling an exodus of cheap labor from Mexico's heartland. From 1990 the population of Juárez swelled from just under 790,000 to 1.3 million.[3]

Despite infrastructure spending, trade agreements, and governance assistance, public services could not keep pace with the massive population influx. While Juárez's shantytowns proliferated largely unregulated, urban planning concentrated on creating shopping, lodging, and business facilities for American investors and consumers. Changes aimed at forging one metropolis within a free-trade area marked the start of a diversion of fortunes between El Paso and Ciudad Juárez.

Juárez on the Frontline

The city's attributes as a transit hub for legal commerce also made it ideal for trafficking in illegal drugs and people. Juárez's reversal of fortune in the 2000s was in part due to its capture by cartels that exploited these advantages. In 2006, the new center-right Mexican president, Felipe Calderón, unleashed his so-called war on drugs against the growing power of the drug cartels across Mexico. Calderón's election also created a power vacuum that severed existing patronage deals between cartels, security forces, and city officials.[4] In March 2008, the frontline of the war on drugs moved to Juárez, where leaders of the Sinaloa and Juárez drug cartels competed to establish new parallel structures within the city administration and security services and to control cross-border drug-trafficking routes.

The president deployed five thousand troops in *Conjunto Chihuahua* (Joint Operation Chihuahua), two thousand to Ciudad Juárez itself, and 180 military vehicles, three aircraft, ten operating bases, and nearly fifty mobile checkpoints.[5] Far from imposing order, the presence of soldiers quickly made the violence worse.

Descriptions of military vehicles patrolling the city, soldiers in face masks, checkpoints, and closed streets reminded observers of the Green Zone in Baghdad. The police force barricaded themselves in local hotels to avoid attacks by gangs of criminals, citizens were left to protect themselves, shops and businesses closed.[6]

Calderón's war on drugs in many ways mimicked the practices and rhetoric of the GWOT launched by George W. Bush. It was an attempt at swamping city streets with military might and weaponry, checkpoints, de facto curfews, and random house-to-house searches.[7] As in Iraq and Afghanistan, the federal government went after high-value targets, decapitating the drug cartels by capturing their senior leaders.[8]

Violence plumbed new depths. Murder in Juárez had been staged previously as public display. The 1990s murders of women had resulted in bodies left on waste ground as a warning to others. After 2008, the brutality and depravity of drug killings was an essential part of the morphology of the violence. Assassinations took place at traffic intersections, and bodies were left in public parks, hanging from bridges, or dumped at public statues, accompanied by warning messages. Media coverage fed into this pornography of violence with lurid descriptions and photographs of corpses.

Border Security

The confluence of events that engulfed Juárez after 2007 has been described as a "perfect storm."[9] At the same time that flows of goods, drugs, and people surged, civic authority weakened, opening power struggles within and among both criminal and civic elites. Juárez was in the crosshairs of a double war: against drugs and against terrorism. Both changed the attitude of U.S. authorities toward the border. Rather than being viewed as a benefit to economic growth, the Mexican frontier began to be portrayed as a source of insecurity, an Achilles heel in the fight against global terrorism, and a channel for illicit traffic. Construction of the border fence beginning in 2005 was the symbolic and physical marker of an expanding regime of national security and the alienation of outsiders, which included redefining Juárez as a threat to the American nation. The U.S. Border Patrol, previously a checkpoint contingent, became reconstituted as guardian of the nation's frontline and protector of "the American people against terrorists and the instruments of terror."[10]

War on Terror

The GWOT strategy of preemption and deterrence found an echo in new border procedures. A 2002 agreement with the United States called "Intelligent Frontiers" formalized anti-terror cooperation between the countries, including the exchange of information and strengthened U.S. legal control of three key border points, including the one between Juárez and El Paso. The logic of the new regime was "enforcement through deterrence," and it was implemented through increasing use of technology and a dramatic escalation in the provision of resources.[11]

The Border Patrol in El Paso consists of eleven stations and six checkpoints. Three forward operating bases are located closer to the border. with agents in residence and rotated every ten days. Not only is the terminology of the operation deliberately militarized, but many of the 2,600 agents, male and female, are predominantly army recruits who receive military-type training, including marching and squad drills and in firearms. Job ranking is along army lines. Teams patrol in pairs in marked SUVs, follow strategic plans, and rely on advanced surveillance technology that includes sensors, cameras, and FLIARs (forward-looking infrared systems).

Since 2003, the number of U.S. border agents has doubled to more than 20,000, and a system of fourteen watchtowers and fifty-two cameras was installed. Most illegal traffic is people; only 15 percent of illegal immigrants are drug traffickers, and despite the high-tech efforts, border guards estimate they catch only 20 percent of those who cross.[12] All illegal crossings are routinely investigated by the FBI as a potential security issue.[13]

Global Warriors at the Mexican Border

Juárez also sits in the shadow of Fort Bliss, the largest inland military site in North America; there the U.S. Army carries out basic training, war gaming, and communications development. The area includes an Air Force base for bombers and drone testing and the White Sands missile range. It is the hub for military deployments in the GWOT, with regular rotations to the Middle East and Afghanistan, handling 10,000 active troops and more than 30,000 reservists. Between 2005 and 2011, the U.S. Department of Defense invested $6 billion on facilities to service the nearly 90,000 residents, including military families, attached to the base. The local economy around El Paso boomed as a result.

After 9/11, the United States brought together twenty-three domestic agencies, including the U.S. Customs Service and elements of the Immigration Service, into a comprehensive border security agency. The resulting Customs and Border Patrol (CBP) was as an arm of U.S. National Security Strategy and counterterrorism. CBP includes the Air and Marine Operations Division and the Intelligence Group. This consists of 500 people who not only monitor activity at the border but also track aircraft movements. CBP uses a wide range of listening and surveillance technologies as well as human intelligence to monitor movements of cartels and people traffickers from the Gulf Coast to Honduras and Guatemala. Preference is given to recruits who have experience of long tours in Afghanistan or Iraq.

The Intelligence Group sees ISIS "as a current threat to border security."[14] There are periodic rumors that Middle Eastern jihadists have penetrated drug-trafficking routes into Texas.[15] Most locals dismiss the claims as fanciful, and Border Patrol agents interviewed said they had never found any sign of foreign groups attempting to use the crossing.

The GWOT culture securitized border management and wider U.S.–Mexican relations. In 2007, the U.S. government agreed on the Merida Initiative, a $2.5 billion package of assistance and a military response to support President Calderón's war on drugs.[16] From 2008 to 2015, the United States spent $1.3 billion as part of the initiative on training, equipment, and technical assistance, including aerial surveillance drones, effectively managing Mexican security policy.[17]

National Security

U.S. national security concerns did not simply foment a culture of border security that centered on the threats from terrorism and that has evolved in the Trump populist discourse into raising the cultural, social, and criminal threats posed by immigration. Security fears also began to shape Mexican responses to the violence in Juárez, which framed cartel activity as a war and focused on the mounting homicide rate. The decision to deploy the army reinforced the sense of a military battle, with the cartels portrayed as a threat to Mexico itself, an existential challenge to state power.

This rhetoric ignored the social and domestic political roots of violence and depravity in the poverty, unemployment, and lack of public services, including the chronic failure of law and order in a city, in a country where over 93 percent of murders still go unpunished and largely uninvestigated.[18] The rhetoric sought to cast not only perpetrators but also victims as subversive agents who were attacking the integrity and stability of the state. As Melissa Wright argued, the government's response not only cut off public safety from national security, but the two were "inversely related as a dualistic binary."[19] Those who were killed or abducted were seen as complicit in their tragedies, part of an underclass that was prone to suffer violence.

The Mexican military response produced exactly the opposite result to the one intended: the annual murder toll rose from 316 in 2007 to 1,607 in 2008. By January 2009, the dispatching of several thousand federal police was accompanied by a further jump in deaths to 2,643. The government claimed that the rising murder rate was proof that the strategy was working and that pressure on the cartels had led to their killing each other.

According to local commentator Victor Quintana, writing in a Mexico City newspaper,

> Either Calderón is mistaken or he intends for us to be mistaken: the army and the federal police in Juárez were not part of the solution, as he claims, but part of the problem. Not only did they convince a number of small criminal groups to unite and to arm themselves in defense against them, or to ally themselves with them, escalating the level of violence, but they also committed countless abuses of human rights: forced disappearances, arbitrary detentions, torture.[20]

Both the violence and the military response overwhelmed the city. Street crime and turf battles between the lower echelons of the drug cartels and street gangs added to the toll on public safety. Soldiers and federal police demanded extortion payments and invaded private homes, claiming they were hunting down cartel leaders. The security presence generated fear and disrespect: "In El Paso if I have a car crash I call the police. In Juárez I would give a guy on the street $8 to look the other way and not call the police. If I get pulled over by the police at two in the morning I am praying."[21]

An estimated 450,000 of the population of 1.3 million fled the city between 2007 and 2011, leaving residential areas abandoned. Those who could not afford to leave began erecting walls around housing developments and barbed wire around children's playgrounds. Juárez's civic identity, built around street gatherings, drinking, and partying, unraveled. Office workers in El Paso who typically crossed the river for their lunch in one of the many restaurants at the Mexican end of the bridges stayed away. Queues at the bridges lengthened as weapons inspections were stepped up. Fearing being caught in shootings at traffic intersections or picked off the street as random kidnap victims, residents stopped going anywhere that might suddenly turn into a killing zone. They swapped anecdotes about how to avoid violence: being fair-haired could ensure you stood out and so were not targeted as part of a drug cartel. On the other hand, if you appeared Mexican and dark might mean you were not noticed at all. Belonging to an organized group carried risks as much as it offered safety and solidarity.

> There are five hundred to nine hundred street gangs now of armed, murderous, unschooled, and unemployed young people. . . . Nothing can immediately roll back the violence, because it is now part of the fabric of the city, a place where in two years twenty-five per cent of the houses have been abandoned, forty per cent of the business shuttered, at least a hundred thousand jobs lost, and where a hundred and four thousand people have fled.[22]

The violence forced a retreat into segregated and gendered spaces: the increase in private security guards and closed neighborhoods made it particularly difficult for women to go outside.

Carola Chavez lives in Juárez and commutes daily to El Paso to work in an American bank.

Between 2008 and 2010 it was drastic. People didn't leave their houses. The streets were empty. There were a lot of house parties. You heard horror stories—usually about people who were drug trafficking, but then it also happened to random people. Everybody knew someone affected. Now you can sense the difference. We are traumatized. That seed of fear has been hard to shake off even though new places are opening up and the parks are full again.[23]

Juárez's migration history has always tested citywide social cohesion. A population that comprises so many people passing through the city emphasizes fluidity over fixity. Organized civic resistance often has been muted and civil society groups marginalized. A group of human rights workers described the weakness of public security in Juárez:

> We need programs that have to do with everyday life. There is also a problem of culture. We don't get a response from the government or society [to human rights abuses]. With so many migrant communities we have different types of solidarity, and we need the resources of outside experts and a more professional approach.[24]

The government's attitude toward public safety, portraying the violence as within and between cartels, was abruptly challenged in January 2010, the year the murder rate peaked. On one Saturday night, four SUVs pulled up outside a working-class *colonia* in Juárez. Two dozen men with assault rifles entered a house where a group of teenagers were having a birthday party. The massacre left fifteen dead. The Villas de Salvácar shootings became a new benchmark of insecurity in the city. Not only were innocent children killed, but it turned out to be a case of mistaken identity, as some of the teenagers belonged to a football team called AA, the same initials as *Artistas Asassinatos*, a gang affiliated with the Juárez cartel. The massacre highlighted the failure to protect citizens even in their own homes. Residents described living in the city after the massacre as living in a blanket of fog, from which it was impossible to imagine a way out.[25]

The city's topography also contributes to its problems. On the desert floor, Ciudad Juárez sprawls in all directions. It is crisscrossed by large freeways, which allow easy access to the border bridges but that bisect communities. Dust is everywhere, blighting attempts to create green spaces. Downtown the streets are long lines of broken windows, derelict buildings, and boarded facades. Once you turn off the main freeways, most roads are unpaved, and street lighting is sporadic.

Casa Amiga stands out in the middle of densely packed rows of houses. It is smart, freshly painted in bright colors. This women's refuge is a unique landmark in a city where there is a chronic lack of public services. It is also a bellwether of the city's social turmoil. When the drug violence spiraled and the army arrived, Casa Amiga began to see more cases of domestic abuse, and it suffered direct attacks by the army. Its then-director, Irma Casas, describes receiving threatening telephone calls at night and Molotov cocktails lobbed over the wall: "Fifteen soldiers would arrive with arms and take it on themselves to burst in." Casa Amiga receives no support from city funds but relies on foreign companies, churches, and mostly U.S. donors to survive. Ms. Casas says that government security policies ignored the city's social problems, were short-term, and militarized the situation.[26]

Neoliberal Security

The third security culture in Juárez is rooted in its economic identity. The phenomenon of the *maquiladora*, a plant that produces manufactured goods for export, began in 1966 as a result of an agreement between the U.S. and Mexican governments that removed tariffs on finished goods sold in the United States. Juárez's *maquila* economy is the city's most distinctive physical and symbolic feature, producing a landscape of vast, gated low-rise industrial plants within reach of the international border. Many of the plants make electronics for the global car industry. The "citizens" of the *maquila* economy are names such as Bosch, Honeywell, Panasonic, and Lear Corporation, for whom security is a set of values and operating practices geared to maximizing the competitive efficiency of manufacturing, in the face of threats such as violence, corruption, dysfunctionality, and increased border controls. Their tools include private guards, cheap female labor (women have smaller hands and skills based on sewing, which can be adapted to the detailed work of electronic components), and a private transport network of buses that convey workers to and from the plants at the start of each shift. The city's road system is also designed in a way to create so-called industrial corridors for delivery trucks.

The neoliberal security culture seeks to safeguard business interests, protect the free market, and ensure continuity and expansion of manufacturing despite an environment permeated by violence, corruption, and conflict. The culture frames threats in terms of loss of competitiveness, investment, and global market share. The free market must be protected as the principal guarantee of the city's survival, the representation of its capabilities, and the ultimate weapon against insecurity.

Neoliberal security is not merely about private forms of security, although its practices assume private means rather than dependence on public policy. Its scope is more profound than privatizing security, in that it draws on discourses of globalization and presumed connections between security and development to advance a premise of economic growth as the indispensable driver of the city's security.

Although neoliberal security replicates the private enclaves familiar in many violent cities, such as the hermetically sealed factories and offices and the gated executive housing in El Paso, Juárez's manufacturing plants promise not only physical safety but also zones of exception to normal urban rules.[27] The *maquiladoras* benefit from a permissive attitude by government authorities and civil society that enables them to act exclusively without restraint from or reference to the norms and regulations of life elsewhere in the city.

One effect of the violence in Juárez was to erode the usual distance between business and security concerns. In its place emerged a security culture that, while retaining a culture of exceptionalism for businesses, sought to fuse manufacturing interests and the security agenda. International companies (in contrast to small businesses, which are forced to make *cuotas* or extortion payments) remained largely free of direct attacks by either cartels or security forces. However, the spike in violence after 2007, and particularly the way it was reported outside Mexico, threatened to damage the city's reputation, deterring international investment and jeopardizing manufacturing growth.

Drug violence in Juárez surged at the same time as global recession and increased competition from China after it joined the World Trade Organization. More than ninety thousand regional jobs disappeared between 2007 and 2010. The *maquiladoras* lost 52,637 jobs in 2008 alone. Most business accounts of the period emphasized the threat from recession and competition rather than from drug violence. They portray the industrial zones as safe havens from the city's killing spree and, indeed, a bulwark against corruption and organized crime. The narrative of the neoliberal security culture suggests that failure of the cross-border regional economy presented as much of a risk to civic stability as the drug war.

There has always been an economic dimension to insecurity in Juárez. Young women who supplied labor to grow the *maquiladoras* were murder victims in the 1990s because they defied cultural prejudices that saw women's place as in the home. The rapid growth of the *maquila* economy made the city vulnerable to global economic swings, boom and bust, and the fortunes of a few leading firms.[28] Average manufacturing wages of $422 per month are almost the lowest of any production center along the U.S. border or in the interior of Mexico, with women earning an average of $300.[29] Resilience to the economic cycle as well as corruption and violence is weak.

At the core of the neoliberal security culture in Juárez is a form of external intervention by global companies, which generates transactional dynamics between locals and outsiders that is infused by an asymmetry of power. As part of this dynamic, locals attempt to mitigate their insecurity through working with and for the internationals and conforming to their norms, while companies leverage their power as investors and employers to exact favorable terms, including bespoke security provisions from civic, federal, and international authorities. As well as special rights of passage, foreign companies have a privileged voice and access to governing elites that allows them to promote their own agendas on security, civic organization, and urban planning. In Juárez, this influence is amplified further as companies are also able to appeal to U.S. policy makers—at federal and state levels—on the grounds that what is good for business in Juárez is also in the interests of U.S. national and regional economics.

An important element in the vocal business constituency are the consultancy firms that specialize in onshoring, providing advice and attracting foreign investors on the basis of Juárez's favorable fiscal regime—the equivalent of an offshore tax haven. Manuel Ochoa is a senior director of Tecma, a leading onshoring consultancy. From his office in El Paso he describes how he helped to reassure nervous foreign investors during the peak violence:

> We are not the target [of the cartels]. None of the killings have happened inside the industrial parks. We had violence and global recession, but companies already there kept the engine running. It meant people were not looking for other sources of revenue and joining cartels.[30]

In contrast to border security, the practices of neoliberal security culture rely on desecuritizing the frontier and liberalizing cross-border flows. Business has negotiated privileged rights at the border crossings, which mitigates the increased security introduced after 2005. The FAST (Free and Secure Trade) program prescreens commercial traffic in order to expedite deliveries of goods. Government rhetoric and policy link security with economic development. In 2014, the government said that the new national police force "would be placed at the disposition of private companies and [that] it would be activated [sic] based on three threats, one of which includes threats to production or sources of income."[31]

To protect entrepreneurs and reassure visitors, the city government created a heavily policed green zone for businesses in December 2010. Under the plan, 120 federal police maintained a twenty-four-hour guard on a small commercial area close to the border. Checkpoints were positioned every five hundred meters to inspect cars and keep an eye on racketeers.

Urban planning in Ciudad Juárez also serves the economic and business agenda. In the 1960s an area close to the border was redeveloped as a so-called global economic vision to cater to the growing business community and the influx of U.S. tourists and businesspeople. The Zona Pronaf was modeled on a U.S. shopping center and was designed to offer a "solid example of actual Mexico: progressive dynamic, working."[32] Until the worst of the violence in 2010, it was seen as one of the most secure areas in the city.

The power of the manufacturing plants not only enables them to bypass the restrictions of border security but also produces contradictory outcomes for citizens' security. The top three firms in the city—Lear, Delphi, and Foxconn—combined operate twenty-six plants and employ forty-seven thousand workers, allowing these companies to dominate the local economy and keep wages low. As violence increased and household poverty rose, their plants also acted as safe havens for workers who preferred to spend long hours inside factories, which have no windows (to avoid distracting workers), but provide heating and lighting rather than be on the street or go home. Thus there are hidden and perverse forms of symbiosis between a city where business, crime, and violence all have reached high levels of organization.[33]

Responses to Violence: The Retaking of Ciudad Juárez

In the aftermath of peak violence, city, state, and national authorities sought to reimpose order and mobilize the population against the drug cartels. Troops were withdrawn in 2010, and federal police detachments followed a year later. Municipal police authorities were strengthened, and police officers were retrained and professionalized.[34] New civic plans attempted to give citizens more say in reforms and promoted urban rehabilitation schemes in which the key themes were transparency of public administration and the refurbishment of public amenities, from education to sport and culture.[35] As well as top-down initiatives, there were coalitions of civic groups such as *Ciudadanos por una Mejor Administración Publica* (Citizens for a Better Public Administration) and the *Alta La Voz* (Raise Your Voice) campaign, which produced two thousand proposals for policy changes.

The most ambitious rehabilitation scheme was *Todos Somos Juárez* (TSJ), or "We Are All Juárez," which targeted social problems with a holistic approach to addressing diverse aspects of insecurity. Actions focused on economic development, employment, education, health, and public security, as well as coordination among federal, state, and municipal authorities. For each policy area a civic council was created, and TSJ was promoted as a forum by which the city's inhabitants could speak against the violence. The program led to hundreds of individual policy actions and programs and over $400 million in federal spending in 2010 and 2011. Around three quarters of the budget was directed to investments in health, education, culture, sports, and recreation. The government also emphasized that improving the business climate was a key element in improving life in the city.[36]

TSJ was a novel approach for the Mexican authorities: it acknowledged that violence had deep social roots, and it sought to regenerate a sense of civic solidarity, despite a legacy of fear; citizens were still afraid to gather publicly and suspicious that their neighbors might be affiliated with gangs or cartels. Ex-President Calderón, initiator of the war on drugs, was the architect of TSJ. "We have achieved positive results, because we not only listened to the people of Juárez but also got them on board to solve this problem with us."[37]

To critics, TSJ was little more than a few government slogans. Civil society groups described it as an exclusive program to improve a few districts of the city. Some regarded it as social cleansing. Among the business community, there was a new engagement with civic authorities. Business leaders were determined to play a dominant role in coordinating public and private initiatives. However, the private sector was also prepared to challenge the agenda of public agencies, and it persisted in promoting its vision of manufacturing strength as a force for security and social change, claiming its aim was to raise living standards on both sides of the border. Acknowledging that "in 60 percent of meetings [with foreign investors], security was top of their concerns," business also continued to play down the extent of the violence and argued that it was somehow uncivic to dwell on the murder rate and drug killings. In the neoliberal narrative, the so-called real Ciudad Juárez was a city of endless economic possibilities—a global powerhouse, not a local killing ground.

Companies also demanded changes in education and public services to secure a more reliable and effective workforce, and they increased pressure on U.S. and Mexican government officials to ease border controls. The frontier now became a contested space in the rescue of Juárez. "Wait times are the challenge for 2015. The longer a vehicle waits, the more revenue is lost. We are not saying don't secure the border, but don't do it in a way that impedes traffic."[38]

New alliances were formed—for example, programs such as Sister Cities and Resilient Cities—to leverage the influence of companies on both sides of the border and to connect Juárez with not only other business communities but also centers of art and culture. In trying to minimize the significance of the border as a physical barrier, businesses also sought increased internationalization of the city, in the words of one executive, "to put us on the global map."[39] The Borderplex alliance is one example: formed in 2012, it includes forty to fifty leading companies in Juárez and El Paso. Privately funded, the Borderplex alliance undertakes initiatives in education, arts, public affairs, and management training. It framed drug violence as a regional and global concern and attempted to create practices of security that could reach beyond municipal, state, and federal agendas to international and transnational levels.

Business-funded campaigns such as *Orgulloso Ser Juarense* (Proud To Be from Juárez) and *Adelante Juárez* (Forward Juárez) used development consultants, public opinion polling, and public relations firms to refurbish Juárez's image as a turnaround city.

The public security culture responded to the drop in the murder rate by citizens reclaiming public spaces, occupying deserted houses, and returning to restaurants and bars, while maintaining pressure on civic authorities to keep their promises of urban regeneration. Consumers rediscovered the al fresco, spontaneous sociability that had been the city's hallmark. "There was a clear shift. . . . people started sticking together. Once the security forces left we had a clear change in our sense of commonness. We are a lot less trusting, but we have learned to watch for ourselves and for each other."[40] In 2016, Pope Francis visited Ciudad Juárez, preaching solidarity across the frontier. His visit inspired a campaign to attract tourists. When I entered the Web site "Visit Juárez," it was an empty page.

There is a recurring pattern in Juárez. Despite reform attempts, security remains partial, sectional, and individual rather than a shared public concern. Businesses see new problems arising from poor coordination between public and private initiatives and confusion from the proliferation of rehabilitation programs. Civil society sees continued marginalization and exclusion of groups such as migrants as well as women and young people. Security culture—whether based on the border, business, or the citizenry—shares a common assumption, though: that of the "relatively absent state."[41]

Shake the kaleidoscope, and new patterns begin to emerge. The crisis for Ciudad Juárez has abated, in the sense that murder rates have continued to fall until recently. The downtown area once again is lively with restaurants, bars, and local businesses. Some residents even talk of the city's "renaissance."[42] Yet Trump's insistence on a border wall, coupled with his rejection of the terms of the NAFTA treaty, once again challenges the delicate relationship between these two interdependent cities, Juárez and El Paso. These actions also undermine the neoliberal security narrative that is at the heart of what connects the cities. Although murder rates have started to climb again, as all over Mexico, Juárez residents are less fearful that the violence will overwhelm their city, because today it is between drug gangs rather than an epidemic of killing and lawlessness that targeted ordinary citizens and daily life. There is perhaps more to fear from the anti-immigration security rhetoric coming from the White House, which seeks to rupture what holds these two historic cross-border neighbors together.

Perhaps the greatest ambiguity to be resolved is how to view the frontier that has shaped so much of Juárez's history and culture. For over a hundred years, decisions about the city have been based on the border "as an unending resource and eternal comparative advantage."[43] This perception was entrenched with the growth of Juárez as a global manufacturing hub. Since 2001, the "border as resource" has been challenged by a counternarrative that presents it as a threat to U.S. and global security, overlooking the economic benefits from proximity to cheap labor on the Mexican side of the frontier and from migrations that have boosted the population resource on the American side.[44]

Trump has rejected both premises and staked his presidency on the counternarrative of threat and harm. *Juaresenses* who sometimes spend hours queuing to pass customs and immigration controls, or who are denied transit altogether, view the border as both an asset and a curse. It is also a reminder of the gulf in welfare between one side of the Rio Grande and the other, which has widened since 2007.

Juárez is a continuously impermanent city. Nowhere better represents this shifting nature than El Chamizal, the park at the border. Once part of Texas, it was fought over as a symbol of territorial sovereignty by both countries. In the worst days of the drug violence, it became notorious as a dumping ground for corpses by the cartels, a reminder of the struggle between organized crime and citizens for control of public space. After 2012, *Juaresenses* began returning to picnic under its trees and to play baseball. When the pope held an open-air mass at the frontier, he was formally greeted by a student chosen by local churches because he lives in Juárez but goes to school in El Paso.

The binomial metropolis might have been fractured and fragmented, riven by inequalities of power and prospects, wealth and security. But its citizens will continue to find ways—illegal and legal—of crossing its divides.

Notes

1. Christopher Power, "U.S. Companies Are Still Rushing to Juárez," *Bloomberg Business* June 10, 2010, bloomberg.com/news/articles/2010-06 -10/u-dot-s-dot-companies-are-still-rushing-to-ju-rez; Nathaniel Parish Flannery, "Big Businesses Boom in an Unlikely Mexican City," *Global Post*, August 23, 2012, http://www.globalpost.com/dispatch/news/regions /americas/mexico/120822/mexican-economy-Juárez-exports-outsourcing -multinationals-business?page=0,0.
2. American Public Health Association, "Public Health Impact of US Immigration Policy," November 9, 2010, https://www.apha.org/policies-and -advocacy/public-health-policy-statements/policy-database/2014/07/30 /13/53/public-health-impact-of-us-immigration-policy (restricted access).

3. Instituto Nacional de Estadística Geografía e Informática, México (INEGI), https://www.inegi.org.mx/.

4. E. Edmonds-Poli and David Shirk, *Contemporary Mexican Politics*. Lanham, MD: Rowman and Littlefield, 2009), 388.

5. Silvia Otero, "Detalla Sedena estrategia del Operacion Conjunto Juárez,' *El Universal*, March, 7, 2008, http://www.eluniversal.com.mx /notas/493387.html.

6. K. Staudt and Z. Y. Mendez, *Courage, Resistance and Women in Ciudad Juarez* (Austin: University of Texas Press, 2015), 99.

7. The militarization of public security has a long history in Mexico. Presidents before Calderón not only turned to the armed forces as a more effective and credible means of combating the drug cartels but also responded to pressure from the United States to stem illegal flows of narcotics across the U.S.–Mexico border. See Jesús A. Lopez-Gonzalez, *Presidencialismo y Fuerzas Armadas en México 1876–2012. Una relación de contrastes* (Puerto Vallarta, México: Gernika, 2012).

8. The arrests failed to detain the criminal leaders. Failure to prosecute narco traffickers has been another symptom of government weakness and complicity with the cartels. The saga of El Chapo, Sinaloa cartel leader Joaquin Guzman, who twice escaped from custody following arrest, reinforced the widespread perception that the government's strategy for addressing organized crime was either incompetent or corrupted. See Ed Vulliamy, "Joaquin 'El Chapo' Guzman: The Truth About the Jailbreak of the Milennium," *Guardian*, July 13, 2015, https://www.theguardian.com/world/2015/jul/13 /joachin-el-chapo-guzman-jailbreak-mexican-drug-lord-escape-prison.

9. Tony Payan, "Ciudad Juárez: A Perfect Storm on the US–Mexico Border," *Journal of Borderlands Studies* 29, no. 4 (2014): 435–47.

10. See U.S. Customs and Border Protection, "Vision and Strategy 2020: U.S. Customs and Border Protection Strategic Plan," http://www.cbp.gov /sites/default/files/documents/CBP-Vision-Strategy-2020.pdf.

11. G. Correa-Cabrera, "Seguridad y Migración en las Fronteras de México: Diagnóstico y Recomendaciones de Política y Cooperación Regional," *Migracion y Desarrollo* 12, no. 22 (2014): 154.

12. Interview with U.S. Border Patrol staff, February 18, 2015.

13. Interview with anonymous employee, El Paso, February 19, 2015.

14. Anonymous interview with an Intelligence Group officer, El Paso, February 19, 2015.

15. "Military Experts: With ISIS in El Paso, Ft Bliss in Danger of Terrorist Attack," *Judicial Watch*, September 4, 2014, https://www.judicialwatch

.org/corruption-chronicles/military-experts-isis-el-paso-ft-bliss-danger
-terrorist-attack/.

16. Clare Ribando Seelke and Kristin Finklea, "U.S.–Mexican Security Cooperation: The Mérida Initiative and Beyond," *Congressional Research Service Report*, May 7, 2015, https://fas.org/sgp/crs/row/R41349.pdf.

17. Ribando Seelke and Finklean, "U.S. –Mexican Security Co-operation, 2; U.S. Department of State, *Congressional Budget Justification for Foreign Operations FY 2010–FY 2016*. Washington, DC: U.S. Department of State.

18. Citizen's Council for Public Security and Criminal Justice, 2017 report.

19. Wright, "National Security Versus Public Safety," 293.

20. Víctor M. Quintana S., op-ed, *La Jornada*, March 1, 2013.

21. Telephone interview with a Ciudad Juárez resident, March 1, 2015.

22. See Edmond Parish Flannery, "Remembering Charles Bowden," September 1, 2014, http://www.forbes.com/sites/nathanielparishflannery/2014/09/01 /remembering-charles-bowden/.

23. Telephone interview in March 2015.

24. Interview with Red Mesa de Mujeres, Ciudad Juárez, February 19, 2015.

25. Interview with volunteers from DHIA, a human rights organisztion, Ciudad Juárez, February 19, 2015.

26. Interview with Irma Casas, Casa Amiga director, Ciudad Juárez, February 20, 2015.

27. A. Ong, *Neoliberalilsm as Exception: Mutations in Citizenship and Sovereignty* (Durham, NC: Duke University Press, 2006); Eisenhammer, "Bare Life in Ciudad Juárez."

28. Payan, "Ciudad Juárez: A Perfect Storm on the U.S.–Mexico Border."

29. Compared with its prime economic competitor, China, Juárez has seen salary growth of 65 percent in ten years rather than the 250 percent increase in China. Paso del Norte Economic Indicator Review April 1, 2015; INEGI. See also Abraham Medina, "2015 Ciudad Juárez Labor Market Is Well-Positioned due to Last Year's Gains," *Tecma Trust*, January 18, 2015.

30. Interview in El Paso, February 18, 2015.

31. "Peace in Mexico?" Security Strategies and Human Rights," *Peace Brigades International, Mexico Project Bulletin* (2014): 8, https://pbideutschland.de /fileadmin/user_files/groups/germany/Dateien/150121_Peace_in_Mexico .pdf.

32. A. Bermudez, quoted in M. Rodriguez and H. Rivero, "ProNaF, Ciudad Juarez: Planning and Urban Transformation," *A/Z, ITU Journal of the Faculty of Architecture* 8, no. 1:196–207.

33. Cd Juárez Testimonio de Vida 2011, Mexican American Catholic College http://www.maccsa.org/documents/Immigration%20Authors/JorgeVargas CMF.pdf.

34. H. Alexander, "How Mexico's Most Dangerous City Transformed Itself to Become Safe Enough for the Pope," *Telegraph*, February 17, 2016, http://www.telegraph.co.uk/news/worldnews/centralamericaandthecaribbean /mexico/12155890/How-Mexicos-most-dangerous-city-transformed -itself-to-become-safe-enough-for-the-Pope.html.

35. Plan Estrategico Juarez, http://planjuarez.org/.

36. Federal government, Mexico, "Se Promueve en Ciudad Juarez Recuperacion de la Actividad Economica" (Press Release), Economics Ministry, 2010. http://www.2006-2012.economia.gob.mx/eventos-noticias/sala-de -prensa/comunicados/6417-se-promueve-en-ciudad-juarez-recuperacion -de-la-actividad-economica.

37. F. Calderón, "Todos Somos Juárez: An Innovative Strategy to Tackle Violence and Crime," *Latin America Journal* (February 19, 2013).

38. Interview with Marcus Delgado, Borderplex El Paso, February 18, 2015.

39. Interview with Marcos Delgado.

40. Interview with Carola Chavez.

41. Staudt et al. 2010. See also Sassen 2007, 213–14.

42. Rick Jervis, "As Trump Demands a Wall, Violence Returns to Texas Border in Ciudad Juárez,' " *USA TODAY*, February 17, 2019, https://www .usatoday.com/story/news/nation/2019/02/15/ciudad-juarez-mexico -el-paso-border-security-donald-trump-violence/2878082002/.

43. Payan 2014, 437.

44. Correa-Cabrera et al. 2015.

References

Ainslie, Ricardo. 2013. *The Fight to Save Juárez*. Austin: University of Texas Press.

Angotti, T. 2014. "The Seventh Generation. Social Justice at the Borders." *Progressive Planning* 200 (Summer): 12–15.

Bowden, Charles. 2010. *Murder City*. New York: Nation.

Correa-Cabrera, Guadalupe, Michelle Keck, and José Nava. 2015 "Losing the Monopoly of Violence: The State, a Drug War and the Paramilitarization of Organized Crime in Mexico (2007–10)." *State Crime Journal* 4 (1): 77–95.

Edmonds-Poli, E., and David Shirk. 2009. *Contemporary Mexican Politics*. Lanham, MD: Rowman Littlefield.

Eisenhammer, Stephen. 2014. "Bare Life in Ciudad Juárez: Violence in a Space of Exclusion." *Latin American Perspectives* 41 (2): 99–109.

López-González, Jesús A. 2012. "Civil-Military Relations and the Militarization of Public Security in Mexico, 1989–2010: Challenges to Democracy." In *Mexico's Struggle for Public Security. Organized Crime and State Responses*, edited by George Philip and Susana Berruecos. New York: Palgrave Macmillan.

Payan, Tony. 2014 "Ciudad Juárez: A Perfect Storm on the U.S.–Mexico Border." *Journal of Borderlands Studies* 29 (4): 435–47.

Philip, George, and Susana Berruecos, eds. 2012. *Mexico's Struggle for Public Security. Organized Crime and State Responses.* New York: Palgrave Macmillan.

Red Mesa de Mujeres. 2010. *Cotton Field.* Mexico City: Red Mesa de Mujeres de Ciudad Juárez.

Ribando Seelke, Clare, and Kristin Finklea. 2015. "U.S.-Mexican Security Cooperation: The Mérida Initiative and Beyond." *Congressional Research Service Report* May 7, 2015 (updated June 29, 2017). https://crsreports.congress.gov/product/pdf/R/R41349

Sassen, S. 2007. *Deciphering the Global: Its Scales, Spaces and Subjects.* London: Routledge.

Staudt, K., and Z. Y. Mendez. 2015. *Courage, Resistance and Women in Ciudad Juárez.* Austin: University of Texas Press.

Wright, M. 2011. "National Security Versus Public Safety: Femicide, Drug Wars, and the Mexican State." In *Accumulating Insecurity: Violence and Dispossession in the Making of Everyday Life*, edited by Shelley Feldman, Charles Geisler, and Gayatri A. Menon. Athens, GA: University of Georgia Press.

5

Responding to, or Perpetuating, Urban Insecurity?

Enclave-Making in Karachi

SOBIA AHMAD KAKER

Since the 1980s, Karachiites have lived through and survived phases of extreme murderous violence. Until recently, the ongoing battle between conflicting ethnopolitical groups, criminal gangs, and state security forces had been mostly contained within Karachi's peripheral zones (Gayer 2014). Consequently, news of violent clashes among various criminal groups, their political sponsors, and the armed forces in the peripheral zones of the vast megacity—such as Lyari, Orangi, or North Karachi—often did little to disrupt everyday life in the vibrant central districts that lie within the south and central districts of the city.

However, present-day events have come to challenge this oversimplified popular imagery of the Pakistani megacity as a divided city where urban violence and its related insecurities are almost containable within certain districts.[1] Today, violence is no longer limited to Karachi's politicized and criminalized peripheral zones. It has permeated the previously safe districts of south and central Karachi, which are more developed and deeply integrated within the global economy.

This expansion of violence has become especially evident since the start of the war on terror in 2001 when the Pakistani state became an ally to the U.S. and NATO forces fighting against al-Qaeda and the Taliban. Although the theaters of conflict lie in Afghanistan and the tribal frontier regions across the Pakistan–Afghanistan border, the ongoing conflict and related displacement of populations from the region has deeply affected urban life and security in Karachi. In the last few years, new criminal actors such as jihadist groups and extortionist gangs working to raise funds for al-Qaeda's nefarious activities have added strength to the city's existing ethno-political-criminal nexus (Yusuf 2012; Mezzera 2011; Rehman 2013).

With the arrival of these actors, conflict among various ethno-political-criminal gangs has intensified, and the number of felonious activities that victimize ordinary Karachiites has spread across the city. Irrespective of where they live, work, or circulate, Karachiites live under the constant threat of extortion, armed robberies, kidnapping for ransom, muggings, and vehicle snatching. Added to this, citizens are increasingly frightened by the relentless terrorist attacks that target government and military offices, foreign consulates, luxury hotels, and busy shopping districts within the administrative districts of Saddar Town and Clifton Cantonment (Yusuf 2012; Anis, Anthony, and Mangi 2014). Against this background Karachi has gained notoriety as "one of the most dangerous cities in the world" (Khan 2013; Magnier 2013).

In this environment of heightened insecurity at the time of this research, the bid to restore order and safety led ordinary residents to bunker down in what Caldeira famously described as fortified enclaves, which are essentially "privatized, enclosed and monitored spaces for residence, consumption, leisure, and work" (Caldeira 1996, 303). As illustrated in figures 5.1 and 5.2, ordinary spaces such as parks, offices, residential neighborhoods, and

Figure 5.1 Community Watch (in Blue Uniforms) Stand Watch in an Enclosed Ethnopolitical Enclave in Azizabad, North Karachi.

Source: Photograph by author (2013).

Figure 5.2 Port Grand.

Source: Photograph by author (2013).

commercial zones and malls were closed off to the public and fortified with the help of gates, barriers, razor wire, and armed private guards. Karachi became emblematic of a so-called new military urbanism; that is, a condition whereby cities that are not formal sites of war are securitized through military logistics (Graham 2010, xiv).

Unlike what is common in other global cities characterized by rampant insecurity (Caldeira 2000; Jürgens and Landman 2006; Hook and Vrdoljak 2002), such visible and spatial forms of privatization, security, and enclosure are not normal for Karachi. Although detached homes have traditionally enjoyed privacy through boundary walls, lifestyle communities and collectively walled and gated security parks have not been traditional forms of residential development in the megacity. Prebuilt gated enclaves exist in the form of military officer colonies in designated cantonment lands, but the construction and marketing of privately developed gated communities that commodify security is a recent phenomenon. Given the limited supply of such securitized housing estates, and the fact that it was difficult for many settled homeowners to relocate within the new gated enclaves, between 2010 and 2014 residents from all walks of life in central and south Karachi started collectively organizing to convert their otherwise open-plan neighborhoods into retrofitted fortified enclaves. They started practicing what I call *enclavization* to ensure neighborhood-level security.

I use *enclavization* to denote the processes through which enclaved spaces are constructed and continuously enacted. This is different from the term *enclave*, which merely refers to an urban format of enclosure and/or separation (such as gated communities or ethnic enclaves).[2] Whereas *enclave* refers to a fixed or static physical form, enclavization denotes the process of enclave-making. Processes of enclavization are therefore the ongoing means—material and/or discursive—through which enclaves are created and upheld. In Karachi, these include some or all of the following elements: private armed security guards, community watch groups, discursive construction of the neighborhood as private property, and/or installing security artifacts such as street barriers, CCTV cameras, and metal detector gates. The primary aim of such enclavization is to ensure collective security and create distance between those living inside and the wider city outside.

During my fieldwork in Karachi, even though I heard that residents and government officials found that enclavization was an effective means of managing urban insecurity, I found the practice to be highly problematic. This is mainly because the practice rests on a false premise that everyday urban interactions and circulations can be segregated neatly to produce security. Enclave-making actually intensifies urban interactions between the rich and the potentially dangerous poor. This is especially the case because private security guards from the city's so-called dangerous slums come to work in shifts to secure affluent enclaves. The resulting interactions between those working, living, and managing enclaves on an everyday basis showcase how paradoxical everyday practices of enclavization actually are. By exacerbating existing inequalities and urban marginality in a city that is already highly polarized, practices of enclavization in fact work to perpetuate urban insecurity.

In the rest of this chapter, I elaborate on this problematic to argue that in Karachi, processes of enclavization work to securitize particular people and places unevenly. The related processes of securitization are productive of political subjectivities and difference in a city that is already violently divided along the lines of social class, ethnicity, and religion. As a result, I argue that such processes of enclavization generate extreme marginality and vulnerability for the urban poor, who are forced to turn to their own forms of community protection and preservation in the face of elite-led violence and state terror.

To elaborate these arguments, I first address the broader context of enclavization in Karachi and explain the structural factors and climate of governance within which present-day enclavization is taking place. Next, I elaborate how processes of enclavization in the unequal and sociospatially polarized megacity are relational and self-perpetuating. Following that elaboration, I provide particular examples from everyday interactions between residents, workers, and visitors and guards in enclaved spaces to highlight the impossibility of separation between inside and outside spaces, and how the very processes of enclavization that aim to isolate and segregate generate increased circulations. I conclude the chapter by highlighting how processes of enclavization generate paradoxes of security and insecurity in a highly complex urban system that is already wrought with stark social, material, and political inequalities and interactions.

The evidence presented in the sections that follow is based on research conducted for my PhD thesis, "Enclaves as Process: Space, Security, and Violence in Karachi." The project was informed by six months of ethnographic fieldwork conducted in Karachi between 2011 and 2013.

Urbanization and Enclavization in the Divided City

Karachi is Pakistan's largest city and is home to approximately 20 million residents. It is also widely recognized as one of the fastest-growing megacities in the world (Kotkin and Cox 2013; Birch and Wachter 2011). Karachi's phenomenal growth is not new; the bustling port city has attracted and absorbed successive waves of migrants continuously since its annexation by the British East India Company in 1839.

The biggest population surge in Karachi came after the creation of Pakistan in 1947, when Muslim migrants from India thronged into Karachi to start a new life in the newly created country. Census records show that between 1941 and 1951, Karachi's population more than doubled. As the political, economic, and financial capital of the new country, Karachi continued to attract unskilled and semiskilled laborers from all over Pakistan—but especially ethnic Pashtuns from the underdeveloped northwestern regions of the country (Hasan 1999). Further waves of migration occurred in the 1970s and 1980s, when refugees displaced by conflict in Bangladesh and Afghanistan moved to Karachi to seek refuge and rebuild their lives. As a result the city's population surged from 3,426,310 in 1972 to 5,208,132 in 1981.

At the last official census in 1998, the city's population was recorded as slightly more than 9 million people. In the absence of any census since then, in 2007 the city government estimated the population to have grown by 56 percent, or up to 14.5 million. The megacity has continued to grow at an alarmingly rapid pace. In the last decade, Karachi has attracted migrants from conflict-ridden areas that lie along the frontiers of the war on terror in Pakistan and Afghanistan, as well as internally displaced populations from the flood-prone regions in Sindh and Punjab. As a result of these continuous waves of migration, the world's fastest-growing megacity is also Pakistan's most ethnolinguist-cially diverse city, with its population consisting of people from all major ethnic groups in Pakistan, such as Mohajirs, Pashtuns, Punjabis, Sindhis, and Balochis.

As is common in other postcolonial cities across the global south, Karachi is unevenly developed and sociospatially polarized. This is not only a function of colonial practices of land planning and development through which the city was divided into white and native neighborhoods but also due to informal land development and migrant settlement over successive years (Gayer 2003). Between 1941 and 1961, Karachi's population increased by a staggering and unprecedented 432 percent (Gayer 2003), leaving the city governors to cope with an exponentially growing housing demand. In these circumstances, post-Partition migrants settled in refugee camps and squatter settlements within the city center, and the ongoing demand for low-income housing was met informally by a nexus of community elders and settlers, entrepreneurial land developers, political patrons, and corrupt officials (Gazdar and Mallah 2011; Budhani et al. 2010). Poor urban migrants settled in inner-city squatter settlements and informally developed *katchi abadis* (irregular settlements) along drainage channels, marshlands, or transport arteries across the city's central districts, or on illegally subdivided land in the city's peripheries (Hasan 1999; Hasan and Mohib 2003).

As a result of such processes of land development and populational settlement, the present-day megacity is wrought with stark material inequalities. More than 50 percent of Karachi's 20 million residents live in *katchi abadis*, the majority of which are spread outward into the city's peripheries (Hasan and Mohib 2003). However, the densest *katchi abadis* remain in central and south Karachi and are tightly nestled in the midst of key government offices, the global financial district, five-star luxury hotels, and elite spaces of residence and consumption. In map 5.1, the latter are labeled in black and prominent *katchi abadis* are circled in white.

Even though these *katchi abadis* provide essential housing for laborers and service workers who are integral to the functioning of the global city, over the past few years, these areas have gained a reputation in local and international media as being places that

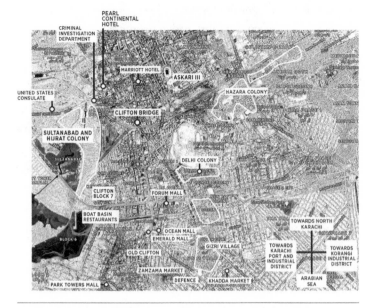

Map 5.1 South Karachi. Dense *katchi abadis* (outlined in white) are nested within affluent spaces (annotated).

Source: Google Earth (2019).

breed criminality and are hotbeds of violence (Raja 2013; Khan 2013; Breman 2012). This reputation is not entirely unfounded: when ethnopolitical tensions are high in the city, politicized ethnic clusters within Karachi's *katchi abadis* become increasingly volatile. Their residents not only become subjects of violence, but they also perpetuate it in tit-for-tat killings across rival ethnopolitical clusters in other *katchi abadis*.

This violence, however, is tied to politicization that occurred as a result of the vote bank politics in which *katchi abadi* residents participated to ensure security of tenure and access to basic infrastructure such as water, electricity, and waste management within otherwise illegal settlements (Gazdar and Mallah 2011).

Most of Karachi's *katchi abadis* have been able to flourish under the protection of community leaders who are either supported by political patrons or are members of powerful ethno-militant political parties or of notorious criminal gangs (Budhani et al. 2010; Gazdar and Mallah 2011). More recently, some of the *abadis* have come into the spotlight as spaces that are controlled by Taliban groups. Recent arrests of high-profile Taliban militants and other members of the party also have helped to lend a reputation of ethnic clusters within some *abadis* as spaces that have been known to provide refuge to Taliban or Taliban sympathizers (Anwar 2014; Khan 2013; Rodriguez 2010).

Knowledge of the ways in which life in *katchi abadis* is lived and negotiated, coupled with negative media representation of such spaces, results in constructing an image of *katchi abadis* as dangerous places from which crime and violence emanate and spread across Karachi. As a result of these imagined geographies of place, residents in neighboring middle-class areas feel great anxiety about living in close proximity to *katchi abadis*. In interviews, residents responsible for enclave-making in Clifton Block 7 (a middle-class neighborhood that lies close to the Tikri Colony *katchi abadi*), justified their steps toward spatial enclosure. They feared that open-plan neighborhoods gave *katchi abadi* residents an advantage in carrying out crimes and then retreating to their impregnable labyrinth-like settlements. Anwar, a security volunteer in Clifton Block 7 explained:

> Criminals used to come into Block 7, commit crimes, and make off into the *katchi abadi* on the other side. I went once with the police after my maid who stole my wife's jewelery, but we couldn't get to her. They [residents] come out in droves, violently pushing the police away. The only way we have is to prevent crime in the first place. We are safer now—with our guarded barriers, twenty-four-hour patrols, and CCTV cameras!

In discussing the popularity of enclavization as a means to ensure security in Karachi, government officers explained that although the practice was not strictly legal, they allowed middle-class residents to put up guarded barriers and restrict access to the public as a necessary stopgap measure to ensure public security. According to Shahid Hayat, inspector general of Karachi Police, the city police department is understaffed and underresourced and hence unable to secure citizens of the rapidly expanding megacity. "It is not an ideal system," said Imtiaz, a senior Home Office official. "But at the moment we are facing a crisis," he continued. "By helping themselves, those who can afford it are helping us. We can divert resources to where they are most needed."

After facing pressure from urban economic elites, city officials have also conceded to middle-class residents' demands to enclose and securitize their residential neighborhoods (Zamir 2014; Zaheer 2011). Given Karachi's overwhelming significance to the national economy as a key industrial, financial, and trade hub (Budhani et al. 2010), the cost of economic disruption caused by events of mass violence and the ensuing insecurity is significant. A single day of suspended economic activities in Karachi can cost up to $10 billion in lost trade and industrial revenue (Yusuf 2012).

In this context, business lobby groups actively influence urban security policies (*Express Tribune* 2014). As groups that have extensive resources, political reach, and a keen interest in urban security, Karachi's business lobby groups also play an active role as citizen-police liaisons and public security consultants. They head civil society organizations such as the Citizen Police Liaison Committee (CPLC), which both encourage and offer support for enclavization in middle-class and affluent residential areas.

Therefore, the production of enclaves in middle-class residential areas in Karachi is made possible through various intersecting factors. Uneven infrastructural development, socio-spatial inequality, and flexible arrangements of urban security governance have allowed Karachiites to respond to heightened insecurity through enclavization. However, the city government's encouragement of enclavization in Karachi is selective. Although enclavization is implicitly supported in middle-class and upper-middle-class localities, officials do not tolerate similar processes of enclavization in many of the city's lower-income neighborhoods, and especially not in the many irregular settlements.

However, residents of Karachi's *katchi abadis* are equally victims of violence and everyday insecurities, and many attempt to organize into tightly insular enclaves. Nevertheless, government officials are not sympathetic to community-led securitization in such spaces. In news media and policy reports, enclavized *katchi abadis* are negatively portrayed as "no-go" areas for police and security forces. In such spaces, enclavization is seen by state officials as a specific form of territorialization that serves illicit groups that aim to challenge state authority and spread violence and terror in the city.

Thus the right to ensure personal safety through collectively organized enclosure is a privilege not granted to all Karachiites equally. Although city officials consider enclavization in middle-class and affluent residential areas to be an act of necessity, enclavization in *katchi abadis* is criminalized and violently opposed by the state. In the following section, I expand on why this is the case and why such a differentiated policy stance on enclavization across different urban spaces is problematic. In doing so, I showcase how enclavization and insecurity exist in a continuum and how processes of enclavization are relational and self-perpetuating across affluent and poor neighborhoods alike.

The Continuum of Insecurity and Relational Enclavization

The official bias in allowing some citizens to privatize and securitize their neighborhoods while violently opposing similar practices by others stems from past experiences of enclavization and violence in Karachi. In the late 1980s, an alarming rise in ethnopolitical violence in Karachi corresponded to the reterritorialization of the city's disenfranchised, ethnically homogenous neighborhoods along ethnopolitical lines. Police officials recall how in the 1980s, members of the Muhajir Qaumi Movement (MQM)—a militant ethnopolitical party—entrenched themselves in fortified enclaves from which they spread terror and violence across the city in a bid to gain political influence in national politics (Gayer 2014). These enclaves became no-go areas for police and security forces and were forcefully opened up after a brutal protracted military operation that helped weaken the party's political organization (Gayer 2014; Khan 2010).

During the same period, Karachiites who did not directly participate in related violent politics set up barriers and checkpoints at street openings to protect themselves from ongoing violence among and between factions of the MQM and state security representatives. State officials interpreted these actions of privately securitizing the neighborhood as harmless and defensive. Once the military operation against the MQM was successful and peace restored, these enclaves were opened up without any accompanying violence.

Present-day enclavization in Karachi is distinguishable from its historical form by way of context but not by way of its interpretation. Political relations between the state and residents of *katchi abadis* are steeped in mutual mistrust, and once again, state officials view protective enclavization in *katchi abadis* to be a form of territorialization of space that can potentially challenge state authority. Police and security forces often find it difficult to penetrate particular enclaves within densely packed *katchi abadis*. On the surface, it seems that enclave-making in *katchi abadis* is intended to keep police and security officials away from apparent criminal groups and activities. However, deeper ethnographic engagement within *katchi abadis* such as Sultanabad, Hijrat colony, and Railway colony highlight that processes of enclavization within such spaces is a means through which marginal residents negotiate community-level protection from violence within and outside the *abadis*. In fact, practices of enclave-making within *katchi abadis* in central Karachi are related to enclosure and heightened securitization in neighboring middle-class areas and in the rest of the city.

I will elaborate this point through the case of Sultanabad, a multiethnic *katchi abadi* in central Karachi that constitutes various concentrated ethnic clusters. Following the influx of migrants from tribal areas along the Pakistan–Afghanistan border, the settlement has become denser, and residents have become more susceptible to crime. They reported being victims of petty theft of mobile phones, food items, and even monetary savings. They discussed how over the past five years, drug peddling and abuse became increasingly rampant, and that the culture and politics of the settlement started changing. Frustration with the existing political order, sympathies with fellow Pashtuns becoming victims of the war on terror, and successful canvassing by right-wing conservative Pasthun nationalists led young Pashtuns within the settlement to participate in violent politics. With upcoming local elections, resident party workers from Pashtun nationalist parties started to threaten minority groups within the settlement with violence, demanding that they trade votes for protection.

Other than facing such routine forms of violence, residents from the settlement also suffered police brutality. They reported being victims of militarized search-and-arrest operations that aimed to round up suspects involved in crimes that included robbery, illegal drug trading, and terrorism. Many termed themselves as victims of state aggression and urban violence, left to fend for themselves, while the city government and police remained interested only in what one resident called "solving the problems of the 'big people.'"

For Sultanabad's urban poor, the constant violence was an unbearable ordeal. Kausar, a long-time resident complained: "Between the police and the forthcoming elections, I have had enough! Every few days the police come in—I don't know who or what they are looking for. And then all these local party workers come in, looking for votes, sweet-talking and threatening in the same breath!"

Precarious residents within Sultanabad therefore enacted enclavization as a means to protect themselves against everyday insecurity from other groups within the larger settlement and/or from police brutality and injustice. They participated in enclave-making through various means, including physically blocking some streets, deliberately misleading and resisting police officers who were trying to enter particular lanes, and apprehending other unrecognizable outsiders to prevent their venturing into residential alleys within the settlements. Residents of the Balti Mohalla within Sulatanabad went one step further to create separation from the rest of the enclave and to limit access into their enclave from outside by putting up gates at entry points, which they locked from the inside at night, and by setting up a regular community watch. They found such practices especially helpful in protecting themselves against incidents of sectarian and political violence from particular youth groups within and outside Sultanabad.

Conversations with residents of Hijrat colony (a *katchi abadi* close to Sultanabad) revealed that they, too, attempted to restrict so-called outsiders from entering their settlement. Jugnu, a young resident who worked as a sweeper in the city government, mentioned that this was a direct reaction to residents' experiences of high-handedness from police officials at the behest of residents in the neighboring middle-class enclave of Bath Island. "Yes, we don't let the police in—for our own safety!" he said. "You saw how the rangers killed Sarfaraz? How can we let them in when they bypass justice to punish us on the behest of the rich?"[3] In referring to a high-profile case of state brutality against a common thief who belonged to Hijrat colony, Jugnu voiced the common sentiment among *katchi abadi* dwellers who felt unrepresented by state security personnel and victimized by the middle class's security concerns.

Given that enclave creation in Karachi's precarious *katchi abadis* is a response to perceived state abandonment in the face of extremely marginal living conditions, I found the current policy of encouraging enclavization in middle-class neighborhoods while rejecting similar practices of enclosure in the city's *katchi abadis* to be clearly counterintuitive and dysfunctional. In fact, I argue that the phenomenon is not only relational but also self-perpetuating, particularly when one considers how the stark material and sociopolitical inequalities in the megacity push the urban poor into developing ties with violent urban actors so they may gain protection from communal violence as well as state-led violence. Yet the reputation of *katchi abadis* as spaces that house violent urban actors spills over to taint all its residents as potential criminals—even though they themselves may be victims of violence. When moving around the increasingly walled and closed-off city, *katchi abadi* residents are routinely criminalized at checkposts and guarded barriers. The systematic securitization of their bodies exacerbates their already marginal status in a megacity where security and criminal justice are increasingly being privatized.

In addition to the problem of insecurity in the fact that Karachi exists in a continuum and that enclavization is relational, I also found that the practice was doomed to failure in that it created complete separation between the safe enclave inside and the feral city outside. The nature of urban life is inherently about interactions, circulations, and interconnections that are often impossible to fully securitize and filter. In the next section, I elaborate on this argument by showcasing the challenges for guards tasked with securing the enclaves to tightly surveil enclaved spaces and to properly manage security within them.

Urban Interactions and Interconnections and the Failure of Complete Enclosure

Residents' practices of enacting spatial fortification and enclosure, I argue here, signals an environmentally deterministic uptake of enclavization. The emphasis on fortification such as gates, walls, razor wire, checkpoints, and barriers suggests that physical fortification is effective in isolating spaces and protecting the inside from the "feral city" (Norton 2003) outside while enhancing surveillance by hiring private security guards and installing CCTV cameras fetishizes the idea of total security and control. Such a view fails to consider the impossibility of total isolation, visibility, and security in enclaves.

This becomes apparent when considering the everyday performance of security in enclaved spaces. For example, during my fieldwork in Karachi, I encountered the impressive security architectures around the Karachi Sheraton Hotel, which affluent

Karachiites often frequent to enjoy facilities such as restaurants, cafes, spa, and gym.[4] Security checks start well before anyone enters the hotel. Cars line up in a separate lane on the main road leading to the hotel's gate, and security guards screen each car using sniffer dogs, metal and explosive material detectors, angled mirrors, and other means. While vehicles are screened to ensure they contain no explosives or suspicious objects, passengers are questioned to determine that their visit to the hotel is for legitimate reasons. Once these security protocols are satisfied, the vehicle is granted entry. Pedestrians, too, face airport-style security checks: they are made to walk through a scanner gate while placing their bags and metal items in a basket that goes through an x-ray device. Guards stationed at these posts are tasked with identifying suspicious people or items.

This detailed security plan aims to assure customers that risky vehicles and humans are kept from infiltrating the hotel's internal spaces. In fact, however, the security plan is often not foolproof, especially as the labor of ensuring security befalls the very populations who are the referent objects of security: poor urban residents. In addition, the prospect of security is more performative than it is effective. This is especially apparent when considering that private security guards who work on rotating shifts are introduced to the neighborhoods and follow repetitive motions of looking in vehicles, making an arbitrary form of calculation on risk, and opening gates responsively.

This insight became evident through my personal experiences of moving through the pedestrian gate at Karachi Sheraton Hotel and my meeting with Aslam, a private security guard employed there. In carrying out the monotonous labor of monitoring pedestrians crossing the electronic security gates to enter the hotel, Aslam played a key role in performing security. "My presence here shows how strict Sheraton's security is," he said.

"Even if I don't fully check people's bags . . . I take a cursory look anyway. I really have no way of stopping a blast. That is all up to Allah!" Even though he played a small part in the impressive security infrastructure at Karachi Sheraton Hotel (which included sniffer dogs, CCTV cameras, and bomb-detecting machinery), Aslam's role of watching people move through and potentially intercepting them on the basis on his suspicion was integral to the discursive creation of the impregnable enclave. Yet Aslam's very presence in the hotel highlighted how an integral element of enclave-making is productive of circulations between the inside and outside of fortified enclaves.

Such necessary interactions between inside and outside spaces especially came to light during my visit to Clifton Block 7, a privately enclosed upper-middle-class neighborhood. Strategically placed roadblocks and guarded barriers along entry and exit points give an appearance of security and exclusivity to the neighborhood. The street barriers were opened during the day to allow entry into Block 7, and all barriers except one are closed from 10:00 P.M. until dawn. Twenty-four-hour CCTV cameras supplement the guards' scrutiny, and private security guards patrol the neighborhood around the clock for added vigilance. Mobile police units were stationed close outside the main entrance to provide support to the private guards in case an encounter became necessary.

In Clifton Block 7, enclave creation and maintenance was overseen by the Block 7 Residents Association. The association was formed in 2008 by community volunteers who sought neighborhood improvement. Initially, the mandate of the organization covered liaising with the city government to ensure timely rubbish clearance and to lobby for local government funds for street improvement and other such structural development in the neighborhood. However, by 2010, the association responded to an increased incidence in muggings, petty theft, and robberies and expanded its mandate to arrange privately organized neighborhood-level security. As a result, Clifton Block 7 Association members met with Home Office officials to gain sanction to restrict public access to their neighborhood. In addition to receiving this informally sanctioned privilege, they also gained support from the city police in privately apprehending criminals in the area. The city police also have offered their full support to the association members in related investigations, detentions, and trials.

However, as was the case with the Karachi Sheraton Hotel, the security barriers in Clifton Block 7 were mostly performative in nature. Interactions with guards revealed their confusion over whom to secure and against what, as well as a lack of clear direction. When asked to explain his job responsibilities, Mehboob, the guard I encountered earlier, explained, "my job is to open the barriers when the cars come, and close it when they leave." Similarly, Ishaq, another guard, voiced his confusion: "They tell us we should only let members through. But I don't know who are members and who aren't!"

Personal observations and detailed interactions with guards in Block 7 thus revealed that the task of providing security merely produces theatrical distancing between inside and outside. Such symbols effectively relieve residents and make them feel safe. Laila, a long-time resident, said, "I would always fearfully look over my shoulder when I made my way into my driveway. Now at least we are safe from muggings!"

Yet, despite offering some sense of security to residents, the increased presence of guards within these neighborhoods also generated a sense of anxiety for some urban residents, as their watchful eyes made some Block 7 residents uneasy. "I don't like the idea of these guards knowing my daily routine," admitted

Samina, a resident housewife. "I feel more insecure knowing that they are aware of my movements." In fact, the system seems to turn in on itself in multiple ways, especially as enclave managers, too, distrust the very guards who are hired to protect them.

The CCTV cameras installed at the neighborhood's entry and exit points are not there only to supplement the guards' scrutiny; the guards also have come to fear them. Members of the Block 7 Residents Association regularly warn guards that the cameras are watching them as well. Showing me the control room where coverage from neighborhood-wide CCTV cameras was aired, Saleem, a security volunteer at Block 7, proudly stated: "This to ensure that they are doing their job of being watchful—and aren't up to anything [illegal] themselves."

Intensifying Insecurity and Marginality: Enclave-Making in Action

This paradox of insecurity is a crucial aspect of enclavization. It not only showcases how impossible it is to ensure complete separation between the inside and outside of enclaved spaces but also highlights the politicized nature of enclave-making as an activity that produces political subjectivities. The upkeep of the affluent neighborhood and smooth functioning of everyday life within it is dependent on a multitude of service workers who reside in neighboring *katchi abadis*. Numerous maids, cleaners, drivers, gardeners, and household guards work within the palatial houses in Clifton Block 7, while street cleaners, garbage collectors, and other municipal service workers come and go on a daily basis. Despite being heavily dependent on these everyday workers, Clifton Block 7's enclave managers acknowledge that these workers are more commonly found to be linked to petty crime and large-scale robberies, as opposed to unknown outsiders who enter the neighborhood. Although daily workers are deemed necessary, given the lifestyle needs of residents and cultural dynamics within Pakistan, the honesty and loyalty of workers are frequently questioned, which is a constant source of anxiety for employers.

In light of such insecurities, poor urban service workers employed in the enclave are thus made referent objects of security. Enclave managers make recommendations to Block 7 residents to hire domestic workers and private guards only after rigorous background checks. The suggested procedure at the time of hiring domestic workers is to verify the validity of the potential employee's national identity card (also known as the NIC). This can be done using a short message that checks NIC numbers against personal information recorded in the government's database. The next step is to register the NIC with the local police. This enables the police to check whether the applicant has a criminal record; it also provides the police with essential information they might need to locate the employee in case he or she becomes a suspect. Thus, despite being users of enclaved spaces themselves, workers are constantly viewed with mistrust. Quotes from enclave residents and managers such as these are suggestive of the strong suspicions that enclave residents and managers hold against domestic workers: "Having a live-in maid is like inviting a thief to sleep on your porch," or "99 percent of the times, guards are in cahoots with robbers.".

Moreover, in an attempt to, in a sense, sanitize the neighborhood, Block 7 Association members restrict the freedom of maids, household guards, and drivers. Community guards are instructed to discourage loitering around the neighborhood streets and from sitting in the community park at certain times of the day. "They [workers] just sit at street corners and stare at us and our children," said Kamran, a Block 7 resident. "We want to be able to use the streets with some amount of freedom and privacy."

Such rules are resented by domestic workers, who feel constantly policed despite being integral to the smooth running of households within the enclave. Farzana, a long-serving maid working in a house in Clifton Block 7, stated, "Just because a few servants commit crimes, we all have to bear the brunt. They [employers] trust us to watch their children, look after their house, but would easily hand us over to the police if someone robs them." Another domestic worker, Farid, finds these rules contradictory: "These guards—they are poor people like us and they only have the power to stop and question us poor people. You and I both know he wouldn't dare stop anyone who's rich and influential for fear of getting beaten up or even fired."

In light of these comments from Clifton Block 7 residents and workers, I argue that the everyday interactions and circulations that are an essential part of urban life in Karachi create practical difficulties for producing a tightly segregated enclave space that can ensure security for residents. In the case of the Karachi Sheraton Hotel, despite the implementation of strict security protocols, incidents such as terrorist bombings continue to occur. Similarly, in Clifton Block 7, although residents feel much safer driving into the neighborhoods thinking that potential muggers might be unable to follow their car into their driveway, robberies and petty thefts continue unabated. In reality, the production of enclaved spaces heightens insecurities for those who work within them as essential laborers and builds paranoia for residents.

In conclusion, I argue that the stopgap measure of enclavization is not entirely effective in ensuring public safety and security. On the contrary, it exacerbates an ongoing crisis of security by discursively representing the urban poor as potential criminal actors. As poor urban residents working in and moving through middle-class enclaves are made the objects of security, they are stripped of freedoms and rights while being subjected to punitive civilian security systems. Such processes of securitization exacerbate existing urban difference, sociopolitical inequalities, and marginalization—conditions that historically have resulted in urban insecurity and violence in Karachi in the first place.

The continuum of insecurity is perpetuated when marginalized *katchi abadi* residents find protection in their own versions of enclaves, which state officials find threatening for broader urban security. In this way, the evidence presented in this chapter highlights how enclavization and processes of enclave-making in Karachi are both a self-perpetuating and a self-defeating strategy for protecting citizens against insecurity.

Notes

1. Better-off Karachiites used to consider insecurity to be a condition limited to the lived experiences of the urban poor or to parts of the city popularly referred to as "north of the bridge." The discursively constructed urban divide between the city north and south of Clifton Bridge signifies an oversimplification of characteristics that are specific to some zones within north and south Karachi. The central districts, which lie in the administrative zones of central and south Karachi, are popularly regarded by urban residents as the infallible global city, where the hyper-global elite live, work, and are entertained. Meanwhile, through frequent news of industrial action and violent clashes, north, east, and west Karachi have been discursively constructed as the peripheral zones of production, labor, violence, and dissent (Shamsie 2002; Ashraf 2012; Ahmed 2013).

2. More broadly, *enclave* is used to denote segregated spaces that are delinked from the wider city through premium infrastructural networks, exclusive political-legal arrangements with city governments, and a sociology of exclusion through which members are granted rights and privileges superior to those of nonmembers (Glasze et al. 2006; Diken and Laustsen 2005; Atkinson and Blandy 2006). In this literature, the particular focus

on lived enclaves—such as gated communities and enclosed neighborhoods, ethnoracial or sectarian enclaves, and no-go areas—highlights how privatization of space, material fortification, and restriction of mobility are key elements of urban security cultures across crime-ridden and conflicted cities such as Karachi, and how such security cultures affect everyday urban life.

3. Sarfaraz, a 19-year-old resident of Hijrat Colony, was brutally killed by state security personnel for attempting petty crime. A member of the Rangers (urban police force) shot Sarfaraz dead in a park in Clifton after he was caught attempting to mug a couple. The event sparked widespread outrage, especially as a mobile phone video released to the media showed that Sarafaraz was shot in cold blood while he begged for mercy (see Khan 2011).

4. Since 2014, the Karachi Sheraton Hotel has been rebranded as Movenpick Karachi. The security processes in the rebranded hotel, however, are very close to those followed by the Karachi Sheraton Hotel.

References

Ahmed, R. 2013. "The Great Divide." *The News Blog*, August 11, 2013. http://blogs.thenews.com.pk/blogs/2013/04/the-great-divide/.

Anis, K., A. Anthony, and F. Mangi. 2014. "Karachi Joins Chaos with Commerce in Taliban Urban Front." *Bloomberg News*, May 9, 2014. http://www.bloomberg.com/news/2014-05-08/karachi-joins-chaos-with-commerce-in-taliban-urban-front.html.

Anwar, N. H. 2014. "Urban Transformations: Brokers, Collaborative Governance and Community Building in Karachi's Periphery." *South Asian History and Culture* 5 (1): 75–92.

Ashraf, S. 2012. "The Horror of 'the Other Side of the Bridge.'" *Express Tribune Blogs*, http://blogs.tribune.com.pk/story/12021/the-horror-of-the-other-side-of-the-bridge/.

Atkinson, R., and S. Blandy. 2006. *Gated Communities*. London: Routledge.

Birch, E. L., and S. M. Wachter (eds.). 2011. *Global Urbanization*. Philadelphia: University of Pennsylvania Press.

Breman, J. 2012. "The Undercities of Karachi." *New Left Review 76*: 49–63.

Budhani, A., H. Gazdar, S. Kaker, and H. Mallah. 2010. The Open City: Social Networks and Violence in Karachi. Cities and Fragile States Working Paper no. 70, Crisis States Research Centre, London School of Economics and Political Science, March. https://www.files.ethz.ch/isn/113620/WP70.2.pdf

Caldeira, T. 1996. "Fortified Enclaves: The New Urban Segregation." *Public Culture* 8 (2): 303–28.

——. 2000. *City of Walls*. Berkeley: University of California Press.

Diken, B., and C. Laustsen. 2005. *The Culture of Exception: Sociology Facing the Camp*. London: Routledge.

Express Tribune. 2014. "Security Woes: Community Policing a Success in Industrial Zone." *Express Tribune*, June 26, 2014. http://tribune.com.pk/story/727066/security-woes-community-policing-a-success-in-industrial-zone/.

Gayer, L. 2003. "A Divided City: 'Ethnic' and 'Religious' Conflicts in Karachi, Pakistan." In *First Pakistan Seminar* (March): 1–22.

Gayer, L. 2014. *Karachi. Ordered Disorder and the Struggle for the City*. London: Hurst.

Gazdar, H., and H. Mallah. 2011. "The Making of a 'Colony' in Karachi and the Politics of Regularisation." In theme issue "Rethinking Urban Democracy in South Asia," *South Asia Multidisciplinary Academic Journal* 5. https://journals.openedition.org/samaj/3248.

Glasze, G., C. Webster, and K. Frantz. 2006. *Private Cities: Local and Global Perspectives*. London: Routledge.

Graham, S. 2010. *Cities Under Siege*. London: Verso.

Hasan, A. 1999. *Understanding Karachi*. Karachi: City.

Hasan, A., and M. Mohib. 2003. "Urban Slums Reports: The Case of Karachi, Pakistan." Understanding Slums: Case Studies for the Global Report on Human Settlements, Development Planning Unit, University College London.

Hook, D., and M. Vrdoljak. 2002. "Gated Communities, Heterotopia and a 'Rights' of Privilege: A 'Heterotopology'of the South African Security-Park." *Geoforum* 33 (2): 195–219. https://doi.org/10.1016/S0016-7185(01)00039-2.

Jürgens, U., and K. Landman. 2006. "Gated Communities in South Africa." In *Private Cities: Global and Local Perspectives*, edited by G. Glasze, C. Webster, and K. Frantz, 105–22. London: Routledge.

Khan, T. 2010. "Karachi Mafia Seek Political Clout with Land Grabs." World, *The National*, December 30, 2010. http://www.thenational.ae/news/world/south-asia/karachi-mafia-seek-political-clout-with-land-grabs.

——. 2011. "Collateral Murder by Pakistan Ranger." Accessed August 13, 2019. http://www.youtube.com/watch?v=I4Z71buXTgU.

——. 2013. "Where Law Enforcers Fear to Tread: The Entry Fee for These Spots of Karachi May Be Your Life." *Express Tribune*, March 23, 2013. http://tribune.com.pk/story/525035/where-law-enforcers-fear-to-tread-the-entry-fee-for-these-spots-of-karachi-may-be-your-life-karachi-city/.

Kotkin, J., and W. Cox. 2013. "The World's Fastest-Growing Megacities." *Forbes*, April 8, 2013. http://www.forbes.com/sites/joelkotkin/2013/04/08/the-worlds -fastest-growing-megacities/.

Magnier, M. 2013. "In Karachi, Crime Leaves Few Families Untouched." *Los Angeles Times*, November 13, 2013. http://www.latimes.com/world/la-fg-c1 -pakistan-karachi-crime-20131112-dto-htmlstory.html.

Mezzera, M. 2011. "Dante in Karachi: Circles of Crime in a Mega city." open-Democracy, October 10, 2011. https://www.opendemocracy.net/marco -mezzera/dante-in-karachi-circles-of-crime-in-mega-city.

Norton, R. J. 2003. Feral cities. *Naval War College Review* 56 (4): 97–106.

Raja, M. 2013. "Fear Factor: No-Go Areas Scare Policemen, Says DIG West." *Express Tribune*, March 30, 2013. http://tribune.com.pk/story/528453/fear -factor-no-go-areas-scare-policemen-says-dig-west/.

Rehman, Z. U. 2013. "The Pakistani Taliban's Karachi Network." *CTC Sentinel* 6 (5): 1–5.

Rodriguez, A. 2010. "Taliban Militants Find Breathing Room in Slums of Karachi, Pakistan." *Los Angeles Times*, February 28, 2010. http://articles .latimes.com/2010/feb/28/world/la-fg-karachi-taliban28-2010feb28.

Shamsie, K. 2002. *Kartography*. Orlando, FL: Harcourt.

Yusuf, H. 2012. *Conflict Dynamics in Karachi*. Peaceworks no. 82, United States Institute of Peace, Washington, DC. https://www.usip.org/publications /2012/10/conflict-dynamics-karachi.

Zaheer, F. 2011. "Traders Accuse Government of Sheltering 'Bhatta' Mafia." *Express Tribune*, August 9, 2011. http://tribune.com.pk/story/234492/traders -accuse-government-of-sheltering-bhatta-mafia/.

Zamir, H. 2014. "Karachi Traders Seek Effective Security Measures." Money Matters, *News International*.

6

Violent Conflict and Urbanization in Eastern Democratic Republic of the Congo

The City as a Safe Haven

KAREN BÜSCHER

On November 20, 2012, the M23[1] rebel movement entered the city of Goma, provincial headquarters of the North Kivu province in eastern Democratic Republic of the Congo (DRC), while the Congolese army retreated without much fighting. President Joseph Kabila urged Goma's citizens to "resist" the M23 takeover (BBC 2012), at the same time that UN peacekeeping forces were observing the situation without intervening, according to their mandate. After the rebels seized control of the town and held it for eleven days, they withdrew as negotiations were announced in Kampala, Uganda.

In the analyses by journalists, political analysts, and scholars that soon followed this brief rebel occupation, the city of Goma was presented as a "prize city" (Jones 2012) and its takeover as a symbolic victory, bringing the Congolese government to its knees and ready to negotiate. Taking over the North Kivu capital and one of Congo's most vital trade hubs was of strong symbolic significance, shaming the UN force as much as the national elites in Kinshasa. It also drew international attention to the Congo wars—a conflict that had been ongoing since the early 1990s. The *New York Times* described Goma's takeover as "raising serious questions about the stability of Congo as a whole" (Gettleman and Kron 2012).

Although the rebel movement, active in the region since 2012 and through CNDP,[2] its predecessor since 2006, had occupied a series of smaller towns in the province for a long time, the fall of Goma marked a turning point. It was as if by taking Goma, they had crossed the line of what was expected (and maybe, for some, "accepted") rebel behavior. Although few *Gomatraciens*[3] ever doubted the ability of the rebels to take control of Goma, the facts were astonishing: a city of more than one million inhabitants—including a UN peacekeeping mission and extended army and police presence that also hosted a massive amount of international donor, development, and humanitarian agencies—was taken in such a short time with almost no resistance. The so-called Goma takeover, as with the Goma conference in 2008,[4] mark decisive moments in the rebel movement's political claims, demonstrating the crucial position of this urban arena within regional political and military strategies.

Yet paradoxically, despite short episodes of direct rebel presence in the city such as that of 2012, the city of Goma has remained relatively stable during the different phases of conflict in the Kivu provinces. The continued urban economic activities, cross-border movements, and large presence of international staff (in peacekeeping, development projects, and humanitarian aid) are all indicators of this relative stability. As a researcher, even when one could hear the fighting nearby, one rarely felt threatened and in danger in Goma; the proximity of the Rwandan border and the possibility to cross anytime to the other side reinforced this feeling.

Despite the fact that wars have become increasingly urban in nature (Kaldor 2007; Beall and Goodfellow 2014), cities often continue to represent a safe environment in a context of violent conflict (Branch 2013). And although recent global dynamics of violence demonstrate that cities as spatial entities represent many forms of risks and danger, they also represent spatial entities of protection. For cities to provide a haven in civil conflicts is fairly common (Beall, Goodfellow, and Rodgers 2011). The urban features of inclusiveness, freedom, global connections, and cosmopolitanism make cities attractive. One of the effects of this attractiveness in a situation of violence is massive urban growth due to the influx of (rural) displaced people.

The city of Goma offers a fascinating example. During twenty years of war, Goma has been transformed from a small administrative town into a vibrant transborder regional pole (Vlassenroot and Büscher 2013; Pech, Büscher, and Lakes 2018). In this chapter, I focus on the status of cities as zones of protection within a context of protracted violence and insecurity. Based on original qualitative data that I gathered over the past eight years, mainly in Goma, I argue that cities have become crucial safe havens, offering protected areas for internally displaced people (IDP) and international humanitarian actors but also for rebel leaders. This urban status of safe haven determines the role that cities come to play in the broader conflict setting. Different actors, with their particular spatial or political agency, navigate the city as a haven for protection and safety in very different ways. In so doing, they contribute to the emergence of new urbanities, which embody urban capabilities in a context of crisis and violence. In this chapter I illustrate not only how the dynamics of violent conflict influence processes of urbanization but also how cities as critical locations in their turn influence the broader political setting.

Civil War and Urbanization in Eastern Congo

Over the past twenty years, in a context of instability and violence, eastern DRC has become increasingly urbanized (Büscher and Mathys 2018). Cities like Bukavu, Goma, and Bunia have exploded in population. For example, in 2000, at the high point of the second Congolese war, Bukavu (the provincial capital of South Kivu) officially counted 338,689 inhabitants. By 2012, after a period of on-and-off fighting in the Kivu region, this number was estimated at 718,805. At the time of this writing, estimates were at 900,000 (Van Overbeek 2018). In a context of profound informalization and the increased outsourcing by the Congolese state, this population growth has created the uncontrolled expansion of vast spaces that lack planning, infrastructure, and basic services. Congolese refer to this process as *urbanisation sauvage* or *urbanisation anarchique.*

Violent conflict has not only spatially and demographically affected existing urban centers, it has also resulted in new emerging towns in eastern Congo's rural hinterlands (Büscher 2018; Büscher and Mathys 2018). Examples of these boomtowns—urbanized agglomerations with a demographic concentration greater than 10,000 inhabitants—are Hombo (South Kivu), Faradje (Haut-Uele), Nyabibwe (South Kivu), Kitchanga (North Kivu), Rubaya (North Kivu), and Numbi (South Kivu). This dramatic growth can be explained in terms of the interplay between forced displacement and livelihood opportunities (for example, artisanal mining). For instance, since 2000, Nyabibwe has seen a quadrupling of its inhabitants. Much of its growth is directly related to its proximity to artisanal coltan mining sites, which has attracted many miners and entrepreneurs who are active in secondary economic activities. Additionally, Nyabibwe saw the influx of large numbers of IDPs fleeing the violent clashes between various armed groups in the nearby highlands of South Kivu (Büscher, Cuvelier, and Mushobekwa 2014).

Violent conflict is by no means the only explanatory factor behind these processes of rural-urban transformation. Although seeking security and protection is an important driver of (forced) mobility, opportunities for livelihood diversification are equally important in explaining people's movements toward urbanized centers (Bakewell and Bonfiglio 2013). What we observe in eastern Congo is a self-reinforcing cycle whereby conflict dynamics generate human mobility, which, in turn, generates urbanization, which further stimulates mobility (Mathys and Büscher 2018). The urbanities emerging from these secondary boomtowns are often (but not always) conflictual in nature because of the way in which urbanization processes reinforce or produce conflicts over land or political representation. Thus while these urbanities are an outcome of dynamics of war, they also exercise a strong influence on political and military processes in the broader region.

Some of these new boomtowns emerged out of concentrations of IDPs and in a sense owe their urban status to the humanitarian industry that followed. Kitchanga, a town in North Kivu of around 80,000 inhabitants that boomed because of intensified violence in that region from 2008 onward, is a clear example of such a "city of refuge" (Mathys and Büscher 2018). Other urban centers represent economic and political strongholds of armed groups; various towns in North Kivu, South Kivu, and Ituri province have occupied such position over the past fifteen years for a variety of armed groups. A number of cities function, or have functioned, as economic hubs for (mostly transborder) trade. Butembo's and Goma's urban development (in North Kivu) as a consequence of transborder trade controlled by military-economic elites has been documented in detail (Raeymaekers 2014; Vlassenroot and Büscher 2013; Tull 2005).

High-intensity violence in eastern Congo since the 1990s took place mainly in rural areas, while established cities have largely escaped heavy fighting. Exceptions are the so-called six-day war in Kisangani in 2000, the heavy interethnic clashes in Bunia in 1999 and 2002, and the outbreak of violence in Bukavu when dissident general Laurent Nkunda temporarily took over the city (Büscher 2011). In addition, smaller cities such as Rutshuru and Kitchanga have, at times, been theaters of violence over the past ten years. The current situation in Beni[5] is exceptional in the sense that atrocities of this scale, over such a relatively long period have never been observed before in such close proximity to urban agglomerations in the region. Instead of arenas of confrontation, cities in eastern Congo more often represent zones of physical, economic, and political safety. Rural-urban migrants will relate how the city offered them the opportunity to escape poverty, isolation, insecurity, social pressure, or stigma.[6]

Yet these migrants' safety is ambiguous. They face the everyday urban realities of mounting crime, youth unemployment, lack of political representation, and inequality. In Bunia, for example, although the security situation is much better than during the time of overt war in the late 1990s, the city still faces serious socioeconomic problems, including a high level of physical violence, a rise in drug and alcohol abuse, abusive and extractive authorities, illegal roadblocks, and armed robberies (Hoffmann, Vlassenroot, and Büscher 2018).

Moreover, the increasing privatization of security as a result of the declining legitimacy of public security forces has created a multilayered urban security landscape. Apart from fragmented police forces, army soldiers, private security firms, and UN blue helmets, the city also provides an arena for the intervention of informal urban self-defense mechanisms. An example is the Anti-Gang, a group of youngsters operating in Goma in the "twilight zone" between formal recognition and illegality and providing protection to urban inhabitants on a local, neighborhood-based scale (Hendriks 2018). Sometimes international actors collaborate with these nonstate actors to reinforce urban security provision; an example is the CLGP, Comités locaux de gouvernance participative, local civilian security committees that have been logistically and financially supported by a number of international donors (Hoffmann et al. 2018).

The City of Goma: An Attractive Urban Arena for Diverging Agencies

With around one million inhabitants, Goma is the largest urban agglomeration in eastern Congo. The city is often referred to as the "urban heart" of the violent conflict, an image that refers not only to its spatial centrality within the conflict region but also to its crucial position politically (the provincial capital, center of state presence, and spatial embodiment of rebel emergence as well as peace deals), militarily (hosting one of the largest UN peacekeeping forces in the world), and economically (the central node in transborder trade between Congo and broader eastern Africa and an arena of influential economic-military "big men"). The interactions between the international nongovernmental organization workers, young Congolese entrepreneurs, UN staff, state officials, transborder traders, IDPs, security companies, and social movements define the cityscape of Goma as spaces of great diversity and "civic capability" (Kaldor in this volume; Simone 2001). Above all, Goma has become a haven for a variety of actors—a city of refuge for displaced people, a heartland for armed actors, and an urban "aidland."

Ville de Refuge: The Urban Effects of Forced Displacement

History shows us that the city of Goma has always been very welcoming. In 1994 we received the Hutus after the genocide. They were many, but we welcomed them, and today it is still them who make war to us. It's hard. Then the displaced people came, until today. They also create insecurity sometimes. But that does not prevent our city to keep its doors open for those fleeing war.[7]

On August 23, 2013, the *Irin News* (now *The New Humanitarian*) published a short article titled "Goma Is Running out of Space for DRC's Displaced." The article pointed to the critical situation in which the provincial capital of the North Kivu province was no longer able to host vast waves of internally displaced people fleeing the violence in the rural hinterlands in search of security within the city (*Irin News* 2013). The article stated that "Goma is full" and had reached its limits of absorption capacity; by that time, the United Nations Office for the Coordination of Humanitarian Affairs (OCHA) reported 60,000 IDPs in urban camps and 35,000 living with host families (NRC 2014).

No other urban center in eastern Congo has received the multiple waves of IDPs flooding the city as in Goma. In contrast to the city's surroundings, Goma forms a safe haven because of its concentration of the Congolese army and police forces, the presence of the provincial government and administration, and the international donor community and UN peacekeeping forces. Hosted in Goma since 2000, MONUSCO (Mission de l'Organisation des Nations Unies pour la stabilisation en République démocratique du Congo) gradually developed into the largest peacekeeping mission globally, with a total of more than sixteen thousand military personnel (UN Peacekeeping 2019). Through their constant patrolling of white UN jeeps and helicopters, their presence is highly visible in town and, despite strong local cynical feelings toward MONUSCO's presence, still engenders a feeling of safety in its inhabitants.

In the urban context of Goma, trust in national police and army is generally higher than in the hinterland because of a higher level of social and political control, which reduces the possibility of abuse and misbehavior.[8] Further, there is the huge presence of humanitarian organizations in the city. Although their focus is largely outside the city and their actions mainly oriented toward the rural hinterlands, the presence of these organizations further ensures a certain degree of physical security in the city. Finally, the increasing presence of vast numbers of international staff is associated with the increasing development of private security companies.

Goma's status as *ville d'asile* (city of refuge) is much older than the resumption of fighting in the late 2000s. It originated in 1994 in the aftermath of the Rwandan genocide, when Goma experienced the mind-boggling arrival of around eight hundred thousand Rwandan refugees. They were installed in refugee camps in the outskirts of the city and lived in horrible conditions. Soon after their arrival, a cholera epidemic broke out, within one month (July–August 1994) killing more than fifty thousand people (Cooley and Ron 2002). Many *Gomatraciens* still vividly remember this humanitarian disaster, which turned the city into a hell of human misery and left inhabitants with profound psychological trauma. As expressed by the local chief cited earlier, the status of *ville de refuge* since that time has retained the impression of both hospitality and suffering.

IDPs arriving in and around Goma were fleeing mainly the Masisi and Rutshuru territories, and many of them stayed there more than once, sometimes living in a camp for a certain period and sometimes moving in with family or friends. The situation of protracted displacement due to ongoing instability makes the return of IDPs to their home areas extremely difficult. Self-settled IDPs often rely on family or friendship relations to find a host, but these connections can also be strangers.

Patterns of self-settlement in Goma often occur against an ethnic background. As a well-developed study by the Norwegian Refugee Council has demonstrated, the level of solidarity toward IDPs should not be underestimated (NRC 2014). Yet, as with the term "IDP," "host" was introduced through a humanitarian discourse. According to Catherine Brun, these "created" categories in turn created a particular power relationship that is marked by inequalities (Brun 2010). In Goma, this fragile, complex relationship is reflected through access to livelihoods and resources and through local issues of rights, ownership, citizenship, and autochthony. The city forms a safe environment in terms of physical security, but in their urban livelihoods, IDPs are exposed to many other levels of social and economic insecurity. Their urban life is a constant navigation between these different levels of security and risks.

Economically, the influx of IDPs has added pressure on the urban patchwork of livelihoods and also has created a peripheral urban cheap labor market. More importantly, Goma's capacity as *ville de refuge* lies at the basis of the city's emergence as a humanitarian hub, hosting hundreds of international humanitarian organizations. Politically, the IDP crisis evidently has been an important issue on the provincial political agenda. Faced with the pressure of being held responsible for failing to protect its population, the governor of North Kivu applied a straightforward policy of closing down all IDP camps in the vicinity of the city from 2014 onward. Return was being (badly) organized, and within the chaos resulting from this action, many IDPs self-settled within the urban neighborhoods. Culturally, apart from the emergence of new identities constructed around "urban lifestyles" (Büscher 2011, Raeymaekers 2010), displacement waves also left their impact on the ethnodemographic composition of the city, for example, via an important influx of Hutu primarily from Masisi and Rutshuru.

Finally, the sense of cosmopolitanism as a determining feature of contemporary urban constellations in Goma stands out as a direct outcome of the city's being an attractive haven. The dynamics of war and displacement have strengthened the city's significance as a regional point of interaction and exchange, a zone of economic, cultural, and ethnic crossing. And interestingly, it is this inclusive cosmopolitan character that is referred to as a crucial aspect of the city's significance as a safe place.

A Rebel's Haven: Urban Agency of Armed Actors

Between 2008 and 2012, every time the rebels (CNDP or, later, M23) threatened to take over Goma, the urban inhabitants were unimpressed, stating that this would be a *démarche inutile* (useless effort). "The rebels already have the city. What's the need for occupying it with their arms?" Having the city refers to the economic and political influence that armed actors exercise over the city. The significance of Goma as a rebel playground for financial support, recruitment, or political negotiations has been observed more explicitly in particular episodes of the Congolese wars than in others. It already had been set in motion during the AFDL[9] campaign when Laurent Désiré Kabila fought the Mobutu regime in 1996, when Goma was a major military base and recruitment reservoir from which *kadogo* (child soldiers) were recruited to fight for the country's liberation.

The most literal interpretation of a rebel's safe haven was undoubtedly the second Congolese war, when, between 1998 and 2004, Goma became the political and military headquarters of the RCD[10] movement. During the RCD reign, Goma was a good example of a rebellion residence that functioned as the administrative headquarters of the insurgency movement. Although the RCD did not carry out profound changes to the local administration, as it largely relied on the existing structures (Tull 2005), the consequences of rebel rule were apparent at various levels of urban society.

With the booming trade in natural resources (due to spectacular increases in global demands for cassiterite and coltan) taking place simultaneously with an intense militarization of the region and a Congolese state at its weakest, this trade became an important part of financial strategies of local and foreign armed groups. This war economy was based on existing local informal trading networks, with rebel movements trying to control these networks by replacing local actors in the chain of transactions with their own intermediaries (Vlassenroot & Romkema 2002). By this means, economic and military power became strongly intertwined in Goma, resulting in the enforcement of a particularly close relationship between the economic urban elite and the politico-military rebel leadership (Vlassenroot & Büscher 2013).

The influential urban Banyarwanda[11] elite that emerged from these dynamics during the RCD period held control over the main economic activities and capital flows that boomed during the war. This rebel control over the city not only had a profound impact on the local urban landscape, it also drastically changed the city's position in regional trading networks and connection to global markets. From being the food basket of the Congo, Goma was transformed into a regional focal point of transborder commercial activities.

In the later episodes of the violent conflict, rebel forces never regained such direct control over Goma, although several armed groups remain closely connected to urban markets, economic elites. and ethnic associations. The examples of CNDP and M23 rebel movements are most visible and documented given their connection to the former RCD elite, but they are not the only ones. Apart from use of the city and its urban social infrastructure (universities, civil society organizations, ethnic associations) as s base for ideological and political recruitment, Goma was significant as a safe haven for rebel agency, which is most evident in the connection between armed actors and urban economic entrepreneurs. Military-economic alliances between, for example, urban fuel traders and the CNDP or M23 rebel movements can be explained by the need of local traders for protection during their transactions between the city and the (rebel-controlled) hinterlands, and rebel movements' need for financial support. For many urban businessmen, collaboration with the rebels was mainly a question of continuing their activities during times of crisis and instability. Whereas in the rural areas these businessmen would offer the rebels cattle, in the city they would offer cars, urban land, or real estate, for example.

The financial contributions imposed by CNDP on Goma's entrepreneurs are well documented (Scott 2008; Büscher 2011; Spittaels and Hilgert 2008; United Nations Security Council 2008). A system of regular contributions, or *cotisations*, was set up by CNDP, organized by a system of pools that included social support and recruitment. In the first place (but not exclusively), taxes were demanded from wealthy *hommes d'affaires* from the Banyarwandan-dominated sectors in Goma (such as minerals, aviation, and petrol). This ethnic aspect of military-economic alliances is crucial for understanding the different dimensions of safety and protection that urban centers represent.

Yet Goma also represents a safe haven for non-state-armed actors in more banal, everyday obvious ways. The safe urban area remains the best environment to invest, and armed actors' involvement in real estate projects in Goma was no secret. The indirect integration of rebel movements in Goma's urban political and social infrastructures (universities, associations, churches, trade unions) explains what people from Goma mean when they say that even without an armed presence, the armed groups control the city. For a long time, the CNDP and, later, M23 General Bosco Ntaganda was the personal embodiment of the visible rebel presence in town. Before his transfer to The Hague, despite the international arrest warrant, he was circulating freely in town, wining and dining in the same bars and restaurants that Goma's expat staff frequented.

The investment of armed groups in urban infrastructure, real estate, and business is often perceived locally as the main reason these groups have interests in keeping out of cities, leaving them quiet and stable. This can also be observed in other urban case studies such as (Gazdar, Kaker, and Khan 2010). In the town of Numbi, South Kivu, inhabitants explained how they saw the rebel's investments in their town as an indication of safety and "insurance" against future violence: the rebels would never attack the place where they had built houses for themselves and their families.[12] This is how, even in the midst of war, cities often "do well" compared with the rest of the country (Beall et al. 2011).

Urban Capabilities of Peace and Stability

Goma as the Heart of the Peace-Building and Humanitarian Industry

The relative urban stability described in the previous section has attracted large numbers of external actors to Goma, people who are involved in projects and practices of aid, peace building, reform, and development. The presence of donor agencies, international development NGOs, and humanitarian organizations has grown steadily over the years of violent conflict. Goma mainly functioned as the operational and logistical headquarters of all these organizations and emerged as the ultimate regional so-called NGO pole. Most of these international organizations orient their activities toward the rural areas, so their urban engagement or "entanglement" is realized more indirectly by their presence than directly by their programs or actions.

The focus and nature of these actors involved has changed over time from humanitarian to peace-building narratives and from emergency aid workers to a jumble of NGO workers, consultants, researchers, volunteers, blue helmets, and political analysts. Goma has evolved from an urban "aidland" (Mosse 2011; Fechter and Hindmann 2011) to an urban "peaceland" (Autesserre 2014). The significance of Goma as an urban peaceland has been analyzed in detail by Autesserre (2014) and Jennings (2014). Although often perceived as an enclosed expat world, a bubble with its own time, space, economy, and culture, this peaceland (like the former aidland) does not involve only expatriates, of course. The huge numbers of local NGOs—an emerging "market" that is evolving simultaneously with the humanitarian and peace-building industry—is also part of the trend, as are the local project managers, brokers, and other staff.

The relationship between the presence of these international actors and the city as a safe haven is complex. On one hand, the city has demonstrated that it is safe enough to become a laboratory of all kinds of externally driven experiments with regard to humanitarian, development, and peace-building actions. It is clear that for many involved in the aid and peace-building sector, Goma represents an island of safety in the volatile North Kivu region. Because of its infrastructure and security provision,

Goma is the preferred base for many international NGOs. While the rural hinterlands are the so-called "field of action," the city is the safe and calm home to which to return when coming from the field. The idea of the city as the safe home can be seen in the extensive tourist and leisure infrastructure (in the form of bars, restaurants, lively expat social scene, etc.). On the other hand, this does not mean that urban insecurity in itself is being ignored; strict rules apply for international staff in terms of where in the town one can and cannot go.

The concentration of international humanitarian and development organizations in itself is perceived as contributing to Goma's safety and stability. Another element contributing to this image is the growing market of private security companies that evolved simultaneously with the increasing presence of international organizations. Since the end of the 1990s, these foreign companies have played an important role in the protection of private houses, NGO offices, company offices, hotels, banks, and other structures.

Safety, protection, and stability are the key concepts in narratives of humanitarian aid and peace-building initiatives. But in contrast to the huge concentration of humanitarian and peace-building organizations in Goma, only recently has attention been paid to the urban context. Because the city is perceived as a safe haven, few humanitarian organizations actively engage with the city. The recent projects involving assistance to urban IDPs is an exception. With regard to security sector reforms, the donor-sponsored deployment of a *Police de Proximité* is another rare example of foreign support of specific urban agency.[13]

The peace-building actors in particular seem to have become more interested in capitalizing on urban opportunities. As forms of urban capabilities, the everyday interethnic interaction and socioeconomic ties emerging from collective urban agencies increasingly have been discovered by external actors as a potential vehicle for peace and change. Many donor agencies have specifically supported transborder social and economic initiatives, symbolically uniting Congolese and Rwandan youth, female traders, sports associations, musicians, and more, capitalizing on their daily transborder, transethnic interactions to construct a counternarrative to violence and war.

Another example is the support provided in Goma by external actors to the local urban-based, multiethnic civil society organization and protest movement *la Lucha*. External partners saw a potential force for urban bottom-up pressure on the Congolese government for change. A final example is the (partly) donor-sponsored Amani festival.[14] Organized yearly by uniting urban youth around music, dance, and performance, this festival is a colorful celebration of the city of Goma and its resilience in a context of violent conflict.

Finally, no actor better represents the international community's engagement in Goma as an urban safe haven than the international peacekeeping mission MONUSCO. More than any other external actor, MONUSCO symbolizes the international community's engagement in the construction of the safe city, despite the fact that its presence, legitimacy, and (in)actions are a constant subject of fierce debate among Goma's inhabitants.

The Urban Catalyst of the Productive Power of Violent Conflict

A violent volcano eruption in 2002 that destroyed large parts of Goma's city center strongly added to the common perception of Goma as a "city of risk" (Oldenburg 2010); some dramatically claimed Goma was "the world's most dangerous city"

(York 2010). This perception largely stems from the city's central position in a region that for decades has been characterized by war and humanitarian emergency. Yet, this image stands in sharp contrast to the impression one gets after staying in Goma for a longer time. From interactions with students, businessmen, artists, traders, or NGO workers, the identity of the capital city of North Kivu emerges as an ever-booming, flourishing, and cosmopolitan economic and cultural hub characterized by several unexpected opportunities.

The city's boom in the midst of the protracted conflict is at minimum impressive and offers an extremely rich setting to investigate what conflict researchers have referred to as the transformative and productive power of dynamics of conflict and violence (Vlassenroot and Raeymaekers 2004, Duffield 2001; Cramer 2006). Without romanticizing this productive power or denying the devastating impact of violent conflict on certain livelihood assets, long-term perspectives, or dreams of human security, urban centers in eastern Congo clearly also show the capabilities of turning crisis into opportunities. Goma's booming real estate market, its humanitarian tourist infrastructure, transborder trading networks, and vibrant urban civil society are demonstrations of the fact that violent conflict not only benefited warlords, entrepreneurs of violence, or criminal profiteers (Collier 1999), it became a source of creativity, offering openings through which different local and foreign urban actors could find new forms of exchange and accumulation.

The capacity of cities to provide these openings is integrally linked to their role in war-torn eastern Congo as safe havens, making possible a stable environment and protection for a variety of actors to engage in the urban space. As such, the city unfolds as a laboratory of diverging agencies and imaginations, in turn creating new possibilities and opportunities. The urban influx of IDPs has provided Goma with its multiethnic, cosmopolitan image; the emergence of Goma as an urban aidland and peaceland has resulted in a variety of new economic markets, and the urban anchoring of war economies has offered unexpected forms of capital accumulation. New identities emerging from these dynamics are a celebration of the urban, representing global connections and change.

As safe havens, cities in eastern Congo not only display the profound transformative effects of violent conflict, but they also embody critical locations of transformation themselves. Analyzing the political, spatial, and socioeconomic evolution of urban centers such as Goma reveals the crucial position and influence of cities in broader regional dynamics of war and peace.

Notes

1. Mouvement du 23 Mars (referring to the signing of a peace treaty between the Congolese government and M23's predecessor CNDP) emerged in 2012. The group, led by General Bosco Ntaganda, operated mainly in the North Kivu province.

2. Congrès National pour la Defense du Peuple, a rebel movement led by General Laurent Nkunda, was established in 2006. Between 2007 and 2009, intensive fighting between CNDP and the Congolese army caused massive waves of forced displacement in the Kivu provinces.

3. *Gomatraciens* is the term used locally to refer to Goma's inhabitants. Sometimes the term *Goméens* is also used.

4. The Goma Conference (Conférence sur la Paix, la Sécurité et le Développement du Nord et du Sud Kivu) took place on January 6, 2008. During the event CNDP committed to disarm and integrate into the national Congolese army. This conference is often perceived as an important moment of reference with regard to armed groups' political ambitions, given that through this conference, CNDP gained access to a number of important political and military positions.

5. For a detailed background on the violence in Beni, see "Who Are the Killers of Beni?" Congo Research Group (blog). http://congoresearchgroup .org/new-report-who-are-the-killers-of-beni/.

6. Based on interviews in Goma (2009–10), Nyabibwe (2014), and Numbi (2014).

7. Interview with former chef de quartier Keshero, Goma, February 4, 2008.

8. Survey and focus group discussions with students at UNIGOM (Goma, June 19, 2010); focus group discussions with inhabitants of Keshero District (Goma, December 7. 2009).

9. Alliance des Forces Démocratiques pour la Libération is a rebel movement led by Laurent-Désiré Kabila and backed by Rwanda, Burundi, and Uganda to overthrow the Mobutu regime.

10. From August 1998 to July 2003, the second war ("*guerre de rectification*") was fought between President Kabila and the Rassemblement Congolais pour la Démocratie (RCD), largely supported by Congolese Tutsi populations and backed by Rwanda and Uganda.

11. Literally "those from Rwanda," a term used locally to indicate people from Hutu and Tutsi ethnic origins in North Kivu.

12. Based on fieldwork in Numbi in 2014.

13. The *Police de Proximité*, deployed in several cities all over the DRC, is funded by DFID and UNDP and is part of the larger international sponsoring of police reform in the DRC.

14. *Amani* is Kiswahili for "peace." This festival was organized in 2014 (https://www.amanifestival.com,/en/).

References

Autesserre, S. 2014. *Peaceland: Conflict Resolution and the Everyday Politics of International Intervention*. New York: Cambridge University Press.

Bakewell, O., and A. Bonfiglio. 2013. "Moving Beyond Conflict: Re-Framing Mobility in the African Great Lakes Region." Working Paper for the African Great Lakes Mobility Project. Oxford: International Migration Institutes, University of Oxford.

BBC 2012. "Goma: M23 Rebels Rapture DR Congo City." *BBC News*, November 20, 2012. http://www.bbc.com/news/world-africa-20405739.

Beall, J., and T. Goodfellow. 2014. "Conflict and Post-War Transition in African Cities." In *Africa's Urban Revolution*, edited by S. Parnell and E. Pieterse. London: Zed.

Beall, J., T. Goodfellow, D. and Rodgers. 2011. "Cities, Conflict and State Fragility." Crisis States Working Paper no. 85. London: London School of Economics and Political Science.

Branch, A. 2013. "Gulu in War . . . and Peace? The Town as Camp in Northern Uganda." *Urban Studies* 50 (15): 3152–67.

Brun, C. 2010. "Hospitality: Becoming 'IDP' and 'Hosts' in Protracted Displacement." *Journal of Refugee Studies* 23 (3): 337–55.

Büscher, K. 2011. "Conflict, State Failure and Urban Tansformation in the Eastern Congolese Periphery: The Case of Goma" (PhD dissertation, Faculty of Political and Social Science, Ghent University). https://biblio.ugent.be /publication/2092391/file/4335807.pdf.

——. 2012. "Urban Governance Beyond the State: Practices of Informal Urban Regulation in the City of Goma, Eastern D.R. Congo." *Urban Forum* 23: 483–99.

——. 2015. "Ongoing Crisis in Eastern D.R. Congo: The Need for an Urban Perspective." *UrbanAfrica.net* (blog), August 11, 2015. http://www .urbanafrica.net/urban-voices/on-going-crisis-in-eastern-d-r-congo-the -need-for-an-urban-perspective/.

——. 2016. "Reading Urban Landscapes of War and Peace: The Case of Goma, DRC." In *Spatializing Peace and Conflict: Mapping the Production of Places, Sites and Scales of Violence* edited by A. Björkdahl and S. Buckley-Zistel. London: Palgrave Macmillan.

——. 2018. "Urbanisation and the Political Geographies of Violent Struggke for Power and Control: Mining Boomtowns in Eastern Congo." *International Development Policy* | Revue internationale de politique de développement 10: 302–24. https://journals.openedition.org/poldev/2769.

Büscher, K., and G. Mathys. 2018. "War, Displacement and Rural-Urban Transformation: Kivu's Boomtowns, Eastern D.R. Congo." *European Journal of Development Research* 30 (100): 1–19.

Büscher, K., and K. Vlassenroot. 2013. "The Humanitarian Industry and Urban Change in Goma." Open Democracy, March 21, 2013. https:// www.opendemocracy.net/opensecurity/karen-büscher-koen-vlassenroot /humanitarian-industry-and-urban-change-in-goma.

Büscher, K., J. Cuvelier, and F. Mushobekwa. 2014. "La dimension politique de l'urbanisme minière dans un context fragile de conflict armé; le cas de Nyabibwe" Annuaire de l'Afrique des Grands Lacs, 2013–2014." http:// congomines.org/system/attachments/assets/000/001/275/original/La _dimension_politique_de_l'urbanisation.pdf?1502278923.

Collier, P. 1999. *Doing Well Out of War*. London: World Bank.

Cooley, A., and J. Ron. 2002. "The NGO Scramble. Organizational Insecurity and the Political Economy of Transnational Action." *International Security* 27 (1): 5–39.

Cramer, C. 2006. *Civil War Is Not a Stupid Thing: Accounting for Violence in Developing Countries*. London: Hurst.

Duffield, M. 2001. *Global Governance and the New Wars: The Merging of Development and Security*. London: Zed.

Fechter, A. M., and H. Hindman. 2011. *Inside the Everyday lives of Development Workers: The Challenges and Futures of Aidland*. Sterling, VA: Kumarian.

Gazdar, H., S. Kaker, and I. Khan. 2010. "Buffer Zone, Colonial Enclave or Urban Hub? Quetta: Between Four Regions and Two Wars." Crisis States Working Paper 69. London: London School of Economics.

Gettleman, J., and J. Kron. 2012. "Congo Rebels Seize Provincial Capital." *New York Times*, November 20, 2012. http://www.nytimes.com/2012/11/21/world /africa/congolese-rebels-reach-goma-reports-say.html.

Giustozzi, A. 2009. "The Eye of the Storm: Cities in the Vortex of Afghanistan's Civil Wars." Crisis States Working Paper 62. London: London School of Economics.

Goodfellow, T., and A. Smith. 2013. "From Urban Catastrophe to 'model' city? Politics, Security and Development in Post-Conflict Kigali." *Urban Studies* 50 (15): 3185–202.

Hendriks, M. 2018. "The Politics of Everyday Policing in Goma: The Case of the Anti-Gang." *Journal of Eastern African Studies* 12 (2): 274–89.

Hoffmann, K., K. Vlassenroot, and K. Büscher. 2018. "Competition, Patronage and Fragmentation: The Limits of Bottom-Up Approaches to Security Governance in Ituri." *Stability* 7 (1): 1–17.

Irin News (The New Humanitarian). 2013 "Goma Is Running Out of Space for DRC's Displaced." *The New Humanitarian*, August 23, 2013. http://www .thenewhumanitarian.org/news/2013/08/23/goma-running-out-space -drc-s-displaced.

Jansen, B. 2011. *The Accidential City*. Wageningen, Netherlands: Wageningen University.

Jennings, K. 2014. "Service, Sex and Security: Gendered Peacekeeping Economies in Liberia and the Democratic Republic of the Congo." 45 (4): 313–30. https://doi.org/10.1177/0967010614537330.

Jones, P. 2012. "Negotiating with the DRC Rebels: First as Tragedy, Then as Farce?" *Think Africa Press*, December 14, 2012. http://allafrica.com/stories /201212150029.html.

Kaldor, M. 2007. *New and Old Wars*. Stanford: Stanford University Press.

Mathys, G., and K. Büscher. 2018. "Urbanizing Kitchanga: Spatial Trajectories of the Politics of Refuge in North Kivu, Eastern Congo." *Journal of Eastern African Studies* 12 (2): 232–53.

Moser, C., and D. Rodgers. 2005. "Change, Violence and Insecurity in Non-Conflict Situations." Working Paper 245. London: Overseas Development Institute.

Mosse, D. 2001. *Adventures in Aidland: The Anthropology of Professionals in International Development*. Studies in Public and Applied Anthropology, vol. 6. Oxford: Berghann.

NRC (Norwegian Refugee Council). 2014. "Living Conditions of Displaced Persons and Host Communities in Urban Goma, DRC." Oslo: NRC. https://www.nrc.no/globalassets/pdf/reports/living-conditions-of-displaced-persons-and-host-communities-in-urban-goma-drc.pdf

Oldenburg, S. 2010. "Under Familiar Fire: Making Decisions During the 'Kivu Crisis' 2008 in Goma, DR Congo." *Africa Spectrum* 45 (2): 61–80.

Pech, L., K. Büscher, and T. Lakes. 2018. "Intraurban Development in a City Under Protracted Armed Conflict: Patterns and Actors in Goma, DR Congo." *Political Geography* 66: 98–112.

Raeymaekers, T. 2010. "Not Going Home: Displaced Youth After War." *Forced Migration Review* 36: 21–2.

———. 2014. *Violent Capitalism and Hybrid Identity in the Eastern Congo: Power to the Margins*. New York: Cambridge University Press.

Robinson, J. 2006. "Inventions and Interventions: Transforming Cities—An Introduction." *Urban Studies* 43 (2): 251–58.

Scott, S. A. 2008. *Laurent Nkunda et la rébellion du Kivu*. Paris: Karthala.

Simone, A. 2001. On the Worlding of African Cities. *African Studies Review* 44 (2): 15–41. https://www.african.cam.ac.uk/images/files/articles/simone

Spittaels, S., and F. Hilgert. 2008. "Mapping Conflict Motives: Eastern DRC." Antwerp: IPIS.

Tull, D. 2005. *The reconfiguration of political order in Africa. A case study of Noth Kivu (D.R. Congo)*. Hamburg: RFA Institut für Afrika-Kunde.

UN Peacekeeping. 2019 "MOSUSCO Fact Sheet."

UN Security Council. 2008. *"Rapport Final du Groupe d'Experts sur la République Démocratique du Congo."* New York: United Nations. https://undocs.org/fr/S/2019/469.

Van Overbeek, F. and Tamas, P., 2018 "Autochthony and insecure land tenure: the spatiality of ethnicized hybridity in the periphery of post-conflict Bukavu, DRC." *Journal of Eastern African Studies* 12 (2): 290–309.

Verhoeve, A. 2004. "Conflict and the Urban Space: The Socio-Economic Impact of Conflict on the City of Goma." In *Conflict and Social Transformation in Eastern Congo*, edited by K. Vlassenroot and T. Raeymaekers, 103–22. Ghent: Academia.

Vlassenroot, K., and K. Büscher. 2013. "Borderlands, Identity and Urban Development: The Case of Goma (Democratic Republic of the Congo)." *Urban Studies* 50 (15): 3168–84.

Vlassenroot, K., and T. Raeymaekers. 2004. *Conflict and Social Transformation in Eastern D.R. Congo.* Ghent: Academia.

Vlassenroot, K., and H. Romkema. 2002. "The Emergence of a New Order? Resources and War in Eastern Congo." *Journal of Humanitarian Assistance* (October 28. Accessed on August 14, 2019. https://www.jha.ac/a111/.

Vogel, C. 2014. "Congo-Kinshasa: The Amani Festival Shows Off Goma's Fun Side." AllAfrica, March 3, 2004. http://allafrica.com/stories/201403040613.html.

Walraet, A. 2011. "Displacement in Post-War Southern Sudan: Survival and Accumulation Within Urban Perimeters." MICROCON Research Working Paper 57. Accessed on August 14, 2019. http://papers.ssrn.com/sol3/papers.cfm?abstract_id=1965634.

York, G. 2010. "Welcome to the World's Most Dangerous City." *Globe and Mail*, April 5, 2010. http://www.theglobeandmail.com/news/world/welcome-to-the-worlds-most-dangerous-city/article4313597.

7

Navigating Security in Bogotá

**JOHANNES RIEKEN, EFRAÍN GARCÍA-SÁNCHEZ,
AND DANIEL BEAR**

ogotá, a city once ravaged by decades of military,
socioeconomic, and political strife, has become a
model for a new approach to security. This significant change provides two distinct understandings of what can
function as sources of security. One is a conventional understanding of security that highlights the importance of physical structures and institutions directly charged with creating
security. The other is an alternative that emphasizes the role of
bogotanos as citizens, public transport systems, parks, and neighborhood groups can develop urban capabilities that provide a
more secure environment than walls, checkpoints, and security
guards. Bogotá provides examples of both side by side.

This distinction also might be conceptualized in terms
of security, either as a good that can grow when communally
shared or as an expensive, often privately purchased commodity afforded to only a few. Extending this line of reasoning,
the privatized commodity-based approach to security tends to
result in the formation of enclaves and the compartmentalizing
of cities, whereas the basis of a communal approach to security
is the idea of mobility. To build shared security, all city dwellers

must be enabled to move about their city comfortably. The aim is to create a virtuous circle whereby when *bogotanos* enjoy the benefits of transportation, their security is increased as places once desolate are given life. This increased sense of security encourages additional movement that is less constrained by fears of victimization.

This chapter starts with an overview of the context and history of the security situation in Colombia and Bogotá and a review of the distribution of crime in Bogotá. The purpose is to illustrate how security has developed into a commodity in Colombia, as well as the consequences of this process. We then examine the package of reforms that aim to reverse this process through a communal approach to security. Finally, we discuss how all the reforms play a pivotal role in the development of Bogotá's distinct security framework. On the one hand is the implementation of tougher and more sophisticated measures to control organized crime, and on the other hand is the promotion of communally based approaches that strengthen not only citizenship security but also coexistence and well-being.

We conclude that Bogotá reflects a noteworthy case of how a city has built urban capabilities to deal with conflict and crime, although it still faces challenges, including new scenarios to come from the Colombian postconflict era.

The Colombian Context and the Configuration of a Multilayered Conflict

To understand Bogotá today it is important to take into account the recent history of security and safety in Colombia. Despite its resurgence as a country, Colombia still carries the stigma that it earned through the toxic mixture of narco traffickers and insurgent forces that turned the streets of every major Colombian city into battlegrounds between the mid-1970s and the early 2000s.

Background Factors: The Wars

Since the conflict between left-wing groups and the Colombian military began in 1958 (later incorporating conflict between narco traffickers and the state), more than 177,000 civilians have been murdered, 31,000 police and military members have been killed, and more than 27,000 have been abducted (Centro Nacional de Memoria Histórica 2012). The kidnapping problem was so bad that the BBC named Bogotá the "kidnap capital of the world" (BBC 2001). In total, 7.38 million individuals have been victims of the conflict that saw Colombia fight for its survival against insurrectionists and *narcotraficantes* (Centro Nacional de Memoria Histórica 2012). The focus of many of the crimes committed by these two groups were against government employees (e.g., politicians, members of police and military, etc.) and wealthy individuals and prompted the development of elaborate private security systems, closed housing complexes, private security guards, and other security mitigation strategies that reflect a physical separation of the spaces and the people (Gutiérrez 2012).

In parallel with the armed conflict in the 1980s, the increase of *narcotráfico* (drug trafficking) and the fight against drug cartels represented an open confrontation between organized crime and the public institutions (especially against law enforcement officials) through what was called *narcoterrorismo*.[1] Antidrug activities had expanded rapidly in Colombia after U.S. President Ronald Reagan declared an intensified effort to eradicate drugs because he believed that "Drugs are menacing our society.

They're threatening our values, and undercutting our institutions. They're killing our children" (Reagan 1986). U.S. support rapidly modernized the Colombian law enforcement system, but emphasis was put on developing state security forces that would be more capable of attacking armed guerrillas and paramilitary forces than in protecting citizens' security. The funds from Plan Colombia were directed largely toward law enforcement activity, including the use of herbicides delivered via aerial spraying (Rincón-Ruiz and Kallis 2013). Many farmers found their fields, homes, and drinking water contaminated by the spraying and had no choice but to leave (Beckett and Godoy 2010). These antidrug activities are essential for understanding the broad scope of internal displacement in Colombia, with many of these uprooted individuals ending up in the main cities, such as Bogotá.

In short, the insecurity long felt in Bogotá is the result of many years of violent attacks that have rocked the capital and, indeed, all parts of Colombia for more than fifty years. These include attacks by the left-wing guerrilla group M-19 against the country's Supreme Court in 1985; bomb attacks on the Departamento Administrativo de Seguridad (DAS) in 1989 ordered by narco cartels; several car bombs detonated in various commercial and political influence zones in the 1990s; and bomb attacks on the police headquarters in 2002. Additionally, the Club El Nogal was attacked by the FARC in 2003, *Caracol* radio station in 2010, and a mortar attack on the presidential inauguration in 2002.

Such attacks have lessened in recent years but continue, with attacks on police and civilian targets. In the first month of 2018 there were eight terrorist attacks in Colombia, often directed against police and military but also injuring civilians (*El País* 2018). These repeated victimization and large-scale attacks have left an indelible imprint on the consciousness of *bogotanos*.

Colombia's multilayered conflict includes the armed conflict between state security forces and guerrillas groups, the violence perpetrated by drug cartels, the emergence of paramilitary groups, and the actions by organized crime groups. Each of these has fed key aspects of urban development—law enforcement systems, public transport, public spaces, citizenship culture, and more—aimed at the challenges created by forced displacement, housing problems, insecurity, and the making of enclaves.

Moving from Privatized to Community-Based Security?

Bogotá's efforts to improve its security and civic spaces in the past two decades, pushed through by liberal-minded mayors, have received much attention and praise. This praise stems from the city's seeming ability to square the circle, that is, to not sacrifice civil liberties for more security. It has promoted security precisely by strengthening democratic values. A focus on a culture of citizenship, the redevelopment of public spaces, and wide-ranging improvements to the transportation systems to connect the people with and through the city—all these aspects illustrate the concept of urban capabilities cited in the introduction to this volume. Through such measures, Bogotá's urban capabilities were constructed on the basis of democratized public space (transport included) to promote inclusion and to improve the quality of life of all citizens.

Former Bogotá Mayor Enrique Peñalosa outlined this new vision for the city when he said, "An advanced city is not one where even the poor use cars, but rather one where even the rich use public transport" (Peñalosa 2013). In other words, for policies and infrastructure projects geared toward creating security through citizenship to be meaningful, they need to have active impacts on the ways in which Bogotá inhabitants "practice their city."

Indeed, the story of Bogotá's transformation is largely about the reorganization of transport; that is, the public means provided to move through spaces. It is important to reiterate that mobility is not only a question of convenience but key to a communal approach to security based on the notion that all citizens should be comfortable moving through their city.

The story of Bogotá is one of violence and inequality but also of impressive reform efforts, economic growth, crime reduction, and cultural transformation (Beckett and Godoy 2010). Bogotá is one of the largest capital cities in Latin America and one of the most attractive investment locations in the region (Universidad del Rosario 2014). Institutional, economic, political, and social investments have aimed at improving security and civility at both the national and the local level. The city has witnessed a sharp reduction in crime rates, with particularly dramatic reductions in the homicide rate. In 1993, the homicide rate stood at 80 homicides per 100,000 population but declined to only 14 per 100,00 by 2017, which was well below the 24 per 100,000 for the country as a whole (Instituto Nacional de Medicina Legal y Ciencias Forenses 2017). Bogotá's security infrastructure was centered on the making of new public spaces, an innovative public transport system (called Transmilenio), and the development of what one former mayor referred to as a "*cultura ciudadana*" (culture of citizenship).

However, Bogotá city also faces other issues that challenge the security improvements reported earlier. High levels of economic inequality and a widespread perception of insecurity still plague the city. Bogotá is a highly unequal city located in one of the most unequal countries of the world (UN-Habitat 2010). Such inequality threatens the defense of public interests (citizenship security) and governance at the expense of the benefits of a few powerful elites (Stiglitz 2015; Piketty, 2014).

In 2017, 50 percent of Bogotá inhabitants reported that insecurity had risen in the last few years (Cámara de Comercio de Bogotá 2017), whereas 95.2 percent of residents thought they needed to be careful with other people (just 4.1 percent reported that most of the people can be trusted) (World Values Survey 2018). Thus privileged groups that felt insecure still might have reason to seek out privatized ways to deal with their own security, even at the expense of supporting public efforts to invest in an open and inclusive city.

Arguably one of the reasons that Bogotá had such potential to improve its security situation through developing a shared sense of citizenship is precisely because its population is economically so unequal. Put differently, purchasing security privately as a commodity has a long and entrenched history in Colombia for certain segments of the population. The communal approach to security provision is new and relatively fragile but has many potential beneficiaries who are unable to afford sufficient levels of security through private spending. Although it might be difficult to scale up private security efforts such as personal bodyguards, underground parking garages, and large homes, there exists an opportunity to build security through the creation of safe public spaces ruled by prosocial groups instead of law enforcement officials. However, even with significant efforts to improve Bogotá's transportation system, in 2017 between 54 percent and 78 percent of the population saw public transport—taxi and Transmilenio services—as insecure (see Cámara de Comercio de Bogotá 2017).

The Privatizing of Security: Socioeconomic Inequality

Although we cannot prove that Bogotá's high levels of inequality (UN-Habitat 2010; Valencia 2015) is a causal factor in its insecurity, large economic inequalities do have an impact resulting in higher rates of violence, poor public health, high incarceration levels, lack of interpersonal trust, education problems, and more (Wilkinson and Pickett 2010). Therefore, although causal relations between economic inequality and security are complex, empirical research shows that inequality is pervasive in areas with insecurity problems (Rufrancos and Power 2013). Inequality is both a challenge for cities and a condition that reshapes them (Sassen 2012).

Urban space in Colombia is officially divided into socioeconomic strata to ensure fairness regarding public services (drinking water, electricity, sewage system, gas, and phone) and taxes (DANE 2015). Socioeconomic stratification, based on the costs and settings of housing, divides the city into six levels, ranging from very high to very low (Secretaría Distrital de Planeación de Bogotá 2011). This system cements the link between urban space and economic inequality, with taxes depending on which of the six levels one lives in.

Bogotá is divided into 19 *localidades* (localities), which are defined by socioeconomic strata. Map 7.1 shows that half of the population and territory of Bogotá is concentrated in the two lowest levels. The highest two levels account for under 5 percent of the population (Secretaría Distrital de Planeación de Bogotá, 2011). These divisions stereotype social classes and can lead to segregation, discrimination, and marginalization (Uribe-Mallarino 2008). Privatized security is an integral part of this mix of policies, habits, and built environments that marks Bogotá's social texture.

One effect of the division of the city by socioeconomic strata is that criminality is also unevenly distributed in Bogotá. Most homicides are concentrated in the south of the city, home to the poorest neighborhoods; Map 7.2, left side), whereas robbery is

Map 7.1 Socioeconomic stratification in Bogotá.

Source: Secretaría Distrital de Planeación de Bogotá (2018).

more intense in the north and center, home to the richest neigh-borhoods; Map 7.2, center). Victimization is concentrated in the city's center and the commercial downtown (Map 7.2, right side).

Although we lack direct empirical evidence correlating socio-economic conditions with insecurity in Bogotá, polls show that 44 percent of citizens think rising insecurity is caused by

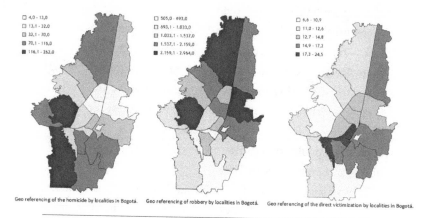

4,0 - 13,0	505,0 - 693,0	6,6 - 10,9
13,1 - 32,0	693,1 - 1.033,0	11,0 - 12,6
32,1 - 70,0	1.033,1 - 1.537,0	12,7 - 14,8
70,1 - 116,0	1.537,1 - 2.159,0	14,9 - 17,2
116,1 - 262,0	2.159,1 - 2.964,0	17,3 - 24,5

Geo referencing of the homicide by localities in Bogotá.   Geo referencing of robbery by localities in Bogotá.   Geo referencing of the direct victimization by localities in Bogotá.

Map 7.2 Geo-referencing of crime in Bogotá.

Source: Drawn by the authors based on data from Cámara de Comercio de Bogotá (2015).

socioeconomic conditions and that insecurity has risen, especially in public transport (57 percent) and on streets (45 percent; see Cámara de Comercio de Bogotá 2015).

A Distinct Path: Creating Community-Based Security Through Urban Capabilities

Bogotá's success in leaving behind the earlier extreme violence is attributed in part to national-level reforms (the law enforcement system and the war against drug cartels; see Casas and Gonzalez 2005; Llorente & Guarín 2013). Also impactful were the measures implemented by Bogotá's mayors between 1995 and 2013 that focused on the making of a *cultura ciudadana* (citizenship culture) based on civility, prevention, education, participation, improvements, and promotion of public spaces and mobility (Acero 2013). Because both approaches coexist, it is difficult to establish their respective independent effects on security. Most likely it will be an ideological choice as to which one can be attributed the current successes. However, Bogotá mayors Mockus and Peñalosa are internationally recognized for addressing insecurity with an education and prevention approach that involved the whole community. Promoting respect among citizens, increasing the use of public spaces, and enhancing public transportation to democratize the city were pillars of these mayors' success.

Key to these reforms was understanding security as a cultural issue. Bogotá's improved security could not have been achieved through strengthening law enforcement, diminishing socioeconomic inequalities, or modifying laws. It took working on the beliefs, interests, and emotions involved in people's behavior (Mockus et al. 2012). This project sought to improve citizens' moral development by emphasizing legality, morality, and culture as part of citizens' autonomy. It avoided instilling fear of law through monitoring and punishments. Security became a function of the way people relate to one another.

However, the program was not without its shortcomings. Poor citizens were portrayed as living in crime-breeding slums and saw their neighborhoods razed to build parks and new infrastructure. The effort to remove insecurities in Bogotá promoted the idea that fighting crime was akin to defeating terrorism, though such efforts, unsurprisingly, led to the stigmatization of some communities (Zeiderman 2013a, 2013b).

A variety of local reforms helped to create effective law enforcement mechanisms based on the needs of citizens. This included the *consejos locales de seguridad* (local councils of security) to help improve public accountability and management of security practices. Community policing with neighborhood and problem-oriented aims was implemented and supported by *frentes locales de seguridad* (similar to a neighborhood watch group) with neighbors supporting local security through solidarity practices. *Zonas seguras* (small mobile police stations built into a van or bus) were a program to decentralize the security infrastructure away from police stations (Mockus et al. 2012) and to encourage citizens' cooperation with authorities and participation in the solutions, a process known as *responsibilization* (Garland 2001). The strategy entails improving relations not only between communities and local authorities but also among citizens through local activities and the recovery of public spaces. It also included *tarjetas ciudadanas* (citizen cards) to address football hooliganism and general uncivil behavior; for example, "mimes and zebras" to teach how to use public spaces and pedestrian sidewalks, and *pico y placa* to improve mobility through the promotion of public transport and the restriction of private cars on the road, including carless days—*días sin carro*. These policies suggest that in Bogotá, mobility is more than just convenience of movement; it is a key part of the city's communal security.

The core of this program of security through mobility included several integrated transportation policy developments, the most visible of which was the restructuring of the city's bus system. Improvements in the Transmilenio bus system—which included special lanes for buses, new high-efficiency loading platform areas, and other improvements—enabled the system to carry more than 1.5 million people per day (Gilbert 2006). Although the new system showed great promise and achieved many of its goals for a short time, it is currently in a state of disrepair, plagued by inefficiency and a growing sense of insecurity. By giving all residents the ability to travel in well-functioning public infrastructure, it was hoped that a democratizing effect would support the city's efforts to reduce incivility and crime (Beckett and Godoy 2010).

Peñalosa, the mayor renowned for invigorating the communal approach to security, was reelected in 2015 for a four-year term and continues the struggle to keep the system functioning as designed. Bogotá is still trying to upgrade the public transport system and is considering implementing an underground metro system.

The strategies implemented in the city combined security and culture concepts using public spaces and transportation. The infrastructure investment was complemented by considerable efforts to promote new practices and relationships between people and the city, which opened a variety of opportunities for change. Future researchers should consider how individuals create narratives about the geographical manifestations of competing modes of security through ethnographic methods.

We have taken a mostly descriptive approach to presenting the complex security situation that characterizes Bogotá. Security is a topic with a long history and many layers in Colombia, and we have worked our way through them from the national down to the local context. In this way we have attempted to make it apparent that Bogotá's approach to security policy developments break with many long-standing practices. This approach can be described as turn away from a conventional understandings of security as an expensive, often privately purchased commodity in the form of guards, walls, and checkpoints that create enclaves, to a communal approach to security that aims to integrate citizens across divides so that they can give each other security.

The latter approach is tied to public transport and places a shared responsibility on citizens to own and be responsible for themselves. This idea would be considered somewhat radical in most contexts, but is especially significant as a policy development in a city such as Bogotá, which spent more than forty years trying to combat violence through ever-increasing law enforcement activity and is characterized by a high level of inequality.

Although the transportation system at the heart of this reconsidered approach to security languishes due to underfunding, even the moderate success visible in this new approach should encourage all policy makers to consider how they might seek to engender a culture of citizenship to promote security in their own communities. Going forward, the success of these efforts will not be judged on crime rates alone but on the establishment of a communal sense of security that will cast off a half century of victimization and turbulence. Such outcomes will be visible in the economic, cultural, and communal vibrancy of a Bogotá that is accessible to all her citizens.

Note

1. The term *narcoterrorismo* gained prominence after the 9/11 attacks in the United States as part of an effort to delegitimize FARC insurgents and link them to the wider narrative of terrorism to garner U.S. support for the fight against such groups (Borja-Orozco et al. 2008).

References

Acero, H. 2013. *Respuesta al estudio "Colombia: éxitos y leyendas de los 'Modelos' de Seguridad Ciudadana: Los casos de Bogotá y Medellín"* [Reply to the study "Colombia: successes and myths about the Models of Citizenship Security: the cases of Bogotá y Medellín"]. Accessed on August 14, 2019. https://www.wilsoncenter.org/sites/default/files/Respuesta al estudio de Llorente y Guarin_0.pdf.

BBC. 2001. "Colombia: Kidnap Capital of the World." *BBC*, June 27, 2001. http://news.bbc.co.uk/2/hi/americas/1410316.stm.

Beckett, K., and A. Godoy. 2010. "A Tale of Two Cities: A Comparative Analysis of Quality of Life Initiatives in New York and Bogotá." *Urban Studies* 47 (2): 277–301. http://usj.sagepub.com/content/47/2/277.

Borja-Orozco, H. et al. 2008. "Construcción del discurso deslegitimador del adversario: gobierno y paramilitarismo en Colombia" [Building a Discourse to Delegitimize the Opponent: Government and Paramilitarism in Colombia]. *Universitas Psychologica* 7 (2): 571–84. http://www.scielo.org.co/pdf/rups/v7n2 /v7n2a20.pdf.

Casas, P., & P. Gonzalez. 2005. "Políticas de seguridad y reducción del homicidio en Bogotá: mito y realidad" [Policies of security and reduction of homicides in Bogotá: myth and reality], in *Seguridad urbana y policía en Colombia*, ed. P. Casas, Á. Rivas, P. González, & H. Acero, 236–89 (Bogotá: Fundación Seguridad y Democracia).

Cámara de Comercio de Bogotá. 2015. "Atlas interactivo económico y social" [Economic and Social Interactive Atlas]. http://recursos.ccb.org.co/ccb /Atlas-interactivo-de-seguridad/Atlas-Bogotá-ano-2014/Reporte_2014 /atlas.html.

———. 2017. "Encuesta de Percepción y Victimización en Bogotá Primer semestre de 2017" [Survey of perception and victimization in Bogotá. First semester 2017]. Accessed on August 15, 2019. http://bibliotecadigital.ccb.org.co /bitstream/handle/11520/19393/Presentación Encuesta de Percepción y Victimización I semestre de 2017.pdf?sequence=1&isAllowed=y.

Centro Nacional de Memoria Histórica. 2012. *Basta Ya! Colombia: Memorias De Guerra y Dignidad* [It's enough! Colombia: Memoirs of war and dignity]. Bogotá, Colombia: Centro Nacional de Memoria Historica. Accessed on August 15, 2019. http://www.centrodememoriahistorica.gov.co/micrositios /informeGeneral/index.html.

DANE (Departamento Administrativo Nacional de Estadística). 2015. Estratificación Socioeconómica: Generalidades [Socioeconomic stratification: Generalities]. DANE. Accessed on August 15, 2019. https://www.dane.gov .co/index.php/servicios-al-ciudadano/servicios-informacion/estratificacion -socioeconomica.

El País. 2018. "En 2018, ya se han registrado 8 actos terroristas del ELN en territorio nacional" [In 2018, 8 terrorist acts perpetrated by the ELN have already been registered in the national territory]. Colombia, *El País*, January 29, 2018. http://www.elpais.com.co/colombia/en-2018-ya-se-han-registrado-8 -actos-terroristas-del-eln-en-territorio-nacional.html.

Garland, D. 2001. *The Culture of Control: Crime and Social Order in Contemporary Society*. Oxford: Clarendon.

Gilbert, A. 2006. "Good Urban Governance: Evidence from a Model City? *Bulletin of Latin American Research* 25 (3): 392–419.

Gutiérrez, F. 2012. "Una relación especial: privatización de la seguridad, élites vulnerables y sistema político colombiano (1982–2002)" [A special relationship: privatization of security, vulnerable elites, and the colombian political system]. *Revista Estudios Socio-Jurídicos* 14 (1): 97–134.

Instituto Nacional de Medicina Legal y Ciencias Forenses. 2017. *Forensis 2016.*

Datos para la vida: Herramienta para la interpretación, intervención y prevención de lesiones de causa externa en Colombia [Forensis 2016: Data for life: Tools for the interpretation, intervention, and prevention of injuries caused by external factos in Colombia]. Bogotá, Colombia: Fiscalía General de la Nación. Accessed on August 15, 2019. http://www.medicinalegal.gov.co /documents/20143/49526/Forensis+2016.+Datos+para+la+vida.pdf.

Llorente, M. V., S. Guarín. 2013. "Colombia: Éxitos y leyendas de los 'modelos' de seguridad ciudadana: los casos de Bogotá y Medellín" [Colombia: Successes and myths of the Models of Citizenship Security: the cases of Bogotá and Medellín]. In*¿A dónde vamos? Análisis de políticas públicas de seguridad ciudadana en América Latina*, ed. C. Basombrío, 169–202. Washington, DC: Wilson Center Latin American Program.

Mockus, A., H, Murraín, and M. Villa (Eds.). 2012. "Antípodas de la Violencia. Desafíos de cultura ciudadana para la crisis de (in)seguridad en América Latina" [Antipodes of the violence: Challenges of citizenship culture to deal with (in)security in Latin America]. Washington, DC: Inter-American Development Bank. https://publications.iadb.org/es/antipodas-de-la -violencia-desafios-de-cultura-ciudadana-para-la-crisis-de-inseguridad -en-america.

Peñalosa, E. 2013. "Why Buses Represent Democracy in Action." Filmed in September 2013. TED video, 14:06. http://www.ted.com/talks/enrique _penalosa_why_buses_represent_democracy_in_action.

Piketty, T. 2014. *Capital in the Twenty-First Century.* Cambridge, MA: Harvard University Press.

Reagan, R. 1986. "Address to the Nation on the Campaign Against Drug Abuse. Accessed on August 15, 2019. https://www.reaganlibrary.gov/research/speeches /091486a.

Rincón-Ruiz, A., and G. Kallis. 2013. "Caught in the Middle, Colombia's War on Drugs and Its Effects on Forest and People." *Geoforum* 46: 60–78.

Rufrancos, H., and M. Power. 2013. "Income Inequality and Crime: A Review and Explanation of the Time-Series Evidence." *Sociology and Criminology* 1 (1):1–9. https://www.longdom.org/open-access/income-inequality-and-crime-a -review-and-explanation-of-the-timeseries-evidence-2375-4435.1000103 .pdf.

Sassen, S. 2012. "Bridging Divides: Enabling Urban Capabilities." Working Paper, World Bank Group Open Knowledge Repository. Accessed on August 15, 2019. https://openknowledge.worldbank.org/handle/10986/17600.

Secretaría Distrital de Planeación de Bogotá. 2011. "21 Monografías de las localidades. Distrito capital 2011, Bogotá" [21 Monographies of Bogotá localities].
Accessed on September 19, 2019, https://bit.ly/2kQPuQ7.

———. 2018. "Estratificación Socioeconómica de Bogotá" [Socioeconomic stratification of Bogotá]. Accessed on September 19, 2019, http://www.sdp.gov.co
/gestion-estudios-estrategicos/estratificacion/estratificacion-por-localidad.

Stiglitz, J. E. 2015. *La Gran Brecha* [The great divide]. Madrid: Taurus.

UN-Habitat, 2010. "State of the World's Cities 2010/2011. Bridging the Urban
Divide." London: United Nations Human Settlements Programme (UN-
HABITAT). http://unhabitat.org/books/state-of-the-worlds-cities-20102011
-cities-for-all-bridging-the-urban-divide/.

Universidad del Rosario. 2014. "Ciudades latinoamericanas más atracti-
vas para la inversión en 2014" [The most attractive Latin American cities
for investment]. Accessed on August 15, 2019. http://www.urosario.edu.co
/getattachment/d893902a-a9db-4680-9e9d-dc6b5a3f9740/Ciudades
-latinoamericanas-mas-atractivas-para-la-i/.

Uribe-Mallarino, C. 2008. "Estratificación social en Bogotá: De la política
pública a la dinámica de la segregación social" [Social stratification in
Bogotá: From public policies to the dynamics of social segregation]. *Universitas Humanística* 65(January–June): 139–71.

Valencia, A. M. 2015. "Persiste la alta desigualdad en la distribución de los
ingresos en Bogotá" [High economic inequality on the income distribution
in Bogotá persists]. Observatorio de Desarrollo Económico, Secretaría
Desarrollo Económico de Bogotá. Accessed on August 15, 2019. http://
observatorio.desarrolloeconomico.gov.co/din%C3%A1mica-econ%C3%
B3mica-y-distribuci%C3%B3n/persiste-la-alta-desigualdad-en-la
-distribuci%C3%B3n-de-los-ingresos-en.

Wilkinson, R., and K. Pickett. 2010. *The Spirit Level. Why Greater Equality
Makes Societies Stronger.* New York: Bloomsbury.

Zeiderman, A. 2013a. "Living Dangerously: Biopolitics and Urban Citizenship in Bogotá, Colombia." *American Ethnologist* 40 (1): 71–87. https://doi
.org/10.1111/amet.12006.

Zeiderman, A. 2013b. "Securing Bogotá." *OpenDemocracy*, February 14, 2013.
Accessed on August 15, 2019. https://www.opendemocracy.net/en/opensecurity
/securing-bogota/.

8

"On the Margins of All Margins"

Explaining (In)Security in Novi Pazar, Serbia

VESNA BOJICIC-DZELILOVIC

The region of Sandzak—a land strip at the crossroads connecting Serbia, Montenegro, Bosnia-Herzegovina, and Kosovo—has been described as "the last piece of the Yugoslav puzzle." That description refers to the inexorable process of disintegration of former Yugoslavia's multiethnic, multiconfessional social tissue that began in the early 1990s. Along with its main city, Novi Pazar, Sandzak thus remains something of an exception in having avoided identity-politics-fueled violent conflict between its two main ethnic communities, the Serbs and the Bosniaks.[1] In 1991–1995, parts of Sandzak in Serbia, which include the city of Novi Pazar, became active sites of a brutal regional conflict. Yet despite years of armed violence pursued to recast the political geography of former Yugoslavia by creating new states in Sandzak's proximity, including a partition of Sandzak between Serbia and Montenegro and extended military presence of Serb forces in and around Novi Pazar, the city was spared from becoming a battlefield and the site of human and physical devastation to which its Bosnian and Kosovar neighbors had succumbed. Rather, and somewhat counterintuitively, Novi Pazar thrived economically amid regional conflict and was able to preserve interethnic peace.

Some fifteen years since the end of Yugoslavia's succession wars, Novi Pazar is a peaceful but unsettled place. Interethnic tensions, which exist alongside deep rifts within the Bosniak community and occasional overt violence fueled by cultural radicalization and divisive politics, have become prominent features of everyday life in Novi Pazar. Although the city is suffused with widespread poverty and marked by forms of everyday insecurity, the precarious balance sustained by Novi Pazar is also a testament to its resilience and remaining civic capabilities.

In attempting to explain the manifestations of insecurity in postwar Novi Pazar, as well as its causes and how the city dwellers cope with it, it is worth recalling an episode from the wartime years. This serves to demonstrate the city's urban capabilities at the time and provides insight that animates the investigation in this chapter of why and how the city's security predicament has changed.

During the Serbian armed forces' siege of Novi Pazar, local businessmen, irrespective of their ethnic backgrounds and despite rising tensions in interethnic relations, joined forces to negotiate with the commanding officers and prevent the onslaught on the city that would have decimated their businesses and endangered their livelihoods.[2] Local residents, in a similar show of solidarity, made huge efforts to assist Serbian military personnel by furnishing their every request[3] in exchange for protecting the city from attacks. This kind of solidarity in the face of adversity has long faded in the people's daily experience; their everyday concerns revolve around a lack of stable livelihoods and welfare protection, which are the main source of everyday insecurity in Novi Pazar.

The argument I make in this chapter is that although civic capabilities are critical in explaining the relative absence of violence, they are difficult to sustain in the long term in the context of broader interrelated dynamics of economic decline, war-induced demographic change, and political and religious radicalization. The emergence of new actors as well as changing norms and identities triggered by the multiple transitions from war and a Socialist-era development model have affected and disturbed urban relationships and processes and engendered widening social and spatial divisions in the city. In the search for security, citizens have turned to various authorities—following their ethnic, party, or religious affiliation—or resorted to the private sphere. The ability to mount a joint response to resolve common issues of concern, as captured by the foregoing example of businessmen and citizens acting together for a common good during the city's worst moments in recent history, has shrunk as a consequence. However, they have by no means vanished.

This chapter is an attempt to capture local people's understanding of the social processes in the city and how those processes relate to specific manifestations of insecurity as articulated by Novi Pazar residents. It draws on sixteen interviews conducted in Novi Pazar in spring 2015 with a cross-section of local businessmen, civil society activists, experts, journalists, and city government officials and informal follow-up interviews with a number of respondents over the Internet. It opens with a description of Novi Pazar's transition from war and a Socialist-era development model that traces economic, political, demographic, and cultural changes that have shaped the particular ways in which the city transformed socially.

The following section focuses on how physical and social spaces have been transformed in response to the processes of social change that accompanied transition from war and the Socialist regime. I also discuss those transformations in relation to specific manifestations of insecurity. The penultimate section looks at why maintaining the city's urban capabilities has been difficult, and I offer examples of remaining civic capacities that illustrate the city's resilience. Finally, in the conclusion I reflect on the dual dynamics of disintegration and reconstitution of Novi Pazar urbanity.

Transitions and Social Transformation in Novi Pazar

Novi Pazar was established by the Ottomans in the fifteen century and was the second-largest city after Sarajevo, the present capital of Bosnia-Herzegovina and a point of reference in the redefinition of contemporary identity among Novi Pazar's Muslims. Historically, Novi Pazar (meaning "new market") was the administrative and commercial hub in that part of the Ottoman Empire. During Socialist times in former Yugoslavia, Novi Pazar underwent a process of modernization through a state-coordinated industrialization policy. This ushered in an era of relative economic progress in the 1970s based on an industry dominated by labor-intensive textiles and leather processing. This type of industry would both spur the city's economic boom during the wars in the region and become its economic "death bed" during the transition to a market economy.

In retrospect, those were the golden days in the recent history of the city and its local economy. Its dynamism attracted an influx of workers—low-skilled and educated alike—from various parts of Serbia, alongside significant rural-urban migration, giving the city its distinct urban profile (Lyon 2008; Interview with Nusret Nicevic 2015).

The relative economic prosperity in a city that was still classified as one of Serbia's less developed municipalities was reflected in the change in the urban landscape and sociocultural processes in the city. The Socialist era saw the construction of several of the city's urban landmarks, including the Vrbnik Hotel—known locally as "Novi Pazar's beauty" and perched above the Raska river, which traverses the city center—and *lucna zgrada*, the sprawling building consisting of block housing for workers from local factories and overlooking one of the city's main thoroughfares. The high-rise apartment blocks mix with the Ottoman-style architecture that is typical of much of the old town and other cultural and religious landmarks, such as the St. Peter and Paul orthodox church. Taken together, these buildings were visible signs of the city's ethnic and cultural diversity (ICG 2005). This diversity was also manifested in a thriving cultural and sporting scene, which was maintained despite the remnants of conservative structures that the Socialist promotion of modern, secular ways of life had failed to completely erase and which, arguably, provided a fertile ground for the upsurge in religious radicalism in the 1990s.

The city's economic demise began in earnest during former Yugoslavia's final decade and at the onset of war in Bosnia-Herzegovina—a milestone event in Sandzak's recent history. In 1992, the city was facing economic meltdown. Yugoslavia's descent into war was inextricably linked to Serbia's increasingly hostile attitude toward Islam and Muslims, including those living within its own borders in the Muslim-majority Sandzak (Biserko 2010; ICG 2005; Morrison and Roberts 2013). The Milosevic regime implemented a systematic policy of repression and fear in Sandzak in response to the 1991 political initiative hatched in Novi Pazar to pursue an agenda of self-determination for Sandzak that was linked to the broader Muslim (Bosniak) "question".[4]

During the war in its neighborhood, Novi Pazar experienced a change in economic fortunes due to the imposition of international sanctions on the rump state of Yugoslavia (then a Serbia-Montenegro union), which came into effect in May 1992. The production of jeans and footwear (including counterfeit items) boomed, benefiting from the exploitation of local entrepreneurs' transnational connections with the Sandzak diaspora in Turkey. Truckloads of goods were transported across the Balkan war zones and their (supposedly) internationally policed borders throughout the Serbian interior and farther afield (Kostovicova 2003; ICG 2005; Muminovic 2005). In many factories, the production cycle continued uninterrupted during the NATO shelling of the city.[5]

In a fluid legal context created by the absence of an effective state presence at the local level, much of the illegal business relied on trust and existing social bonds nurtured within the confines of this small city, which often crisscrossed ethnic demarcation lines, as well as local and transnational space.[6] The city hosted a bustling foreign exchange market fueled by illegal trade, including weapons, drugs, and people. Conducted by organized crime groups, the trade flourished under the war economy, which was thriving in this border region (Morrison and Roberts 2013, 162). Amid a hubbub of thriving informal commerce, the Socialist-era factories—once the pride of the city and its economic lifeline—lay idle and neglected, their former skills base repurposed for the needs of a booming (privately owned) informal economy that connected Novi Pazar with the global flows of commerce.

The illegal commerce benefited Bosniak and Serb entrepreneurs alike, many of whom were former employees of state-owned company who had lost their livelihoods with the collapse of the city's formal economy. The economic boom helped to foster wartime intergroup relations in the city, which had begun to strain under the regime's targeting of Bosniaks.[7] Meanwhile, the Serbian regime turned a blind eye to the illegal flows that involved breaches of the state-sanctioned regulations and international embargoes because the proceeds were needed to replenish empty government coffers. For the regime, keeping Sandzak peaceful was also instrumental in deflecting international criticism over its support to the Bosnian Serbs in their anti-Muslim agenda (Biserko 2010).

Local political dynamics, however, pulled in the opposite direction. The Bosniak political leadership pressed on with its self-determination agenda to redefine Sandzak's status and demanded greater autonomy in the form of more decentralized and regionalized governance. The leading political figures at the time aligned themselves with the Bosniak leadership in Bosnia-Herzegovina, which they formally endorsed as the Sandzak Bosniaks' kin state. The range of actors influencing the city's trajectory in a struggle for a different position in new, post-Yugoslav Serbia consequently expanded beyond city and national borders. The plight of Sandzak's Bosniaks with regard to political autonomy was perceived, and discursively framed, in the Serbian media and political circles as part of an Islamic resurgence in this part of Europe, which allegedly carried the risk of Sandzak's secession (ICG 2005; Lyon 2018; Morrison and Roberts).

Meanwhile, on the ground, the self-determination agenda resonated with incidents of discrimination and oppression toward those Bosniaks whom the Serbian regime perceived as disloyal. Furthermore, the regime's use of force to stem the Bosniak political movement fed the regime's fear and resentment. In an ICG account (2005, 13), for Bosniaks the message of the 1990s was that, owing to "state-sanctioned crimes and official legalized discrimination," they were now "second-class citizens, who no longer enjoyed the protection of the state; an unwanted and harmful foreign organism whose life and property had no value before the law."

Although this discrimination might have served the purpose of legitimizing the Bosniak political elites' fight for self-
determination, the agenda was not endorsed unequivocally by
either Sandzak's Bosniaks or the citizens of Novi Pazar, and
resistance against the tide of resurgent nationalism continued
throughout the war. Many Bosniak residents of Novi Pazar
cherished the idea of brotherhood and shared identity with their
Serbian neighbors, which was forged following the antifascist
struggles during World War II, and resented the political agendas being pursued in their name. At the same time, Novi Pazar's
Serbs, caught between Belgrade propaganda and aggressive
Bosniak politics, pledged allegiance to the main Serbian political
parties and to the Serbian regime as the protector of their security. The ensuing rift among Novi Pazar residents allowed for the
emergence of a new form of authority and new allegiances which
would only deepen over time (Morrison and Roberts, 2013).

Besides this changing economic and political context, the
city's wartime patterns of migration were another potent factor in shaping social transformation during this period. Novi
Pazar experienced major population movements starting in the
first half of the 1990s. An outpouring of the local population—
Bosniak along the traditional migratory routes toward Bosnia-
Herzegovina and Turkey, and Serb toward Belgrade—was coun-
teracted by inflows of mostly refugees of Muslim faith from
Bosnia-Herzegovina, Croatia, and Kosovo and an influx of the
Muslim populations from neighboring villages seeking refuge
among the city's ethnic kin population.

The city received some ten thousand people over the ten years
between 1992 and 2002, including some six thousand refugees
(Joksimovic et al. 2012). These demographic changes had a huge
impact on the cultural and urban fabric already disrupted by
the strains of post-Socialist transition, as newcomers to the city

often embraced different worldviews and espoused more aggressive ways of communicating and interacting.[8] This new kind of migration was different from the economically motivated migrations of the 1970s in that it was a part of a pattern of ethnic homogenization triggered by the dissolution of Yugoslavia; by default, it was aggressive, exclusionary, and antagonistic in asserting its presence in the city.

The transition to peace following Kosovo's independence was, in equal measures, economically, politically, and socially turbulent in Novi Pazar. Reassertion of the state's oversight of the economy, coupled with the enforcement of regional borders, mostly brought to an end the informal market in textiles and footwear.[9] However, for a number of years the transport sector continued to exploit the unregulated border between Serbia and Kosovo and benefited from a buoyant informal trade in that area (Bjelic et al. 2012).

According to some accounts, during this time Novi Pazar became an important drug-smuggling point on the route from Turkey to Western Europe. The wealth generated in the process was subsequently used in corrupt business activities that dominate the city's toxic political economy (Morrison and Roberts 2013). Meanwhile, the ailing Socialist-era economy continued to flounder. Many workers, the majority of whom were women, lost their jobs, businesses closed, and an economic recession set in, pushing most Novi Pazar residents into poverty.[10]

The political gap between the Bosniak political leadership and the Belgrade regime has since centered on the issue of minority protection in the context of Serbia's European Union accession. The Party of Democratic Action's (SDA) wartime monopoly over Bosniaks' political representation has been challenged not only by other majority Bosniak parties, principally the Sandzak Democratic Party (SDP),[11] but also by the party established by the Sandzak mufti Muamer Zukorlic,[12] which has caused further divisions among Novi Pazar residents. As well as being a religious leader, Zukorlic has become one of the most influential political and economic actors in Novi Pazar, adding to the panoply of new actors that has emerged over the course of the city's changing moral, economic, and normative orders. At the same time, the contribution of national authorities to Novi Pazar's economic and welfare needs has been negligible. The city has remained on the margins of development, deprived of much-needed infrastructural and other investment. Out of sight of the national state—except for the purpose of consolidating Serbian nationhood—many Novi Pazar residents have been forced to rely on their own devices in the search for security.

Manifestations of Insecurity in Novi Pazar and the City's Urban Reconfiguration

Novi Pazar is surrounded by mountains and resembles a cauldron at whose base are clusters of tightly packed buildings in irregular patterns, crisscrossed by narrow streets that lead in and out of the city via the mountain slopes. Entering the city from any direction involves a long journey through the mountains, which amplifies a sense of the city's physical isolation and distance from Serbia's capital, where political and economic power is concentrated. The overcrowding resulting from a city built to meet the needs of some ten thousand people—now home to more than ten times that number—is visible on its streets (Joksimovic et al. 2012). Standoffs of cars and pedestrians are frequent due to the sheer volume of traffic and poor road signage. Other physical infrastructure is similarly strained; only the city center benefits from regular water and electricity supply. Outlying neighborhoods, many of which were built illegally during the 1990s waves of immigration, experience frequent electricity and water shortages and poor waste disposal services; many of these settlements are connected to the city by unpaved or only partly paved roads.[13] In some of the refugee settlements, living conditions are particularly dire; except for sporadic assistance mostly from nongovernmental organizations, these communities have seen little by way of local government engagement. [14]

The failures of governance also are reflected in the fact that illegal construction is not exclusive to refugees and rural immigrants in the city's purlieus. Some of the most elegant homes of Novi Pazar's new elites, and some business premises in the city's prime locations, have been built without following the planning process.[15] In some cases the buildings have no water pipelines or electricity connections, which results in electricity theft, a practice that largely goes unsanctioned. In other cases, apartment buildings with no car-parking facilities have been inserted into city center neighborhoods.

Contributing to this sense of disorderly urbanization—a consequence of demographic pressure, weak legal enforcement, tax evasion, corrupt practices, and a sluggish economy against which liberal market transitions have continued apace—are numerous unfinished facades scattered throughout the city.[16] They are often situated next to rundown houses whose owners cannot afford maintenance costs, or next to Socialist-era housing blocks, which no longer enjoy the maintenance once provided by the state. This is the fate that has befallen Hotel Vrbnik, the "Novi Pazar beauty," left to dereliction by its new owners. These physical markers on the city's landscape are vivid reminders of its troubled and uncertain transition. They also draw the invisible social lines of division that crisscross the city.

The city's economic decay, reflected in its physical landscape, is especially glaring in what used to be its industrial zone. This is now a quiet place with empty business premises still covered in faded advertisements of the fashionable clothes once produced there for foreign markets, a poignant image of the times when the lives of local residents were more secure and protected. It is a landscape of so-called dead capital trapped in buildings and idle equipment, a somber addition to a vast stock accumulated through the unsuccessful privatization of state-owned companies,[17] which is in large part responsible for the city's economic downfall. Most of the former female workforce (some 70 percent of total registered unemployment) now belongs to Novi Pazar's army of unemployed; many live in the outlying city suburbs with no alternative employment opportunities and no regulated welfare provision. Not just poverty but physical violence has been on the rise[18] in the local community, making women one of the most vulnerable groups in Novi Pazar.

For company owners who are still in business, keeping afloat is arduous in an unstable local and regional political and economic context, and in the absence of supportive state policies, including infrastructure investment.[19] Even among successful entrepreneurs, there is a sense of concern and sometimes desperation and a fear that years of investment in developing their business ultimately could count for nothing.[20] The squeeze produced by the transition to a liberalized economy is palpable in the many shops that are clustered in the main market in the city center a stone's throw from Hotel Vrbnik and the main city square, which see little business these days and no longer act as the city's gathering places.

Poverty is widespread: Novi Pazar has been described by the World Bank as an "actively impoverished area"(Korisnici prava za socijalnu zastitu 2014). One-third of Novi Pazar's citizens cannot afford a telephone connection fee; this contributes to a general sense of vulnerability and deprivation among certain sections of the population, particularly among the elderly and infirm, who are dependent on outside help.[21] In the remote suburbs and the neighboring villages, the lack of infrastructure limits the economic activity of their residents and is an obstacle to access to the city for other needs. This creates additional incentives for rural-urban migration, with all its problems in a malfunctioning city.

Security in Novi Pazar has been punctuated by occasional episodes of physical violence, foremost connected to the power contestation among the two majority Bosniak political parties (the SDA and the SDP) and Mufti Zukorlic, whose supporters have clashed on the city streets. The vitriolic anti-Serb rhetoric served up for years by the leaders of the two Bosniak parties, accompanied by unprincipled collaboration with subsequent Serbian governments, have strengthened the religious pull and Zukorlic's standing.

The consequence is a perception of an increasing "Islamization" of the city encouraged by the Wahhabi and Salafi supporters alongside more moderate local variants of Islam. Salafis, in particular, practice outside the mosque, in private houses fringing the narrow streets in the old city center, which have become virtual exclusion zones for those opposed to this kind of worship, including both Bosniaks and Serbs. Likewise, the biggest mosque in the old city hosts a religious school and a kindergarten, where the pupils' dress code is in stark contrast to that of the nearby secular school. After school, even in the case of the secular school, children no longer hang around with their schoolmates but instead hurry to their homes and neighborhoods—a telling sign of an unyielding border that is separating the Bosniak and Serb communities in their quest for security. [22]

There has never been pronounced spatial polarization in Novi Pazar. There were only a couple of fairly ethnically homogeneous neighborhoods. The Socialist-era housing blocks were a micro-cosm of former Yugoslavia's multicultural tradition whereby difference and diversity were managed through a tradition of maintaining good neighborly relations. But over the years, many non-Muslim residents either have left the city or relocated to so-called ethnic neighborhoods; in fact, there are very few Serbs still living in the city center.[23] Similarly, a process of gradual ghettoization operates in public spaces.[24] Novi Pazar, like many cities in the former Yugoslavia, always had a central city prom-enade where youths in particular used to gather for an evening stroll. The city promenade no longer exists, but an alternative one opened in the Serb-majority Varos *mahala* (neighborhood), frequented primarily by Serb youth.[25] This is only one example of the two communities' increasingly socializing in isolation from each other.

In a symbolic encroachment of public space, with a simi-larly divisive effect among Novi Pazar's ethnic communities, the central city square is dominated by a building in which the university—whose president is Mufti Zukorlic—has its offices. The building includes a ground-floor bookstore displaying in its windows both religious works and books on the subject of al-Qaeda, jihad, wars in Iraq and Afghanistan, and the like. Success in recruiting fighters for those wars, including the top student from Novi Pazar grammar school, who was killed in Syria in 2014, [26] has been a source of apprehension among residents who do not share the ideology behind such recruitment. The Serbian regime has used the information on Wahhabi activities in Novi Pazar and the recruitment of local youth to reinforce its stance toward the Bosniak political leadership.

On the Broken City Contract and Civic Capabilities

In March 2015 a newborn baby on the journey from Novi Pazar to Belgrade to receive life-saving treatment died when a helicopter carrying the baby and all members of the crew crashed near Belgrade airport. The helicopter was sent to the rescue because a mudslide had blocked the main road connecting the two cities. There was a hospital and an airport close to the site where the ambulance was stopped, but the helicopter was not permitted to use the airport.

In the local commentaries following this incident, bitter remarks were made about Serbia's world-champion tennis player having access to that airport for his private jet. If the helicopter had been allowed to use the airport, perhaps the baby could have been saved. There was also condemnation of Novi Pazar's hospital director, who was perceived as prioritizing his political career over the needs of the local community through his neglect of the already poor local health care facilities, which had necessitated the 290-km trip to Belgrade to try to save the infant.[27] My interviewee said: "In this city, no one is safe."[28] The story poignantly sums up the broken city contract.[29]

Since the overthrow of Milosevic's regime in 2000, Novi Pazar's city government has consisted of various coalitions led by one of the two major Bosniak parties, as noted earlier: the SDA and the SDP. Historically, the Serbs have been represented disproportionately in the local public administration and government institutions such as the courts, police force, and health and education services. Given Novi Pazar's scarce job opportunities,[30] this pattern has been difficult to break. The main parties' revisiting of the ethnic makeup of official institutions—the police in particular—has contributed to local mistrust of the state.[31]

Even more disturbing is the inability of the Bosniak political elites to formulate a shared vision for the city because of
their different positions regarding the solution to the so-called
Bosniak minority question in Serbia. The official focus on high-
level politics and the struggle for power have resulted in the total
neglect of the needs of Novi Pazar's residents, as evidenced in the
city's dilapidated physical infrastructure, inadequate health care
facilities, social welfare, and so on.[32] As one of my informants
articulated, underlining the state-society distance as manifested
in Novi Pazar: the "elite agenda is about autonomy, motorway,
the airport—in contrast, citizens' concerns are water, electricity,
and sewage."[33]

In a void created by the absence of local and national state
welfare and public goods provision, Novi Pazar, over the years,
has experienced the ascendancy of a new type of welfare provision from Wahhabi followers.[34] The Wahhabis organize the city's
street cleaning, provide allegedly superior education and child-
care compared with those provided by mainstream institutions,
and help ordinary people with tasks such as house painting,
wood cutting for fuel, and other assistance.[35] However, these services come at a price, which may be the requirement for women
to cover their heads in the Islamic tradition or to refuse help
from mainstream nongovernmental organizations, or maybe a
less explicit demand for non-Bosniak residents to refrain from
objecting to an increasing Wahhabi presence in the city.

Ultimately, the effect of these new allegiances attributed to
the city's creeping Islamization is to reinforce social polarization among Novi Pazar's citizens. As many of my informants
argued, the Wahhabi presence is disconcerting not least because
it goes beyond simply religious influence. One argued that
Wahhabism in Novi Pazar "is also a lifestyle."[36] Its members,
very few of whom hold jobs, show visible signs of wealth; they

drive top-of-the-line cars, sport the latest mobile phone models, and can afford sophisticated electronic equipment in their homes—a far cry from the reality of most impoverished Novi Pazar residents.

Speculation is rife that this wealth comes from foreign donations and murky business deals involving land acquisition, linking those actors who seemingly embrace tradition and local life with broader regional and transnational actors and processes. Their appeal, particularly among the poorer sections of Novi Pazar youth, is strong; many Wahhabi followers hail from the city's immigrant communities, the display of wealth transmits a message of success and social ascendance that is not necessarily underpinned by a strong work ethic.

Among the local businessmen and a number of other respondents in this study, there is a concern about the changing business culture promoted by a new type of unscrupulous businessmen—labeled "the wrong kind of entrepreneurs" by one of my interviewees—seeking quick profits, often involving money-laundering schemes and privatization of state-owned enterprises. This kind of entrepreneur shies away from legal means of trading and instead opts for informal and often criminal channels. These means and practices find fertile ground in the messy reality of local governance based on the zero-sum politics of the local political and religious leaders, which thrives on divisions and embraces patronage and clientelism (Cvejic 2016) while undermining the social cohesion of local communities.

Local governance has been permeated by clientelistic relations and allegations of corruption and crime surrounding local government officials. Loyalty to political and religious leaders prevails over all other criteria for access to business and other opportunities, which, arguably, is one of the main reasons for Mufti Zukorlic's strong standing in the local community.

The political divisions among the city's Bosniak political elites (Zukorlic included) also can be understood in terms of competition about control over resources and the private logics and personal profit-seeking agendas of the elites. It is an open secret that the mufti's business affairs involve breaches of law, but they go unsanctioned because of his power and influence and the protection from the sections of the Belgrade political establishment that he allegedly enjoys.[37] One of my interlocutors commented on this changing moral universe that has suffocated Novi Pazar's commercial zeal, citing the old local saying that the "mufti can only hail from the city thoroughfares and not the village mud."[38] This alludes both to the moral decay and the greed of those responsible for the local community's well-being as well as to the pernicious impact that war-induced rural immigration has had on the city's urban reconfiguration.

Commercial actors who are interested in investing in legally regulated production have been a victim of this toxic political economy, which is entwined with the identity politics in a kind of double helix pattern. They are routinely subjected to discrimination in accessing business funding, securing urban locations, or receiving other types of services that might improve their commercial prospects[39] and the economic fortunes of the city to the benefit of wider public. Local government officials are an important active part of this toxic local political economy, as excessive government inspections of the legally registered businesses often serve to extort bribes.[40]

The provision of symbolic goods also has been affected by the way in which city governance operates. The choice of public holidays, for example, has been a contentious local governance issue. There was a strong push against retaining secular tradition, such as New Year's Eve celebrations, which in the past were marked by citywide parties hosted by Hotel Vrbnik and other venues. Instead, the marking of the Islamic tradition of boys' circumcision is a public holiday in Novi Pazar, as is the Muslim holiday of Bajram, when the streets are emptied of Bosniaks, who celebrate in their own homes, and Serbs, who consider it inappropriate to go out. Many public sporting events are timed to coincide with important dates in the Islamic calendar and have been named appropriately; for example, a Ramadan athletic race and a month-long Ramadan football tournament. This applies also to cultural events, such as the Islamic music and Islamic poetry and fiction festivals, which tend to receive much more prominent media coverage than other cultural manifestations that traditionally attracted regional and international participants and a mostly urban audience. Multicultural manifestations with a long tradition in Novi Pazar have been affected by the changing politics as well as by lack of funding from impoverished former donors.

At the same time, there is evidence of resistance to aggressive assertion of particular worldviews, practices, cultures, and values that underwrite the perception of growing social distance among Novi Pazar's citizens amid failures of the city governance to work in their common interest. In January 2015 a local youth theater staged a play entitled *Beton mahala*,[41] in which six Bosniak and two Serb actors took part. Although the play was closed down after only two nights, allegedly because the local political establishment did not like the content dealing with the city's problems, including interethnic relations,[42] it is a testament to the city's resilience. Because local (like national) media is politically controlled—Mufti Zukorlic, for example, owns two TV stations, a newspaper, and a weekly magazine, and a number of other outlets are controlled by the SDP leadership—the play incident was portrayed in ways that accentuate differences and tensions among the city's residents. Yet despite one of the actors being threatened by a lawsuit, the group did not give in and searched for alternative performing venues outside the city.

There are other innate aspects of the city's urbanity that work as a counterforce to the divisive effect imparted by the city's governance. Novi Pazar is a city of youth; 15–25-year-olds account for 33 percent of its population, and its three universities enroll some six thousand first-year students annually. However, its youth are increasingly inhabiting parallel city spaces.[43] The insistence on minority rights protection resulted in the introduction of the Bosnian language in schools in 2013, an action that has not only separated children into different classrooms but represents a step toward the reshaping of their respective identities.

The enforcement of an alcohol ban in the city center has been one of the factors contributing to changing the city's street life and has driven many non-Bosniak young people away from that area. However, this measure has been only partly successful. Occasional visits to bars in the Serb neighborhoods by Bosniak youths for a round of drinks still happen, in a display of urban defiance against the attempted imposition of new rules.

The remnants of the city's civic capability to pursue its own methods of social ordering can be gleaned in other ways, too. Under a shop window of a jewelry store in the old city is a graffito that publicly shames a couple for not repaying the shop owner the money they borrowed and bans them from entering the shop. For those Novi Pazar citizens who consider themselves "true" urban subjects, this is a way to compensate for weak provision of justice to address the city's changing moral universe that resonates with their experience and knowledge of the city.

The nongovernmental sector in Novi Pazar is feeble and has received far less international support than elsewhere in Serbia. It suffers from strong political interference with some of the newly established nongovernmental organizations (NGOs) that are funded by the political parties and the Islamic community. Nevertheless, a handful of long-standing NGOs remain active and maintain relations with other civil society organizations in Serbia and in the region. Some of their work focuses on issues that are at the core of residents' sense of insecurity in the context of the social change that local communities have undergone. This work concerns, for example, advocacy on gender rights and, more broadly, human rights, particularly for the most marginalized groups, such as the Roma.

Those organizations do not shy away from tackling the issues of interethnic relations and human security; organizations such as Damad have reached out to all local groups, including the local representatives of the two Serbian Islamic communities, to open dialogue on the common interests of the city and its inhabitants.[44] According to Damad's head, the inability to define what is in the common interest of the city is slowly eating into the essence of Novi Pazar's urban spirit and contributing to its slow extinction. This is acknowledged by the owners of small businesses, who try to find ways to circumvent the barriers created as a result of control of the local economy by networks of political and economic entrepreneurs who are driven by private and sectarian agendas. There have been examples of local business owners joining forces to lobby for services, such as the organization of and attendance at business meetings and trade fairs, as a way to create openings for businesses that would not require allegiance to any of the local power brokers.[45]

During the war, Novi Pazar was able to prosper economically and to preserve interethnic peace amid violent regional conflict fueled by exclusive identity politics. Since then, much has changed, and the city is now home to an exhausted community on the edge economically, politically, and psychologically whose residents fearful that life can only become more difficult. The economic dynamism of the 1990s is long gone. Although violent interethnic conflict seems unlikely—especially since two of the three main Bosniak political protagonists joined the incumbent government of Aleksandar Vucic—some locals poignantly say that because intercommunity life no longer exists in the city, multiple lines divide its residents. Most are living insecure lives, dependent on remittances from families living abroad.

The Bosniak majority's aggressive reconstruction of an ethnic identity in response to the Serbian regime's intrusive nation-state-building that privileges the Serbian majority has set in motion processes that are challenging the city's internal community cohesion. Many of the institutions of daily life, such as the work environment and Socialist-era work-related housing, traditionally facilitated the mixing of people and enabled a common experience of living together and managing differences. These no longer exist. The gradual erosion of the city's civic capabilities is being exacerbated by its weakened role as the provider of a public good in the context of a weak economy and weak governance.

At the core of this transformation is a fragmented local political economy, which developed at the interface of the 1990s war economy and the liberalized marketization mandated by national and local government (and their international collocutors), and its capture by various alliances of political, religious, business, and criminal actors. The victim is the city's collective interests, which have given way to various actors' power-driven private and political agendas. In this context, civic-minded individuals faced the choice of siding with those actors or withdrawing from the public sphere and leaving the city vulnerable to the disintegrative effect of this toxic political economy.

Nevertheless, the city has—however feebly—demonstrated its resilience and avoided slipping into an interethnic conflict despite the odds. Novi Pazar citizens believe that if only the economy could turn around, it would be possible to reverse some of the damage caused by intertwining dynamics of new wars and liberal marketization. For this to happen, as one of my informants suggests, political energy needs to be rechanneled toward nurturing the city's legacy of living together. A recognition that no one is safe in the city as it functions at present, shared by many of my interlocutors, is a somber reminder of the consequences of divisive politics that has been pursued by its elites.

Notes

"On the margins of all margins" is the expression my local host, Ms. Bisera Seceragic, uses to describe the socioeconomic reality of Novi Pazar. I owe her a debt of gratitude for sharing her knowledge and insight with me.

1. The name "Bosniaks," denoting the Islamic faith group, entered official use in Sandzak in 1993 following its adoption in Bosnia-Herzegovina to replace the word "Muslims." According to the 2011 census, Bosniaks represent an absolute majority in Novi Pazar, accounting for 77.1 percent of the total population. Another 4.9 percent of citizens declared themselves to be Muslims. http://publikacije.stat.gov.rs/G2013/Pdf/G20134002.pdf.
2. They used bribes and even raised money to build a holiday home for the acting army commander. The officer in question eventually sold the house. Interview with confidential source.
3. Interview with confidential source.
4. In 1992, a local branch of Bosnia-Herzegovina's main Bosniak political party, the Party of Democratic Action (SDA), was established in Novi Pazar under the leadership of Sulejman Ugljanin, a Sarajevo-educated dentist. To this day, SDA remains one of the main political forces in Novi Pazar.
5. Interview with Esad Hamzagic.
6. Interview with Esad Hamzagi and Bisera Seceragic.
7. In addition to official rhetoric from the Serbian political leadership, the regime began a systematic purge of so-called disloyal Bosniaks from public institutions in Novi Pazar (ICG 2005).

8. Interview with Enes Niksic.
9. They include international sanctions on Serbia, an arms embargo in Bosnia-Herzegovina, Serbia's blockade of Kosovo, and the Greek embargo on the FYR Macedonia.
10. Novi Pazar is officially classified as a city with an "actively poor population" (Evropski pokret Srbije Lokalno vece Novi Pazar 2009).
11. The SDA and SDP have participated in all Serbian governments since 2000.
12. There are two rival Islamic communities in Serbia: Islamic Community of Serbia, led by effendi Adem Zilkic, whose seat is in Belgrade; and Islamic Community in Serbia, led by Muamer Zukorlic, whose seat is in Novi Pazar.
13. Often road building in these neighborhoods is timed to coincide with the election campaign, only to be left unfinished once the election is over. According to some sources, one of Novi Pazar's Bosniak political leaders has initiated the building of some one hundred local roads. Interview with confidential source.
14. Interview with Semiha Kacar.
15. It is estimated that there are some ten thousand illegally built houses in Novi Pazar (Biserko 2010).
16. Houses with finished facades are subject to an additional tax (Lyon 2008).
17. Of some fourteen cases of privatization sales in Novi Pazar, only two have been successfully completed: the construction company Putevi and the city's bakery (interview with Bisera Seceragic).
18. Interview with Semiha Kacar.
19. Interview with Esad Hamzagic, Ramiz Paljevac, and Nusret Nicevic; also see Evropski pokret Srbije Lokalno Vece Novi Pazar 2009.
20. Interview with Esad Hamzagic.
21. Interview with Semiha Kacar.
22. Interview with Zibija Sarenkapic; see also Damad 2008, 2015.
23. Interview with Bisera Seceragic.
24. Interview with Zibija Sarenkapic.
25. Interview with Zibija Sarenkapic.
26. Interview with confidential source.
27. Interview with Semiha Kacar.
28. Interview with Sladjana Novosel, Bisera Seceragic, and Semiha Kacar.
29. The phrase "broken city contract" is borrowed from Oberschall 2007, 16. See also Gupta 2016.
30. Rate of unemployment in Novi Pazar stood at 53.7 percent compared with 27.6 percent for Serbia as a whole. (Korisnici prava za socijalna zastitu . . . 2014).

31. Interview with confidential source. The police office's top brass are appointed by the central government in Belgrade.
32. Interview with Easd Hamzagic, Semija Kacar, and Sladjana Novosel.
33. Interview with Zibija Sarenkapic.
34. Other types of nonstate provision from NGOs exist but are inadequate.
35. Interview with confidential source; also see Lyon 2008.
36. Interview with confidential source.
37. Interview with confidential source.
38. My source used the Turkish word *kaldrma*, which means a cobbled road rather than dusty, unpaved rural lanes. Interview with confidential source.
39. Interview with confidential source.
40. Interview with confidential source; also see European movement, ibid.
41. *Mahala* is the Turkish word to describe a suburb harboring a culture of gossip; *beton* is the local name for concrete.
42. Interview with Zibija Sarenkapic. The play is critical of the local politics of division in Novi Pazar.
43. In my interviews I heard stories of Novi Pazar's culture of tolerance and respect. One of my interviewees referred to his mother's stories of how, at the beginning of the last century, girls of different faiths would share the same classroom but huddle in separate groups in the opposite corners of the room to study their respective religious texts (Qu'ran and the Holy Bible).
44. Interview with Zibija Sarenkapic.
45. Interview with Esad Hamzagic.

References

Biserko, S., ed. 2010. Sandzak I evropska perspektiva [Sandzak and European perspective]. Belgrade: Helsinski odbor za ljudska prava.

Bjelic, P. et al. 2012. "Freedom of Movement of People and Goods Between Serbia and Kosovo." Novi Sad: Centre for Regionalism.

Cvejic, S., ed. 2016. *Informal Power Networks, Political Patronage and Clientelism in Serbi and Kosovo.* Belgrade: SeCons.

Damad. 2008. "Stop korupciji-Korpucija I mladi" [Stop to corruption—corruption and youth]. Novi Pazar: Damad.

———. 2015. "Integrated Response of the Community to Human Security Challenges." Novi Pazar; Cultural Centre Damad.

Evropski pokret Srbije-Lokalno vece Novi Pazar (European movement-Local council Novi Pazar). 2009. "Percepcija privatnog sektora Sandzaka o politickom I ekonomskom ambijentu" [The private sector perception of political and economic environment of Sandzak]. Novi Pazar.

Gupta, J. with Commins, S. 2016. "Cities, violence and order: The challenges and complex taxonomy of security provisions in cities of tomorrow." https:// bulletin.ids.ac.uk/idsbo/article/view/2784/ONLINE%20ARTICLE

ICG (International Crisis Group). 2005. "Serbia's Sandzak: Still Forgotten." Europe Report No. 162. Brussels: ICG.

Joksimovic, A., et al. 2012. "Socijalno-ekonomski I bezbjednosni izazovi u Sandzaku" [Socioeconomic and security challenges in Sandzak]. Belgrade: Centar za spoljnu politiku.

Korisnici prava za socijalnu zastitu i socijalne usluge u Novom Pazaru, Sjenici i Tutinu. 2014. Novi Pazar, September 2014.

Kostovicova, D. 2003. "Fake Lewis, Real Threat." Transition online (14.8.2003).

Lyon, J. 2008. Serbia's "Sandzak Under Milosevic: Identity, Nationalism and Survival." *Human Rights Review* 9: 71–92.

Morrison, K., and E. Roberts.2013. *The Sandzak: A History*. London: Hurst.

Muminovic, R. 2005. *Hadzi Murad I Sandzak*. Sarajevo: Blicdruk.

Oberschall, A. 2007. *Conflict and Peace Building in Divided Societies: Responses to Ethnic Violence*. London: Routledge.

Conclusion

Spaces for Tactical Urbanism

SASKIA SASSEN AND MARY KALDOR

Cities are complex systems, but they are incomplete systems. Their urbanized formats vary enormously across time and place. In this mix of complexity and incompleteness lies the possibility of making and remaking the urban—the political, the civic, a history.

One question we need to ask when it comes to the issues raised by our diverse authors is whether such urban capabilities can also operate in war zones. What our authors show is that they can, albeit to a limited extent, and those capabilities are often subject to interruptions.

The yogurt run described in the introduction to this volume is a good example of such capabilities in play, even if that run is reduced when armed conflicts arise. We must recognize that a city's people, as distinct from the military in that city, are going to have to scramble every day for food, water, medications, and shelter. The residents also run the risk of serious injury and worry about children, neighbors, and others. The military, though not always armed groups, are, generally speaking, provided with what they need. A city's residents are mostly not. But it is also in cities—whether at peace or at war—that lies the possibility for those who may have long lacked power to be able to make a history, a politics, even if they do not get empowered. This becomes evident in some of the valiant efforts by those at risk who are described in the various chapters of this book. Powerlessness can become complex in the city, even in the city at war.

Urban Space Becomes Strategic

Against the background of an often acute, even if partial, disassembling of nation-states in war zones, the city can function as a strategic site for the active creation of minor, often temporary "orderings"—orderings that can take on multiple, highly variable, always partial formats. These can include spatial, economic, political, environmental, and cultural conditions and instantiations. In this book, our authors provide multiple diverse, mostly minor cases of such interventions—interventions that for the most part address desperate survival needs. The chapters include examples of urban resistance to war, as in Novi Pazar, or of the way in which the international humanitarian industry intersects with waves of refugees to produce dynamic transborder trade even in the midst of war (Goma), or of self-reinforcing trust between local communities and security forces as in the rural hinterland of Kabul. And in the cases of Bogotá and Ciudad Juárez, we observe imaginative efforts by local authorities to promote new forms of public civic security that are more or less successful.

Such minor or even major survival interventions by the women, men, and children living in cities at war are not often described in analyses of war situations. We have found that it might be worthwhile to consider such interventions, minor as they might be. Rather than seeing these modest efforts as somewhat irrelevant to the analysis of cities at war, we join the growing movement to recover the daily lives of people struggling in a war situation. In addition, we conceive of these practices as a mode of tactical urbanism: tactical because it has to adjust to conditions that vary continuously from day to day and in the most extreme situations, often even hour by hour.

The Urban Map of Terror

Beyond the cases examined in each chapter, we have seen an urbanizing of war over the last several decades—from the attack on the U.S. embassy in Nairobi, to the attack on the Manhattan towers, to the destruction of Aleppo or Mosul, and to terrorist attacks in London, Paris, Mumbai, and Madrid, to name a few. This is in sharp contrast to classical wars, which most often engaged the enemy in vast open spaces—from oceans to skies. In World War II, of course, cities were also hit, or, at the most extreme, purposefully destroyed, with Dresden, Hiroshima, and Nagasaki the key telling historical instances.

In our project the focus is on a range of diverse conflict zones where cities function mostly as key operational spaces. One major reason for this particular difference with classical wars is the fact that today's wars largely involve a combination of networks of state and nonstate actors, and they feature air strikes conducted by governments combined with a range of militias and irregular combatants operating on the ground. The foregoing chapters address cities facing deep insecurity as a consequence of the war on terror, such as Bamako, Kabul, Baghdad, and Karachi. Yet in most cases the war on terror intersects with criminality and ethnic violence; in this respect we observe different combinations in our different field sites—criminality in Bogotá, criminality and the war on terror in Ciudad Juárez, and ethnic violence and criminality in Goma.

What matters for our analysis when it comes to these new types of war is that cities become key strategic ground for armed conflict, because it is mostly in cities that irregular combatants are safest. Yet these chapters show that urban warfare does not exclude other frontiers. Indeed, warfare is a method of remapping geography, as the chapters on Bamako and Karachi vividly illustrate. New internal frontiers involving fences, gates, checkpoints, and private security contractors are constructed within cities through a process of enclavization (Karachi), privatization (Ciudad Juárez), and ghettoization. New so-called frontier zones of remote border areas, deserts, mountains, and the like are also rearing back in force, as explored in the Mali case, in the story of Kabul and its hinterland and of Karachi vis-à-vis the tribal areas.

How can we understand this fragmentation of warfare across both urban and remote domains? How do different scales of warfare and security intervention intersect? To take an example, the cities of Niger and, to some extent, Mali have come to host large foreign counterterror forces and serve as drone bases and thereby link the scale of the city—and local tensions around this presence within the city—to a vast hinterland. Again, this is similar to the case in the fortified parts of Kabul with regard to the U.S. bombardment of Afghan border areas, which also involved other cities and headquarters far from the zone of combat. International security assemblages do not always exacerbate violence; in some places such as Goma, a liberal peace presence can play a relatively benign role.

Nor is it only violence that reshapes urban spaces and remakes precarity and insecurity. The dramatic decline of value-adding production, increased inequalities, and the disassembly of states associated with global neoliberalism compounds the tensions that crisscross the city with which its residents must contend every day.

Returning to the Yogurt Run

The nature of contemporary warfare means that people, more than armies, are a key presence. This marks a rather sharp differentiation from earlier wars. Of keen interest to us is that these conditions for war mobilize the residents of those cities that have become part of the war zone.

Survival in a city that has become part of the theater of war requires its people to adjust to the situation. Some may be able to flee because they have an alternative. But most people in such a city are stuck. The main concern under such conditions will be the search for what is necessary to survive. If survival entails negotiating for food and other critical items, survival will override (if possible) just about all other rules of the game. What we have called the yogurt run is an emblematic case. It tells us, or makes visible, how residents relate to the notion of an enemy. We cannot name the particular cities in play, as that would expose both sides to the wrath of their controlling armies.

War or not, a key priority for urban residents is securing their needs. And if that entails bringing in the yogurt from a city that is on the other side of the armed conflict, that is fine. It is a run that has to cross multiple battle lines—the armed insurgents, conventional militaries, criminal gangs, and ethnic militias that inhabit this new type of warfare. And out of this crossing it may be possible to identify new ways of confronting violence.

Contributors

Ali Ali is a postdoctoral researcher at the Institute for Global Affairs at the London School of Economics (LSE). He is also a Research Associate at the Refugee Studies Centre, University of Oxford, where he was previously a departmental lecturer in forced migration, and a postdoctoral researcher investigating the politics of the Syrian refugee crisis. Before joining Oxford he was a member of the "Security in Transition" team at LSE, researching the socioeconomic implications of armed conflicts in Syria.

Ruben Andersson is an anthropologist and associate professor in migration and development at the University of Oxford. His research is concerned with migration, borders, and security. He is the author of *Illegality, Inc.: Clandestine Migration and the Business of Bordering Europe* (2014) and *No Go World: How Fear Is Redrawing Our Maps and Infecting Our Politics* (2019), both with the University of California Press.

Daniel Bear is a professor in the criminal justice degree program at Humber College, Toronto, Canada. He completed his MSc and PhD in social policy at the London School of Economics and his bachelor's in sociology from the University of California at Santa Cruz.

Vesna Bojicic-Dzelilovic is codirector of the Business and Human Security Programme at the London School of Economics and Political Science. Her main area of research is the political economy of conflict and development with a geographic focus on southeastern Europe.

Karen Büscher is an assistant professor at Conflict Research Group (CRG), Ghent University (Belgium). Her research focuses on the complex relationship between urbanization and dynamics of violent conflict and postconflict reconstruction in the Democratic Republic of the Congo and northern Uganda. Topics that run as research lines through her work include violent conflict, urban governance, rural-urban transformation, forced displacement, urban anthropology, humanitarian urbanism, and urban violence.

Sobia Ahmad Kaker is a lecturer in sociology and criminology at Goldsmiths, University of London. Her research focuses on everyday urban life and insecurity, particularly in the context of global south cities. She adopts a contextual, postcolonial, and ethnographic approach to her work. Sobia completed her PhD at Newcastle University in 2015. Her project, titled "Enclaves as Process: Space, Security, and Violence in Karachi," describes how sociomaterial processes of enclavization exacerbated conflict and violence in the already divided Pakistani megacity.

Mary Kaldor is emeritus professor of global governance and director of the Conflict and Civil Society Research Unit at the London School of Economics and Political Science. She is CEO of the DFID-funded Conflict Research Programme. She is the author of several books on war, human security, and global civil society. Her most recent books are *International Law and New Wars* (with Christine Chinkin) and *Global Security Cultures*.

Mary Martin is a senior research fellow in the Department of International Relations at the London School of Economics and Political Science. She is also director of the UN Business and Human Security Initiative at LSE IDEAS, LSE's foreign policy think tank. Her research interests include the role of corporations in conflict prevention, private security in the international system, local ownership of peace-building, and changing concepts of security.

Johannes Christian Rieken completed his MSc and PhD in social psychology at the London School of Economics and Political Science, where he went on to work as a research officer. He obtained his bachelor in political science at Constance University (Germany) and holds an M.P.A.P. from Rutgers University. He advised government institutions—specifically police services—in the UK, Norway, and

Colombia on topics including training, anticorruption, and technology. He works in organizational development in the private sector.

Efraín García Sánchez is a researcher in the Lab of Social Psychology of Inequality as part of the Department of Social Psychology at the University of Granada. He completed his MSc in psychology of social intervention and PhD in social psychology at the University of Granada, and his MSc and bachelor's in psychology from the University of Valle (Cali, Colombia).

Saskia Sassen is the Robert S. Lynd Professor of Sociology at Columbia University and a member of its Committee on Global Thought, which she chaired until 2015. She is a student of cities, immigration, and states in the world economy; inequality, gendering, and digitization are three key variables running through her work. She is the author of eight books, including *Expulsions: Brutality and Complexity in the Global Economy* and *The Global City*.

Florian Weigand is a postdoctoral fellow in the Conflict and Civil Society Research Unit at the London School of Economics and Political Science. His work is concerned with armed conflicts, insurgencies, international interventions, and transnational crime. His research spans various conflict zones in Asia, including long-term field research in Afghanistan.

Index

Page numbers in *italics* represent figures or tables.

242 ||| Index